CLIMB

STORIES OF SURVIVAL FROM ROCK, SNOW AND ICE

EDITED BY CLINT WILLIS

adrenaline ™

MAINSTREAM
PUBLISHING

EDINBURGH AND LONDON

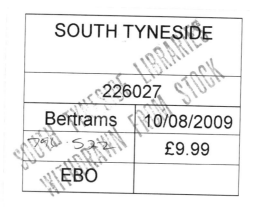
Adrenaline ™ and the Adrenaline™ logo are trademarks of
Balliett & Fitzgerald Inc. New York, NY

An Adrenaline Book™

First published in Great Britain in 2001 by
MAINSTREAM PUBLISHING COMPANY (EDINBURGH) LTD
7 Albany Street
Edinburgh EH1 3UG

ISBN 1 84018 402 7

Reprinted 2004

First published in the United States by
Thunder's Mouth Press
841 Broadway, 4th Floor
New York, NY 10003

and

Balliett & Fitzgerald Inc.
66 West Broadway, Suite 602
New York, NY 10007

Series Editor: Clint Willis
Book design: Sue Canavan
Frontispiece photo: © Corbis/Bettmann

Printed and bound in Great Britain by Antony Rowe, Chippenham, Wiltshire

For Anne and Perry
with all my heart

c o n t e n t s

p h o t o g r a p h s

introduction

When I was eleven years old, I saw Willi Unsoeld give a slide show about his 1963 ascent of Everest, where he'd suffered severe frostbite. The only slides I remember showed some of his toes floating in a jar at a medical clinic or hospital. That was 30 years ago. This morning I heard on the radio that Alex Lowe of Bozeman, Montana has died in an avalanche on Shisapangma in Tibet. The same avalanche has killed cameraman and climber David Bridges; the two men were part of an expedition to climb up and ski down the peak. I briefly talked with Alex several years ago when I was writing a magazine article about climbing guides. Since then, I have read about his efforts to balance his commitment to his family (he leaves a wife and three young sons) with his commitment to the mountains. Once or twice his name or image surfaced in connection with climbs that to me, at least, looked or sounded dangerous as well as difficult.

I remember Alex's voice, which I heard again this morning. The radio program ran some tape; it was recorded recently when Alex was rappelling from Pakistan's Great Trango Tower after a 36-day ascent. He explained that it would take the party days to get down, and noted how odd the whole enterprise must seem: You work so hard to get up a mountain, then you work hard to get down. Alex had just finished what some people have since called the world's biggest rock climb. During this climb he had been knocked unconscious by falling rock, had been laid out with a fever and had taken a 50-foot fall. He sounded delighted to be where he was, confident, relaxed, absurdly strong for someone who had just done and endured all those things. He sounded happy.

A few years ago, a climber friend read a story in a general interest magazine; the piece suggested that climbers climb mainly because they love danger; that they suffer from some kind of death wish. My friend objected to this in a long letter to the magazine's editors. He argued that most climbers climb in spite of the risk. They do what they can to make the activity safe, often taking great pains; that done, they evaluate whatever risk remains. Sometimes – though not always – they accept that risk in pursuit of the satisfactions climbing offers them. Does that make climbers daredevils?

No. In fact, few climbers are willing to take on the hazards of extreme mountaineering in places like Alaska or the Himalaya, where toppling seracs, avalanches, crevasses, altitude and rockfall routinely kill even the most careful mountaineers; instead, most climbers get what they need on safer terrain.

Still, surprising numbers of people go to the big mountains year after year, where they die with shocking regularity; others take big risks on smaller cliffs. And even the most cautious climber must accept a degree of danger: moving unroped to save time; braving terrain that's vulnerable to rockfall or avalanche; trusting that the afternoon thunderstorms will hold long enough for him to get below treeline. Climbers spend much of their time drawing lines – consciously or otherwise – between acceptable risks and unacceptable ones.

Many of the stories, essays and other selections in this book are about danger and its consequences, which include the losses climbers and their loved ones sometimes suffer. John Long contributes two short pieces to the collection. 'The Green Arch' tells how he and his young friends turned to climbing to distinguish themselves, even if it meant putting their lives on the line. Later, as an established hotshot on Yosemite's big walls, Long stumbled upon what he calls 'The Only Blasphemy' in the essay of that name. His revelation occurred on a day when he set out to cover 2,000 feet of hard climbing without a rope, and the discovery was elemental; but was it worth the risk?

David Roberts writes in 'Moments of Doubt' that he has never been happier than he has been in the mountains; yet by age 22, he'd witnessed three climbing accidents that killed a total of four people, all of them people he knew. How did he keep climbing past the first death, let alone the fourth?

Some writers treat these matters as routine or as material for comedy. Hamish MacInnes suffers a skull fracture high on the Bonatti Pillar of the Petit Dru and with a little help from friends finishes the route; neither he nor his companions seem terribly put out. Fellow Scotsman Tom Patey, a strong climber and a very funny man, makes the dangers of the Eiger's notorious North Face seem wildly amusing. Patey died in a 1970 rappelling accident.

This is serious stuff. Jim Wickwire, a leading American mountaineer of his generation (he's 59), published his 1998 memoir under the title *Addicted to Danger*. Wickwire 18 years ago watched a much younger friend slowly freeze to death in a crevasse; could do nothing to help him; swore he'd never climb again; has been climbing ever since. He pondered his struggle as he worked on his book:

> As I recalled my repeated promises to stop climbing and my inability to follow through – despite small children at home and the deaths of several companions – I recognized that I climbed not only for the solitude, beauty, physical exertion or bonds of friendship I found in the mountains, but also because of an attraction to danger. This has been a sobering insight.

• • •

But what's attractive about danger? Here's an idea: Danger makes us face things, which is the same thing as noticing them. The mountains are all the more beautiful at those moments when we realize that sooner or (if we are careful and fortunate) later we will lose them – and with them everything else that we've learned to value and love: family, work, cake, dog, music, comfort, love itself. Maybe we visit the mountains to pay our respects to death, which is nothing more or less than loss – and to life, which likewise amounts to a series of losses: children growing up, friends and acquaintances moving on; parents and spouses dying; even ourselves – this very self! the one that belongs to me! – growing older and eventually ceasing to be.

When I was nine years old, an adult explained to me that time starts to run out the day that we're born; he was right and I knew it; at that age, I couldn't lie to myself with the sophistication required to deny so fundamental and obvious a truth. But it may be that such lies become easier to spin and believe as we get older – or maybe we're more desperate to believe them.

Even so, we spend some of our time looking for what's true, and some of us find it in the mountains. In the mountains we sometimes get so interested in what we are doing that we forget to hide from the truth, which is change, which implies our own death. The mountains sometimes can remind us that this very moment must serve for eternity – and sometimes when we are in the mountains that is enough. I'm saying that a phrase like 'addicted to danger' may be just another phrase for an addiction to seeing things the way things are; to being awake to the facts, which include our inevitable, our continual, losses. Maureen O'Neill writes an essay about losing friends and climbing partners who have died in the mountains; it is in part an essay about what it is like to climb:

> Something inside says yes, yes, I recognize this. I want to see the earth above all with nothing hidden. The same laws that govern this world govern the life of my body and soul and it is a relief, finally, to see violence and beauty erupt, both parts of the whole.

• • •

Often while climbing on hard or dangerous ground there is a temptation to ignore obstacles and hazards; to forge ahead, hoping for the best. If you do that and then arrive safely at the next ledge, you can cite this as proof that you acted wisely; that you did the right thing. But you eventually will pay a price for such self-deception. Here is a passage from a piece New Hampshire climbing guide Michael Jewell gives his students who want to learn to lead (the leader on a rope team goes first, placing protection as he climbs; his risk is thus greater than his partner's):

Although it is possible to substantially limit the risks of leading, learning to lead is a deadly serious game. You must never forget for a moment that even the shortest fall can cause harm. Broken legs, spinal damage and head injuries are real consequences of poor focus, distorted priorities and sloppy management.

The gist of the document, which runs for some ten pages, is simple: If you are leading and you lie to yourself about anything – if you rationalize or pretend – you might get hurt or killed. I find something appealing about an activity that demands such allegiance to the way things are; that so clearly requires you to face your own fragility. There is something stunning and even gorgeous about the fact that a lie can cause you to take a 30-foot fall onto a ledge, maybe breaking an arm and a leg, maybe even dying of hypothermia if it rains and you didn't bring a jacket and your partner gets lost going for help.

These things all happen. Two weeks ago, *Accidents in North American Mountaineering 1999* arrived in the mail. I always read it, for the stories and for the analysis of accidents; trying to learn from other people's mistakes and misfortune. This year's edition brought news of 20 fatalities in reported mountaineering accidents in the United States during 1998. Greg Kowalsky (age unknown) fell 70 feet when a knot came untied. Richard Ladue, 37, was climbing ice without a rope when he fell 100 feet; he died nine hours later during a rescue attempt. An ice avalanche killed Russ Peterson, 40, while he was belaying a friend on a winter climb. Daniel O'Malley, rock climbing in Pennsylvania, dislodged a rock that knocked him off his climb and severed his rope; the fall killed him.

The *American Alpine News* arrived in the same package; its last page was an obituary to Canadian climber Jim Haberl, an avalanche victim last spring on Ultima Thule Peak in the University Range of the Wrangell-St. Elias Park in Alaska. Jim's been dead for six months now, but it came as news to me.

I knew him only slightly; we corresponded when I was compiling the stories for another anthology in 1998. Jim was kind enough to let me include in that book a passage from one of his books: *K2: Dreams and Reality*. The passage describes his 1993 ascent of the world's second-highest mountain. He reached the summit with his friend Dan Culver; but Culver slipped on the way down to their high camp, and fell to his death. Jim watched him fall; now Jim is dead, too. Climber Joe Simpson called his second book *This Game of Ghosts*; seems like a good title for a climbing book.

But ghosts are everywhere, aren't they? Everywhere, the dead outnumber the living. My younger child wants to know if there are cheeseburgers in heaven. Last night I went to a concert; at intermission, I stood in a line of mostly older men filing slowly through a sort of tunnel into the men's room. I suddenly imagined the line ending in darkness; here I was, standing with these old men, all of us shuffling towards the dark, getting closer . . . About twice a year, I wake up in the night alive to my mortality – utterly convinced that everything will end for me some day. It is an intense, fluttery feeling; not terrible, but not comfortable.

I went climbing for a couple of days last week with a friend I'll call Robert. I spent much of the second day frustrated and a little scared; I was practicing skills that were new to me; it was safe, but at moments it didn't feel as safe as it was. That night I described to Robert my fluttery feeling: that sense of being awash in the knowledge of my own death. Robert replied that he has something like it every single night, only stronger: He feels the dark trying to crush him, taking away the light and joy, all that he values and loves – his friends, his climbing, his life.

Maybe that is why Robert climbs more than anyone I know. Climbing is no salve for feelings of mortality; rather, it can help force us to believe them. But in believing, we accept; in accepting, we live; we fill up with whatever light is available to us – the light of the here and the now.

And so Robert has been climbing most days for almost three decades. He turned 50 a while ago, and had his first serious accident; he fell eight feet and broke his leg badly. Three months later he went to the Alps; he had to crawl across talus to get to the base of some of the climbs. Some of my other climbing partners have had worse mishaps: One broke his back; another fractured his skull and lay in a coma for weeks; a third broke his back and shattered both knees. They're all still climbing; the one who fractured his skull did it in the early 1970s; he's 60ish now, and he's been climbing for almost 40 years. Willi Unsoeld, minus the toes in that jar, went back to the mountains until one of them killed his daughter in 1976; he kept going back even then until an avalanche killed him in 1979; he was 52 years old. Some people don't walk away from climbing. They're dragged or they're carried.

Andrew Greig's example might serve as a warning to any non-climber who reads this book or others like it. Greig was a poet and an armchair climber who'd never roped up; then Scottish climber Mal Duff more or less out of the blue invited him to come on an expedition to climb the Karakoram's remote, difficult and dangerous Mustagh Tower. It was a crazy idea, as Greig writes in *Summit Fever*:

> A couple of climbing acquaintances filled me in on the quite astonishing variety of ways of croaking in the Himalaya. Falling off the mountain seemed the least of my worries. Strokes, heart attacks, pulmonary edema, cerebral edema, frostbite, exposure, pneumonia, stone fall, avalanche, crevasse, mountain torrents and runaway yaks – each with a name and an instance of someone who had been killed that way . . . Life was too pleasant and interesting to lose, yet to turn down an experience like this . . .

He went. The trip proved extremely dangerous and by far the most grueling experience of his life to that point. By the time he got back to Scotland, Greig had agreed to take another trip, this one to an even bigger mountain.

Why? Forgive me, but for some reason I think of Fagin in the '60s film version of *Oliver Twist*. When Fagin considers giving up his life of crime (he's seen the consequences; they're not pretty) the old cynic recalls (he's singing this) that his dearest companions have always been villians and thieves . . .

The mountains teach us to love. I think of Charles Dickens; I think of my mother listening to music from *South Pacific* and singing along; I think of my wife and her stepmother on horses; I think of my father dressing (tails) for a Mardi Gras party; I think of my sister down in Louisiana, knitting something warm for her first grandchild (a girl!), who lives in Texas. I think of Harold Brodkey writing or talking about writing, or sending faxes of his drawings to my children. I think of Steve Longenecker at Devil's Courthouse in 1974; I think of my brother in Linville Gorge in 1968; Ian Turnbull in Huntington Ravine; Mike Jewell on Cathedral Ledge talking about birds; my older son on Otter Cliff; his brother, aged ten, crossing a snowfield in Wyoming last July. I think of my dearest companions.

–*Clint Willis*

Moments of Doubt

by David Roberts

David Roberts (born 1943) has written about subjects ranging from Jean Stafford to the Anasazi tribe. He made his early mark with two climbing books (Deborah and The Mountain of my Fear). By age 22, Roberts had witnessed three fatal climbing accidents. His 1980 essay asks whether climbing is worth the risk.

A day in early July, perfect for climbing. From the mesas above Boulder, Colorado, a heat-cutting breeze drove the smell of the pines up onto the great tilting slabs of the Flatirons.

It was 1961; I was eighteen, had been climbing about a year, Gabe even less. We were about six hundred feet up, three-quarters of the way to the summit of the First Flatiron. There wasn't a guidebook in those days, so we didn't know how difficult our route was supposed to be or who had previously done it. But it had gone all right, despite the scarcity of places to bang in our Austrian soft-iron pitons; sometimes we'd just wedge our bodies in a crack and yell 'On belay!'

It was a joy to be climbing. Climbing was one of the best things – maybe the best thing – in life, given that one would never play shortstop for the Dodgers. There was a risk, as my parents and friends kept pointing out; but I knew the risk was worth it.

In fact, just that summer I had become ambitious. With a friend my age whom I'll call Jock, I'd climbed the east face of Longs Peak, illegally early in the season – no great deed for experts, but pretty good for eighteen-year-old kids. It was Jock's idea to train all summer and go up to the Tetons and do *the* route: the north face of the Grand. I'd never even seen the Tetons, but the idea of the route, hung with names like Petzoldt and Pownall and Unsoeld, sent chills through me.

It was Gabe's lead now, maybe the last before the going got easier a few hundred feet below the top. He angled up and left, couldn't get any protection in, went out of sight around a corner. I waited. The rope didn't move. 'What's going on?' I finally yelled. 'Hang on,' Gabe answered irritably, 'I'm looking for a belay.'

We'd been friends since grade school. When he was young he had been very shy; he'd been raised by his father only – why, I never thought to ask. Ever since I had met him, on the playground, running up the old wooden stairs to the fourth-grade classroom, he'd moved in a jerky, impulsive way. On our high school tennis team, he slashed at the ball with lurching stabs, and skidded across the asphalt like a kid trying to catch his own shadow. He climbed the same way, especially in recent months, impulsively going for a hard move well above his protection, worrying me, but getting away with it. In our first half-year of climbing, I'd usually been a little better than Gabe, just as he was always stuck a notch below me on the tennis team. But in the last couple of months – no denying it – he'd become better on rock than I was; he took the leads that I didn't like the looks of. He might have made a better partner for Jock on the Grand, except that Gabe's only mountain experience had been an altitude-sick crawl up the east side of Mount of the Holy Cross with me just a week before. He'd thrown up on the summit but said he loved the climb.

At eighteen it wasn't easy for me to see why Gabe had suddenly become good at climbing, or why it drove him as nothing else had. Just that April, three months earlier, his father had been killed in an auto accident during a blizzard in Texas. When Gabe returned to school, I mumbled my prepared condolence. He brushed it off and asked at once when we could go climbing. I was surprised. But I wanted to climb, too: the summer was approaching, Jock wasn't always available, and Gabe would go at the drop of a phone call.

Now, finally, came the 'on belay' signal from out of sight to the left, and I started up. For the full 120 feet Gabe had been unable to get in any pitons, so as I climbed, the rope drooped in a long arc to my left. It began to tug me sideways, and when I yanked back at it, I noticed that it seemed snagged about fifty feet away, caught under one of the downward-pointing flakes so characteristic of the Flatirons. I flipped the rope angrily and tugged harder on it, then yelled to Gabe to pull from his end. Our efforts only jammed it in tighter. The first trickle of fear leaked into my well-being.

'What kind of belay do you have?' I asked the invisible Gabe.

'Not too good. I couldn't get anything in.'

There were fifty feet of slab between me and the irksome flake, and those fifty feet were frighteningly smooth. I ought, I supposed, to climb over to the flake, even if it meant building up coils and coils of slack. But if I slipped, and Gabe with no anchor . . .

I yelled to Gabe what I was going to do. He assented.

I untied from the rope, gathered as many coils as I could, and threw the end violently down and across the slab, hoping to snap the jammed segment loose, or at least reduce Gabe's job to hauling the thing in with all his might. Then, with my palms starting to sweat, I climbed carefully up to a little ledge and sat down.

Gabe was now below me, out of sight, but close. 'It's still jammed,' he said, and my fear surged a little notch.

'Maybe we can set up a rappel,' I suggested.

'No, I think I can climb back and get it.'

'Are you sure?' Relief lowered the fear a notch. Gabe would do the dirty work, just as he was willing to lead the hard pitches.

'It doesn't look too bad.'

I waited, sitting on my ledge, staring out over Boulder and the deadstraw plains that seemed to stretch all the way to Kansas. I wasn't sure we were doing the right thing. A few months earlier I'd soloed a rock called the Fist, high on Green Mountain above Boulder, in the midst of a snow storm, and sixty feet off the ground, as I was turning a slight overhang, my foot had come off, and one hand . . . but not the other. And adrenalin had carried me the rest of the way up. There was a risk, but you rose to it.

For Gabe, it was taking a long time. It was all the worse not being able to see him. I looked to my right and saw a flurry of birds playing with a column of air over near the Second Flatiron. Then Gabe's voice, triumphant: 'I got it!'

'Way to go!' I yelled back. The fear diminished. If he'd been able to climb down to the snag, he could climb back up. I was glad I hadn't had to do it. Remembering his impatience, I instructed, 'Coil it up.' A week before, on Holy Cross, I'd been the leader.

'No, I'll just drape it around me. I can climb straight up to where you are.'

The decision puzzled me. *Be careful*, I said in my head. But that was Gabe, impulsive, playing his hunches. Again the seconds crept. I had too little information, nothing to do but look for the birds and smell the pine sap. You could see Denver, smogless as yet, a squat aggregation of downtown buildings like some modern covered-wagon circle, defended against the emptiness of the Plains. There had been climbers over on the Third Flatiron earlier, but now I couldn't spot them. The red, gritty sandstone was warm to my palms.

'How's it going?' I yelled.

A pause. Then Gabe's voice, quick-syllabled as always, more tense than normal. 'I just got past a hard place, but it's easier now.'

He sounded so close, only fifteen feet below me, yet I hadn't seen him since his lead had taken him around the corner out of sight. I felt I could almost reach down and touch him.

Next, there was a soft but unmistakable sound, and my brain knew it without ever having heard it before. It was the sound of cloth rubbing against rock. Then Gabe's cry, a single blurt of knowledge: 'Dave!'

I rose with a start to my feet, but hung on to a knob with one hand, gripping it desperately. 'Gabe!' I yelled back; then, for the first time in half an hour, I saw him. He was much farther from me now, sliding and rolling, the rope wrapped in tangles about him like a badly made nest. 'Grab something,' I yelled, I could hear Gabe shouting, even as he receded from me, 'No! Oh, no!'

I thought, there's always a chance. But Gabe began to bounce, just like rocks I had seen bouncing down mountain slopes, a longer bounce each time. The last was conclusive, for I saw him flung far from the rock's even surface to pirouette almost lazily in the air, then meet the unyielding slab once more, headfirst, before the sandstone threw him into the treetops.

What I did next is easy to remember, but it is hard to judge just how long it took. It seemed, in the miasma of adrenalin, to last either three minutes or more than an hour. I stood and I yelled for help. After several repetitions, voices from the Mesa Trail caught the breeze back to me. 'We're coming!' someone shouted. 'In the trees!' I yelled back. 'Hurry!' I sat down and said to myself, now don't go screw it up yourself, you don't have a rope, sit here and wait for someone to come rescue you. They can come up the back and lower a rope from the top. As soon as I had given myself this good advice, I got up and started scrambling toward the summit. It wasn't too hard. Slow down, don't make a mistake, I lectured myself, but it felt as if I were running. From the summit I downclimbed the eighty feet on the backside; I'd been there before and had rappelled it. Forty feet up there was a hard move. *Don't blow it.* Then I was on the ground.

I ran down the scree-and-brush gully between the First and Second Flatirons, and got to the bottom a few minutes before the hikers. 'Where is he?' a wild-eyed volunteer asked me. 'In the trees!' I yelled back. 'Somewhere right near here!'

Searching for something is usually an orderly process; it has its methodical pleasures, its calm reconstruction of the possible steps that led to the object getting lost. We searched instead like scavenging predators, crashing through deadfall and talus; and we couldn't find Gabe. Members of the Rocky Mountain Rescue Group began to arrive; they were calmer than the hiker I had first encountered. We searched and searched, and finally a voice called out, 'Here he is.'

Someone led me there. There were only solemn looks to confirm the obvious. I saw Gabe sprawled face down on the talus, his limbs in the wrong positions, the rope, coated with blood, still in a cocoon about him. The seat of his jeans had been ripped away, and one bare buttock was scraped raw, the way kids' knees used to look after a bad slide on a sidewalk. I wanted to go up and touch his body, but I couldn't. I sat down and cried.

Much later – but it was still afternoon, the sun and breeze still collaborating on a perfect July day – a policeman led me up the walk to my house. My mother came to the screen door and, grasping the situation at once, burst into tears. Gabe was late for a birthday party. Someone had called my house, mildly annoyed, to try to account for the delay. My father took on the task of calling them back. (More than a decade later he told me that it was the hardest thing he had ever done.)

In the newspapers the next day a hiker was quoted as saying that he knew something bad was going to happen, because he'd overheard Gabe and me 'bickering' and good climbers didn't do that. Another man had watched the fall through binoculars. At my father's behest, I wrote down a detailed account of the accident.

About a week later Jock came by. He spent the appropriate minutes in sympathetic silence, then said, 'The thing you've got to do is get right back on the rock.' I didn't want to, but I went out with him. We top-roped a moderate climb only thirty feet high. My feet and hands shook uncontrollably, my heart seemed to be screaming, and Jock had to haul me up the last ten feet. 'It's OK, it'll come back,' he reassured.

I had one friend I could talk to, a touch-football buddy who thought climbing was crazy in the first place. With his support, in the presence of my parents' anguish, I managed at last to call up Jock and ask him to come by. We sat on my front porch. 'Jock,' I said, 'I just can't go to the Grand. I'm too shook up. I'd be no good if I did go.' He stared at me long and hard. Finally he stood up and walked away.

That fall I went to Harvard. I tried out for the tennis team, but when I found that the Mountaineering Club included veterans who had just climbed Waddington in the Coast Range and Mount Logan in the Yukon, it didn't take me long to single out my college heroes.

But I wasn't at all sure about climbing. On splendid fall afternoons at the Shawangunks, when the veterans dragged us neophytes up easy climbs, I sat on the belay ledges mired in ambivalence. I'd never been at a cliff where there were so many climbers, and whenever one of them on an adjoining route happened to yell – even if the message were nothing more alarming than 'I think it goes up to the left there!' – I jerked with fright.

For reasons I am still not sure of, Gabe became a secret. Attached to the memory of our day on the First Flatiron was not only fear, but guilt and embarrassment. Guilt toward Gabe, of course, because I had not been the one who went to get the jammed rope. But the humiliation, born perhaps in that moment when the cop had led me up to my front door and my mother had burst into tears, lingered with me in the shape of a crime or moral error, like getting a girl pregnant.

Nevertheless, at Harvard I got deeply involved with the Mountaineering Club. By twenty I'd climbed McKinley with six Harvard friends via a new route, and that August I taught at Colorado Outward Bound School. With all of 'Boone Patrol,' including the senior instructor, a laconic British hard man named Clough, I was camped one night above timberline. We'd crawled under the willow bushes and strung out ponchos for shelter. In the middle of the night I dreamed that Gabe was falling away from me through endless reaches of black space. He was in a metal cage, spinning headlong, and I repeatedly screamed his name. I woke with a jolt, sat shivering for ten minutes, then crawled, dragging my bag, far from the others, and lay awake the rest of the night. As we blew the morning campfire back to life from the evening's ashes, Clough remarked, 'Did you hear the screams? One of the poor lads must have had a nightmare.'

By my senior year, though, I'd become hard myself. McKinley had seemed a lark compared to my second expedition – a forty-day failure with only one companion, Don Jensen, on the east ridge of Alaska's Mount Deborah. All through the following winter, with Don holed up in the Sierra Nevada, me trudging through a math major at Harvard, we plotted mountaineering revenge. By January we had focused on a route: the unclimbed west face of Mount Huntington, even harder, we thought, than Deborah. By March we'd agreed that Matt Hale, a junior and my regular climbing partner, would be our third, even though Matt had been on no previous expeditions. Matt was daunted by the ambition of the project, but slowly got caught up in it. Needing a fourth, we discussed an even more inexperienced club member, Ed Bernd, a sophomore who'd been climbing little more than a year and who'd not even been in big mountains.

Never in my life, before or since, have I found myself so committed to any project. I daydreamed about recipes for Logan bread and the number of ounces a certain piton weighed; at night I fell asleep with the seductive promises of belay ledges and crack systems whispering in my ear. School was a Platonic facade. The true Idea of my life lay in the Alaska Range.

At one point that spring I floated free from my obsession long enough to hear a voice in my head tell me, 'You know, Dave, this is the kind of climb you could get killed on.' I stopped and assessed my life, and consciously answered, 'It's worth it. Worth the risk.' I wasn't sure what I meant by that, but I knew its truth. I wanted Matt to feel the same way. I knew Don did.

On a March weekend Matt and I were leading an ice climbing trip in Huntington Ravine on Mount Washington. The Harvard Cabin was unusually full, which meant a scramble in the morning to get out first and claim the ice gully you wanted to lead. On Saturday I skipped breakfast to beat everybody else to Pinnacle Gully, then the prize of the ravine. It was a bitter, windy day, and though the gully didn't tax my skills unduly, twice sudden gusts almost blew me out of my steps. The second man on the rope, though a good rock climber, found the whole day unnerving and was glad to get back to the cabin.

That night we chatted with the other climbers. The two most experienced were Craig Merrihue, a grad student in astrophysics, said to be brilliant, with first ascents in the Andes and Karakoram behind him, and Dan Doody, a quiet, thoughtful filmmaker who'd gone to college in Wyoming and had recently been on the big American Everest expedition. Both men were interested in our Huntington plans, and it flattered Matt and me that they thought we were up to something serious. The younger climbers looked on us experts in awe; it was delicious to bask in their hero worship as we nonchalanted it with Craig and Dan. Craig's lovely wife Sandy was part of our company. All three of them were planning to link up in a relaxing trip to the Hindu Kush the coming summer.

The next day the wind was still gusting fitfully. Matt and I were leading separate ropes of beginners up Odells Gully, putting in our teaching time after having had Saturday to do something hard. I felt lazy, a trifle vexed to be 'wasting' a good day. Around noon we heard somebody calling from the ravine floor. We ignored the cries at first, but as a gust of wind came our way, I was pricked with alarm. 'Somebody's yelling for help,' I shouted to Matt. 'Think they mean it?' A tiny figure far below seemed to be running up and down on the snow. My laziness burned away.

I tied off my second to wait on a big bucket of an ice step, then zipped down a rappel off a single poorly placed ice screw. Still in crampons I ran down into the basin that formed the runout for all five gullies. The man I met, a weekend climber in his thirties who had been strolling up the ravine for a walk, was moaning. He had seen something that looked like 'a bunch of rags' slide by out of the corner of his eye. He knew all at once that it was human bodies he had seen, and he could trace the line of fall up to Pinnacle Gully. He knew that Doody and Merrihue were climbing in Pinnacle. And Craig was a close friend of his. During the five minutes or so since the accident he had been unable to approach them, unable to do anything but yell for help and run aimlessly. I was the first to reach the bodies.

Gabe's I had not had to touch. But I was a trip leader now, an experienced mountaineer, the closest approximation in the circumstances to a rescue squad. I'd had first-aid training. Without a second's hesitation I knelt beside the bodies. Dan's was the worse injured, with a big chunk of his head torn open. His blood was still warm, but I was sure he was dead. I thought I could find a faint pulse in Craig's wrist, however, so I tried to stop the bleeding and started mouth-to-mouth resuscitation. Matt arrived and worked on Dan, and then others appeared and tried to help.

For an hour, I think, I put my lips against Craig's, held his nose shut, forced air into his lungs. His lips were going cold and blue, and there was a stagnant taste in the cavity his mouth had become, but I persisted, as did Matt and the others. Not since my father had last kissed me – was I ten? – had I put my lips to another man's. I remembered Dad's scratchy face, when he hadn't shaved, like Craig's now. We kept hoping, but I knew after five minutes that both men had been irretrievably damaged. There was too much blood. It had been a bad year for snow in the bottom of the ravine; big rocks stuck out everywhere. Three years earlier Don Jensen had been avalanched out of Damnation Gully; he fell 800 feet and only broke a shoulder blade. But that had been a good year for snow.

Yet we kept up our efforts. The need arose as much from an inability to imagine what else we might do – stand around in shock? – as from good first aid sense. At last we gave up, exhausted. I could read in Matt's clipped and efficient suggestions the dawning sense that a horrible thing had happened. But I also felt numb. The sense of tragedy flooded home only in one moment. I heard somebody say something like 'She's coming,' and somebody else say, 'Keep her away.' I looked up and saw Sandy, Craig's wife, arriving from the cabin, aware of something wrong, but in the instant before knowing that it was indeed Craig she was intercepted bodily by the climber who knew her best, and that was how she learned. I can picture her face in the instant of knowing, and I remember vividly my own revelation – that there was a depth of personal loss that I had never really known existed, of which I was now receiving my first glimpse.

But my memory has blocked out Sandy's reaction. Did she immediately burst into tears, like my mother? Did she try to force her way to Craig? Did we let her? I know I saw it happen, whatever it was, but my memory cannot retrieve it.

There followed long hours into the dark hauling the bodies with ropes back toward the cabin. There was the pacifying exhaustion and the stolid drive back to Cambridge. There was somebody telling me, 'You did a fantastic job, all that anybody could have done,' and that seemed maudlin – who wouldn't have done the same? There were, in subsequent weeks, the memorial service, long tape-recorded discussions of the puzzling circumstances of the accident (we had found Dan and Craig roped together, a bent ice screw loose on the rope between them), heated indictments of the cheap Swiss design of the screw. And even a couple of visits with Sandy and their five-year-old son.

But my strongest concern was not to let the accident interfere with my commitment to climb Huntington, now only three months away. The deaths had deeply shaken Matt; but we never directly discussed the matter. I never wrote my parents about what had taken place. We went ahead and invited Ed, the sophomore, to join our expedition. Though he had not been in the ravine with us, he too had been shaken. But I got the three of us talking logistics and gear, and thinking about a mountain in Alaska. In some smug private recess I told myself that I was in better training than Craig and Dan had been, and that was why I wouldn't get killed. If the wind had blown one of them out of his steps, well, I'd led Pinnacle the day before in the same wind and it hadn't blown me off. Almost, but it hadn't. Somehow I controlled my deepest feelings and kept the disturbance buried. I had no bad dreams about Doody and

Merrihue, no sleepless nights, no sudden qualms about whether Huntington was worth the risk or not. By June I was as ready as I could be for the hardest climb of my life.

It took a month, but we climbed our route on Huntington. Pushing through the night of July 29–30, we traversed the knife-edged summit ridge and stood on top in the still hours of dawn. Only twelve hours before, Matt and I had come as close to being killed as it is possible to get away with in the mountains.

Matt, tugging on a loose crampon strap, had pulled himself off his steps; he landed on me, broke down the snow ledge I had kicked; under the strain our one bad anchor piton popped out. We fell, roped together and helpless, some seventy feet down a steep slope of ice above a 4,500-foot drop. Then a miracle intervened; the rope snagged on a nubbin of rock, the size of one's knuckle, and held us both.

Such was our commitment to the climb that, even though we were bruised and Matt had lost a crampon, we pushed upward and managed to join Ed and Don for the summit dash.

At midnight, nineteen hours later, Ed and I stood on a ledge some fifteen hundred feet below. Our tents were too small for four people; so he and I had volunteered to push on to a lower camp, leaving Matt and Don to come down on the next good day. In the dim light we set up a rappel. There was a tangle of pitons, fixed ropes, and the knots tying them off, in the midst of which Ed was attaching a Karabiner. I suggested an adjustment. Ed moved the Karabiner, clipped our rope in, and started to get on rappel. 'Just this pitch,' I said, 'and then it's practically walking to camp.'

Ed leaned back on rappel. There was a scrape and sparks – his crampons scratching the rock, I later guessed. Suddenly he was flying backwards through the air, down the vertical pitch. He hit hard ice sixty feet below. Just as I had on the Flatiron, I yelled, 'Grab something, Ed!' But it was evident that his fall was not going to end – not soon, anyway. He slid rapidly down the ice chute, then out of sight over a cliff. I heard him bouncing once or twice, then nothing. He had not uttered a word.

I shouted, first for Ed, then for Don and Matt above. Nothing but silence answered me. There was nothing I could do. I was as certain as I could be that Ed had fallen 4,000 feet, to the lower arm of the Tokositna

Glacier, inaccessible even from our base camp. He was surely dead.

I managed to get myself, without a rope, down the seven pitches to our empty tent. The next two days I spent alone – desperate for Matt's and Don's return, imagining them dead also, drugging myself with sleeping pills, trying to fathom what had gone wrong, seized one night in my sleep with a vision of Ed, broken and bloody, clawing his way up the wall to me, crying out, 'Why didn't you come look for me?" At last Don and Matt arrived, and I had to tell them. Our final descent, in the midst of a raging blizzard, was the nastiest and scariest piece of climbing I have done, before or since.

From Talkeetna, a week later, I called Ed's parents. His father's stunned first words, crackly with long-distance static, were 'Is this some kind of a joke?' After the call I went behind the bush pilot's hangar and cried my heart out – the first time in years that I had given way to tears.

A week later, with my parents' backing, I flew to Philadelphia to spend three days with Ed's parents. But not until the last few hours of my stay did we talk about Ed or climbing. Philadelphia was wretchedly hot and sticky. In the Bernds' small house my presence – sleeping on the living room sofa, an extra guest at meals – was a genuine intrusion. Unlike my parents, or Matt's, or Don's, Ed's had absolutely no comprehension of mountain climbing. It was some esoteric thing he had gotten into at Harvard; and of course Ed had completely downplayed, for their sake, the seriousness of our Alaska project.

At that age, given my feelings about climbing, I could hardly have been better shielded from any sense of guilt. But mixed in with my irritation and discomfort in the muggy apartment was an awareness – of a different sort from the glimpse of Sandy Merrihue – that I was in the presence of a grief so deep its features were opaque to me. It was the hope-destroying grief of parents, the grief of those who knew things could not keep going right, a grief that would, I sensed, diminish little over the years. It awed and frightened me, and disclosed to me an awareness of my own guilt. I began remembering other moments. In our first rest after the summit, as we had giddily replayed every detail of our triumph, Ed had said that yes, it had been great, but that he wasn't sure it had been worth it. I hadn't pressed him; his qualifying judgment had seemed the only sour note in a perfect party. It was so obvious to me that all the risks throughout the climb – even Matt's and my near-disaster – had been worth it to make the summit.

Now Ed's remark haunted me. He was, in most climbers' judgment, far too inexperienced for Huntington. We'd caught his occasional technical mistakes on the climb, a piton hammered in with the eye the wrong way, an ice axe left below a rock overhang. But he learned so well, was so naturally strong, complemented our intensity with a hearty capacity for fun and friendship. Still, at Harvard, there had been, I began to see, no way for him to turn down our invitation. Matt and I and the other veterans were his heroes, just as the Waddington seniors had been mine three years before. Now the inner circle was asking him to join. It seemed to us at the time an open invitation, free of any moral implications. Now I wondered.

I still didn't know what had gone wrong with the rappel, even though Ed had been standing a foot away from me. Had it been some technical error of his in clipping in? Or had the Karabiner itself failed? There was no way of settling the question, especially without having been able to look for, much less find, his body.

At last Ed's family faced me. I gave a long, detailed account of the climb. I told them it was 'the hardest thing yet done in Alaska,' a great mountaineering accomplishment. It would attract the attention of climbers the world over. They looked at me with blank faces; my way of viewing Ed's death was incomprehensible. They were bent on finding a Christian meaning to the event. It occurred to them that maybe God had meant to save Ed from a worse death fighting in Vietnam. They were deeply stricken by our inability to retrieve his body. 'My poor baby,' Mrs. Bernd wailed at one point, 'he must be so cold.'

Their grief brought me close to tears again, but when I left it was with a sigh of relief. I went back to Denver, where I was starting graduate school. For the second time in my life I thought seriously about quitting climbing. At twenty-two I had been the firsthand witness of three fatal accidents, costing four lives. Mr. Bernd's laborious letters, edged with the leaden despair I had seen in his face, continued to remind me that the question 'Is it worth the risk?' was not one any person could answer by consulting only himself.

Torn by my own ambivalence, studying Restoration comedy in a city where I had few friends, no longer part of a gang heading off each weekend to the Shawangunks, I laid off climbing most of the winter of 1965–66. By February I had made a private resolve to quit the business, at least for a few years. One day a fellow showed up at my basement apartment, all the way down from Alaska. I'd never met him, but the name Art Davidson was familiar. He looked straight off skid row, with his tattered clothes and unmatched socks and tennis shoes with holes in them; and his wild red beard and white eyebrows lent a kind of run-down Irish aristocracy to his face. He lived, apparently, like a vagrant, subsisting on cottage cheese in the back of his old pickup truck (named Bucephalus after Alexander's horse), which he hid in parking lots each night on the outskirts of Anchorage. Art was crazy about Alaskan climbing. In the next year and a half he would go on five major expeditions – still the most intense spate of big-range mountaineering I know of. In my apartment he kept talking in his soft, enthusiastic voice about the Cathedral Spires, a place he knew Don and I had had our eyes on. I humored him. I let him talk on, and then we went out for a few beers, and Art started reminding me about the pink granite and the trackless glaciers, and by the evening's end the charismatic bastard had me signed up.

We went to the Cathedral Spires in 1966, with three others. Art was at the zenith of his climbing career. Self-taught, technically erratic, he made up in compulsive zeal what he lacked in finesse. His drive alone got himself and Rick Millikan up the highest peak in the range, which we named Kichatna Spire. As for me, I wasn't the climber I'd been the year before, which had much to do with why I wasn't along with Art on the summit push. That year I'd fallen in love with the woman who would become my wife, and suddenly the old question about risk seemed vastly more complicated. In the blizzard-swept dusk, with two of the other guys up on the climb, I found myself worrying about *their* safety instead of mere logistics. I was as glad nothing had gone wrong by the end of the trip as I was that we'd collaborated on a fine first ascent.

Summer after summer I went back to Alaska, climbing hard, but not with the all-out commitment of 1965. Over the years quite a few of my climbing acquaintances were killed in the mountains, including five close friends. Each death was deeply unsettling, tempting me to doubt all over again the worth of the enterprise. For nine years I taught climbing to college students, and worrying about their safety became an occupational hazard. Ironically, the closest I came during those years to getting killed was not on some Alaskan wall, but on a beginner's climb at the Shawangunks, when I nearly fell head-first backwards out of a rappel – the result of a Karabiner jamming in a crack, my own impatience, and the blasé glaze with which teaching a dangerous skill at a trivial level coats the risk. Had that botched rappel been my demise, no friends would have seen my end as meaningful: instead, a 'stupid,' 'pointless,' 'who-would-have-thought?' kind of death.

Yet in the long run, trying to answer my own question 'Is it worth it?', torn between thinking the question itself ridiculous and grasping for a formulaic answer, I come back to gut-level affirmation, however sentimental, however selfish. When I imagine my early twenties, it is not in terms of the hours spent in a quiet library studying Melville, or my first nervous pontifications before a freshman English class. I want to see Art Davidson again, shambling into my apartment in his threadbare trousers, spooning great dollops of cottage cheese past his flaming beard, filling the air with his baroque hypotheses, convincing me that the Cathedral Spires needed our visit. I want to remember what brand of beer I was drinking when that crazy vagabond in one stroke turned the cautious resolves of a lonely winter into one more summer's plot against the Alaskan wilderness.

Some of the worst moments of my life have taken place in the mountains. Not only the days alone in the tent on Huntington after Ed had vanished – quieter moments as well, embedded in uneventful expeditions. Trying to sleep the last few hours before a predawn start on a big climb, my mind stiff with dread, as I hugged my all-too-obviously fragile self with my own arms – until the scared kid inside my sleeping bag began to pray for bad weather and another day's reprieve. But nowhere else on earth, not even in the harbors of reciprocal love, have I felt pure happiness take hold of me and shake me like a puppy, compelling me, and the conspirators I had arrived there with, to stand on some perch of rock or snow, the uncertain struggle below us, and bawl our pagan vaunts to the very sky. It was worth it then.

How I (Almost) Didn't Climb Everest

by Greg Child

Greg Child (born 1957) went to Everest in 1995, one year before Jon Krakauer. Child's piece reads like a preamble to Krakauer's Into Thin Air. *The crowds, the competition, the incompetence are all in place; casualties are routine, and the stage is set for the 1996 disaster.*

Fifty feet ahead of me and a hundred feet below the summit of Everest, a Sherpa named Ang Babu grunts and pushes at the butt of some French geezer who is tugging with all his might on an old hank of rope hanging over a short cliff. With a mighty heave the Sherpa shoulders his client onto the summit ridge; then they begin the easy home stretch to the top of the world.

It's a windless, cloudless morning near the apex of the North Ridge. On one side of this 2.5-mile fin of ice and rock, starkly backlit clouds lap at Nepalese peaks; on the other, tawny Tibetan hills stretch into a soft, heliotropic haze. I pause to take in the view, then realizing that in a few minutes I'll be on the highest place on Earth, I start sniffling with emotion. Or is it that bloody cold that's been dogging me for weeks?

Wiping my frosted goggles and freeing my oxygen mask of a golfball-size ice cube of drool, I look up at the Frenchman and his Sherpa guide. They move side by side until, after a few paces, the Sherpa inadvertently overtakes his client by a stride – and is sternly stopped by a French mitten backhanded against his chest. The Frenchman has paid a boodle of cash to be escorted up Everest, and he'll be damned if anyone else is going to beat him to this coveted summit.

This display of inverted camaraderie and French neocolonialism squeezes a weary laugh out of me (actually, through my oxygen mask, it sounds more like a dog barking in a rubber echo chamber). Karsang, the Sherpa beside me, drops his mask from his face and gives me an expression that crosses borders of language and says, 'Can you believe that arsehole?' But we humor the Frenchman, and the remaining six of us on the ridge that day – a polyglot group made up from two expeditions – fall into rank behind the imaginary line he has drawn in the snow.

I share those last steps with Bob, a Nebraskan who ropes steers for a hobby, and who, like the Frenchman, is a member of a commercial Everest trip. Unlike the get-there-first Frenchman, who creeps ahead with excruciating slowness, Bob is just happy to be where he is. Bob's summit fantasy includes twirling a lariat to become the world's highest trick roper. When we passed through Lhasa he did rope tricks on a street corner – jumping in and out of the lariat, and lassoing a cheering Tibetan bystander – till Chinese soldiers broke up the crowd. Yeah, Bob is a nice guy, which is why I find it upsetting when he slips on the skating-rink-hard slope, pivots upside down and then slides forty feet to disappear over the 10,000-foot North Face.

It happens lightning quick, a blur to the eyes and the imagination. Aside from my lame shout of 'Stop!' he is gone without a sound. I turn toward Karsang, partly to gauge from his expression whether I have hallucinated all this, but he, too, gapes toward the claw marks of Bob's slide to oblivion.

I gather what wits I can muster at nearly 29,000 feet and crampon toward the precipice. Foolishly I call Bob's name – what's the point, he's a croaker for sure – then I hear a cry for help.

'Dammit,' I think to myself, now imagining the epic of extricating a mangled Bob from the cliffs below the Big One's crown. 'Looks like I won't climb this tit of a hill after all.'

I had always sneered at Everest, snubbed invitations to join expeditions to it, pooh-poohed it as an overrated, overclimbed status symbol. 'Just because it is the biggest shitpile on Earth doesn't mean it is the best shitpile on Earth,' I used to say. But in 1995 I went to the mountain Tibetans call Goddess Mother of Earth. Maybe I went because I was tired of making excuses as to why I had climbed so many Himalayan peaks, but not Everest. Maybe a crack at Everest is just inevitable for anyone silly enough to dub themselves a 'Himalayan climber'. Whatever the reason, as the departure date for Tibet neared, I did feel a growing fascination – okay, call it a dose of Everest fever – to stand on the Earth's highest point. Mostly though, I just wanted to get the bloody mountain off my back.

Shortly before I left for Everest I visited Steve Swenson, a friend who'd climbed the North Ridge in 1994. We'd climbed K2 together five years earlier, and he'd soloed Everest without oxygen. He described the route, showed me slides, and told me about the scene at base camp. 'Expect lots of people, all types of people – a lot of them guided, a lot of them people you or I wouldn't classify as climbers – swarming all over the mountain,' he warned. During his Everest season there had been six ascents and four deaths amid a near-constant climate of hurricane wind and cold. 'Anyway,' he said in conclusion, 'you'll come away with good material for a story.'

I justified selling out my No-Everest principles because I had a project up there: to make a film about climbing the North Ridge with an old friend who is an amputee. Tom Whittaker is a loquacious Brit I had met in Yosemite in 1978 while I was crawling out of a dumpster and he was crawling in. I was scavenging for pop cans stamped with the magic nickel-deposit seal, to cash in so I could buy a new rope. He had two legs back then, and he talked me into climbing the Nose on El Cap with him. Seventeen years later, and after he'd lost his right foot in a car smash with a drunk driver on Thanksgiving night in 1979, he phoned me to suggest another climb. This time I would help him become the first amputee up Everest. 'Why would I want to climb with a one-legged man, Tom?' I asked him bluntly. 'Because it will make us both very sexy,' he replied.

To launch the expedition we needed money, and the best way to get the money was to make a documentary of Tom's attempt. So I faxed Leo Dickinson, the British adventure filmmaker, who, among his seventy films had made a film about ballooning over Everest and crash-landing in Tibet. Leo got on board and persuaded a British TV station to finance the film. After we secured the film deal, *The North Face* helped underwrite the expedition, and we bought into a trip to Everest's Tibetan side. Before we knew it, we were at base camp.

And so were about 500 other people whose eleven base camps dotted the snout of the East Rongbuk Glacier. About half these people were support members, cooks, bottle-washers, and Chinese liaison officers. The rest – some 180 of them – had their eyes on the summit of Everest. Aside from a behemoth Japanese/Sherpa team on the Northeast Ridge, the bulk of traffic was on the North Ridge.

Why the North Ridge? Because it was a climber's bargain, with a peak fee of $15,000 and no limit on team size, as opposed to the $50,000 minimum royalty demanded by the Nepalese for a team of five climbers. It also allowed the four commercial operators on the North Ridge to offer middle-class Everest wannabes packages priced from $18,000 to $25,000. By contrast, a guided ascent of Nepal's South Col route sported the tony price tag of $65,000.

Everesting has always been a separate sport from the rest of climbing. For a certain breed of climber, it is the only mountain they'll ever try, and they'll pay big bucks for the big tick. To quote David Breashears, who has climbed Everest several times and recently made an IMAX film of an ascent, 'Everest is the ultimate feather in the pseudomountaineer's cap.'

'Doing Everest' became possible for people with disposable income in the 1990s, when a few climbers started guiding on the mountain. A cheaper deal than the 'guided ascent' emerged with the advent of the 'commercial trip', on which a team of lead climbers and Sherpas outfit the mountain with camps, oxygen, and fixed ropes and let the punters have at it without a guide. This is the ultimate high-adventure package tour, and the ultimate blind date, as you don't meet your partners till you reach Kathmandu. In my opinion, letting inexperienced people loose on an 8,000-meter peak is like giving a drunk an Uzi with a full clip, but it is astonishing how many people have gotten to the top, either guided or on commercial trips, and have survived the experience. These days, it is also sobering to tally up the number of ingenues who have died on Everest.

Altitude-addled from the drive to base camp at 17,000 feet, I fairly fell out of the jeep. Everest loomed in the distance. The long sweep of the North and Northeast Ridge routes formed the left skyline, the West Ridge the right, and the Great Couloir and Hornbein Couloir formed gashes up the center. I was surprised at how rocky the mountain was – 'black as a snake's arse," the wild-haired Aussie climber Jon Muir had quipped when we'd flown past it, en route to Lhasa.

Through binoculars I scoped the landmarks of the North Ridge route. Above the highest campsite, at 27,000 feet, were the crumbling cliffs of the Yellow Band; I'd read that around there, in 1933, the British climber Frank Smythe had been so discombobulated by altitude he had offered a bite of his lunch to an imaginary partner. Above that, protruding from the ridge, were two rocky humps, the First Step and the Second Step. The Second Step – a stack of rocks culminating in a fifteen-foot vertical cliff – is the technical crux of the route. Here the Englishmen George Leigh Mallory and Andrew Irvine were last sighted during a summit bid on 8 June 1924. Some climbers believe those two summited and beat Hillary and Norgay to Everest's first ascent by nearly three decades, but until their bodies are found and the film in the cameras they carried is restored, the matter of whether or not they reached the summit will always be conjecture. The Second Step is also where Chinese climbers, on the second ascent of the ridge in 1975 (Chinese made the first ascent of it, too, in 1960, but Western observers doubted the claim at the time), erected a ten-foot aluminum ladder to overcome this rocky obstacle.

Rumor had it around base camp that in 1994 some wise guy had cut the ropes securing this rickety old ladder to the wall and hurled it off the mountain. Some climbers in camp looked forward to the challenge of climbing the Second Step by 'fair means'; others were mortified that the aid had been eliminated. Our team considered issuing a spoof press release to the climbing media saying we'd bolted the Second Step – just to piss off the traditionalists.

It was also on the North Face, on the slopes below the curve of the ridge, that Reinhold Messner made his tour de force in 1980 by soloing a new route without oxygen. He had been the only climber on the entire Tibetan side of Everest. His only companion at base camp was his girlfriend. Never again would a climber experience such solitude on Everest.

By early May the expeditions had marched the fifteen miles up the East Rongbuk Glacier to establish Advance Base Camp (ABC), a 200-tent ghetto jammed onto a moraine strip at 21,000 feet, below Everest's bleak, black Northeast Wall. It is well known by biologists that a cage containing a clan or two of lab rats presents a harmonious community, but when the population gets out of control and the cage gets overcrowded, the rats get strange, go crazy, and eat their young. The first sign of antisocial behavior on Everest came when an American team got territorial and encircled their camp with a fence of rope to keep trespassers out. Then on a foul, windy day in mid-April, while I stood below the North Col at 21,500 feet, watching snow plumes stream over the ice-blue crest 2,000 feet above, I met The Man With An Attitude.

All around me, climbers were setting out and then abandoning their journeys to Camp One on the col, driven back by the gale and signs of impending storm. Wind swirled about in a vortex, occasionally sweeping breathable air away and leaving a momentary vacuum that left one with an awful suffocating feeling. While I zipped up my windsuit to keep spindrift out, I noticed Leo locked in conversation with a climber from another team and then watched them march purposefully toward me.

'Er, this fellow says he's going to cut our tents loose from the North Col and toss them off the mountain,' said Leo.

After an introduction I learned the following: The Man With An Attitude was the climbing leader of his expedition; he'd been on Everest a month longer than me and didn't like our intrusion on his ridge; he claimed he'd placed all the fixed ropes himself; if I wanted to use his ropes I had to ask his permission; anyway, it was too late to ask for permission to use his ropes, as he intended to cut them loose so that ingrates like me couldn't use them; and, as Leo said, he planned to slash the ropes lashing our tents to the mountain and let the wind devour them.

It took but a second to identify this character as a dangerous alpine psycho in need of a megadose of Lithium. Leo prescribed different treatment. His heritage was of British bar-room brawls and the use of Don Whillans–style fisticuffs to settle climbing disagreements. While Leo shadowboxed in the background, whispering, 'Hit him, hit him,' I pretended to be a UN negotiator trying to arrange a cease-fire between Serbia and Bosnia.

After a heated discussion in the cold, I got safe passage for us to the North Col by threatening sanctions and reprisals if The Man With An Attitude touched our tents. His threat to destroy our camp was, in his words, 'a non-life-threatening protest to our presence.' 'Well,' I said, 'I've been on twelve Himalayan expeditions, and that's the first time I've heard that one.'

I offer an apologia for The Man With An Attitude: he had been on Everest too long; the mountain was too big for his mind and his body; and he believed the myth of Himalayan solitude – making for a shattered wilderness experience for him when the masses arrived at base camp. His delusions that he'd fixed all the ropes (many teams, including ours, had contributed rope) and that destroying our tents would solve anything, were, however, just plain nuts. As we parted company I wondered how anyone was going to summit with kooks like him around.

But summit people did, in droves.

On 10 May, a thick, warm fog rolled up the glacier. For climbers like Russell Brice, a New Zealander who was our expedition leader and who, during four expeditions to the north side, had known only winds that flatten tents and send rocks frisbeeing through the sky, it was a perplexing omen. 'This either means the worst storm in history is about to hit, or we're about to get perfect weather.' After twenty-four hours the sky was clear.

First to summit, on 11 May, were six members of the Japanese/ Sherpa team on the Northeast Ridge. This was the first time this immensely long route had been climbed in its entirety, though Russell and Harry Taylor had climbed the route, alpine style, to its junction with the North Ridge in 1988.

After the Japanese success the gauntlet was down. Between 11 May and 17 May, about fifty more people summited by the North Ridge. There were first national ascents for Taiwan, Turkey, Latvia, and Rumania.

Russian, American, British, Austrian, and Italian climbers succeeded, too. Reinhard Patsheider, of Italy, set a north-side speed record with a twenty-one-hour oxygenless blitz from ABC to the summit. Britain's Alison Hargreaves made a seemingly effortless oxygenless ascent in 'unsupported' style, meaning that although she was always surrounded by other climbers and had radio contact with base camp, she carried her own gear, established her own camps, and had no Sherpa help (as opposed to climbers like me who were vying for bad-style ascents, who happily paid Sherpas to carry their junk, who sucked the guts out of oxygen bottles, and who hauled themselves up fixed ropes). So independent and style-conscious was Alison that she wouldn't even accept a cup of tea from me while on the mountain, lest it be construed as 'support.' Though hers was the 'best' ascent of the season, her publicity machine in Britain got carried away afterward, variously claiming hers as the first female oxygenless ascent, first-ever female ascent, and that it was all done solo. In fact, on her summit day, she was seldom less than fifty feet behind two Italians (who also climbed oxygenless). As for firsts, Junko Tabei of Japan made the first female ascent in 1975, and Lydia Bradey in 1988 was the first woman up without oxygen (though Lydia's claim was hotly disputed at the time, all but misogynists and Luddites credit her ascent now).

Others were gunning for firsts, too. There were contenders for the youngest ascent (age fifteen) and the oldest ascent (age sixty-three), and there was The Man Who Would Bivy Highest.

A member of a commercial expedition, The Man Who Would Bivy Highest hit the spotlight one morning when a team going for the summit found him shivering below the Second Step, at 28,100 feet. He had survived the night dressed only in his climbing suit. Fearing he'd be frostbitten, two Sherpas gave up their summit bids – and the $300 bonus they stood to earn for helping their clients to the top – to assist The Man Who Would Bivy Highest. Radios buzzed as a rescue was mounted, people moved up the ridge to help, and yaks were assembled for his evacuation down the glacier.

When The Man Who Would Bivy Highest passed my tent at 25,600 feet, he was verbally abusing his Sherpa rescuers from behind an oxygen mask. When I saw his gloves dangling from strings on his wrists, I suggested he put them on his dead-fish-colored hands. This prompted him to launch into a tirade about how everyone on the mountain was overreacting to his plight. 'I'm in control. I don't need rescuing.' He saw no cause to be grateful to anyone for the effort launched on his behalf.

Wary now of alpine psychos, I zipped my tent shut, and from the safety within I suggested to the bivouacker that the world would be a better place if he jumped off the mountain. He stumbled away to impress others with his bonhomie, especially Leo, who, when he handed His Bivouackship a cup of tea at the North Col, had it 'thrown back at him' because there wasn't sugar in it.

Miraculously, the bivouacker escaped severe frostbite. In base camp he bragged that he'd set a record for the highest bivy sans oxygen. He believed his accomplishment would create a media storm when he returned to Kathmandu. Perhaps my attitudes are old-fashioned, but sitting out near the summit of Everest doesn't seem so much a record to break as a fuck-up to avoid. Then the theory emerged that The Man Who Would Bivy Highest had intentionally sat the night out to set his record. An American who'd passed Der Bivymeister at 1 p.m. at the Second Step said he'd given him a full bottle of oxygen. Although there were still seven hours of daylight left, the bivouacker descended no farther. But unbeknown to Mister Bivouack, in 1994 Mark Whetu and Michael Rheinberger had survived a night without shelter even higher on the ridge. When told this, The Man Who Would Bivy Highest faded into the crowds at base camp and was not missed.

During April and May, Tom and I and several score of summit hopefuls reached the wind-ravaged site of Camp Two. For anyone with two feet, this section of the climb up firm, 40-degree snow and scree was easy. But not for Tom, with his spatula-footed, carbon-fiber-ankled, Terminator-like, crampon-adapted, Flexfoot prosthesis. Though he could saunter down a city street with a gait that hinted nothing of a disability, his footing was sketchy on rubble. 'I figure I expend a third more energy than an able-bodied person to climb the same distance,' he said, explaining his slower pace. He couldn't just kick a foot into snow or edge up on rock, he had to eyeball the appendage his stump was slotted into, place it carefully, and ease onto it. He had no ankle rotation, no calf muscle, no toe to spring off. He also had two trick knees he could invert at will. His leg was also sensitive to cold. He combated this with a battery-powered warming device taped to his stump. After a month, he was running out of artificial feet, having damaged two of his four prostheses on the slog between base camp and ABC. He patched the feet with glue and kept going.

With his strange foot, Tom was easily the most conspicuous, but not the most colorful character on Everest. Aussie climber Jon Muir wore a homemade, Cossack-like, fox-head hat and wielded a mummified chicken claw he'd salvaged from a Tibetan restaurant and planned to leave on the summit. 'First chicken-claw ascent. They said it couldn't be done,' he'd cackle to confused punters at base camp. Jon, who'd climbed Everest in 1988, was back again to support his wife, Brigitte, in her attempt at an ascent, but he found it hard to take the 1995 mob scene seriously. When a young Turkish candidate suggested he was 'willing to die' for Everest, Jon nonplussed him by laughing maniacally and waving his chicken claw around.

Then arrived The Feral Kid, an American youth who appeared at ABC one day, vigorously shook my hand, and began a hard-sell pitch to join our team. He'd 'resigned' from his expedition due to irreconcilable differences; now he was a free agent. He rattled out his climbing resume to impress me. It included the ability to whip off one-arm pull-ups, a pointless feat on Everest, where the main use of the bicep is to tie bootlaces. I felt like I was being sold a used car that I didn't want, so I offered this orphan of Everest some advice: 'Don't join a team, just solo the mountain.' When I offered these words I think I was talking to myself, imagining I was in the next valley, on the solitude of the North Face, where there was not a single person. There, away from the complexity of our film and the hordes, a climber might actually be able to consider himself worthy of the name.

The kid disappeared up the North Ridge with two oxygen bottles scavenged from a Latvian team. I envied his escape from the formality of a structured expedition. He was an animal who'd escaped the zoo, gone wild – a feral climber. I never saw him again, though rumors abounded of a lone youth at the high camp, dossing in abandoned tents, digging in the snow for old food dumps, trying to inveigle himself onto summit teams. Maybe The Feral Kid climbed it, maybe not. He was just another face in the crowd.

More conventional yet no less intriguing was George Mallory, eponymous grandson of the late George Leigh Mallory. After young George summited on 14 May, there was little doubt in his mind that his grandfather was the first man up Everest. He based his belief on the fact that in 1924 their teammate, Noel Odell, saw Mallory and Irvine crest the Second Step (in later years Odell seemed unsure of exactly where on the ridge he'd seen them, but in his written dispatches at the time of the disappearance he pinpointed them at the Second Step). Odell sighted them at about 1 p.m. The Second Step is 900 vertical feet and a horizontal half-mile before the summit.

'After that, the route is easy. There is nothing to stop you from climbing to the top,' young George said enthusiastically of the remaining terrain. Indeed, the weather on 8 June 1924, was reportedly good, though cloudy, and Mallory and Irvine were strong climbers and were using primitive oxygen sets. Although young George had found the Chinese ladder intact, he'd checked out the ladderless variation and felt grandpa could have flashed it, or at least stood on Irvine's shoulders. Anyway, the Chinese Wang Fu-Chou had climbed it in 1960 without the ladder. He'd removed his boots and climbed the rock in his socks, freezing some toes in the process. These were later snipped off.

Though nothing concrete is known about Mallory's and Irvine's last hours, they left some tantalizing clues, such as the ice axe found midway between the First and Second Steps by a 1933 British expedition. Did it signify their high point, the site of a fall, or was it just dumped because it was useless on the rocky ridge? One of their bodies seems to have been found in 1975 by a Chinese porter, Wang Hung-bao, who went for a twenty-minute stroll from his camp at 26,600 feet and returned with the tale of finding 'an English dead'. Wang's tentmate on the day of the grisly discovery, Zhang Jun Yan, later confirmed Wang's tale. In 1979 Wang revealed his story to Japanese climbing leader Ryoten Hasegawa, but before they could find the corpse, Wang was killed in an avalanche below the North Col. Tom Holzel, an American, had found the whole mystery so compelling that he'd launched an expedition in 1986 to find the bodies and the cameras. Imagine finding a summit photo that proved Hillary wasn't first up Everest! What a scoop! But Holzel found nothing.

Two weeks after I returned from Everest, Holzel revealed to me the long-kept secret of where Wang had found the body, the location of which he'd learned from Chinese climbers. It was eerie to learn that our high camp lay a stone's throw from the possible solution to climbing's most enduring mystery, and our base camp a few yards from Wang's grave.

As the season wore on, thievery raised its ugly head. It began with allegations that precious oxygen bottles stashed at the high camp had been stolen from one expedition by another. Later, two rogue Sherpas were caught red-handed with tents and sleeping bags they'd liberated from a neighboring expedition, an act that left a Sherpa descending from the summit without a sleeping bag to slumber in that night. Tents on the glacier were ransacked by Tibetan yak-men, then tents were uprooted and stolen altogether by yak-men. Locking your tent didn't help; they just ripped out zippers to get inside. Even my ice axe disappeared from beside my tent at 23,000 feet, though I got it back some days later when I met an Eastern European climber toting it down from the summit. But most disturbing to our team was the disappearance of sixty liters of rum, spirited away from base camp.

Was nothing sacred on Everest? Evidently not. Lawsuits were threatened by clients against guides, fax machines spewed out messages to constantly remind us of the real world, and the concrete blockhouse toilets at base camp filled with shit. One could mangle the phrase 'If power corrupts, then absolute power corrupts absolutely' to 'If mountains corrupt, then Everest corrupts absolutely.'

Then the infamous jet-stream winds returned to sandblast the summit on 18 May. It occurred to me then that I had not climbed the mountain, that I had missed the good weather, and that I probably would not climb the mountain. I tried to take this in my stride, but the threat of failure became a wart on my psyche that I scratched and scratched like a mangy dog. Punters whom I'd helped into their crampons had summited, why not me? I was supposed to be a climber, and these people were – tourists. What was wrong?

The timing was wrong, and getting wrapped up in a film project was wrong, and being trapped in a heavyweight expedition where management decreed when you could climb the mountain and when you could not, was wrong. I'd failed on about half of my eleven Himalayan expeditions, but the failures were always more or less on my terms, an amicable agreement between me and the mountains. Slow learner that I am, I realized at Everest that my self-perceived identity is defined to an unhealthy degree by mountaineering, and I resolved to lighten up, get into the zen of failure, and laugh at the fact that people with minimal mountaineering experience had summited while I was still festering in base camp. But before I could get into any of that feel-good stuff, the weather cleared.

On 25 May, Tom, Russell, Sherpas Karsang and Lobsang, and I hunkered down for the night in the final camp. The summit stood 2,100 feet higher and a horizontal mile in distance southwest of us. At midnight we woke, plugged into Russian-made oxygen masks and set off into the moonless night.

We followed a trail of frayed ropes anchored to the decrepit rock of the Yellow Band. The bulbous muzzles on our faces made it impossible to see our feet. Cold killed our headlamp batteries. We probed about like blind men. It wasn't easy for Tom, but he forced himself on, pulling on the ropes that snaked up a seemingly endless flow of ramps and cliffs. To speed Tom's progress, the rest of us took his load. The weight was ridiculous. Each of us was weighed down by three oxygen bottles. I also carried a video camera, a radio, a still camera, and a liter of water. My food for the day consisted of 200 calories of GU, an energy paste. At the first glow of sunrise at 4.30 a.m., we stopped at about 27,200 feet to assess our progress.

We unanimously judged Tom's pace to be too slow. We had not even reached the crest of the Northeast Ridge. At this speed he could get to the summit, but not till very late. We'd all be out of oxygen by then, and a nocturnal descent with dead headlamps was an invitation to frostbite, falls, and horror. It was an agonizing moment for Tom, but it was the end of the road for him. He returned to the high camp with Russell while I continued up with Karsang and Lobsang.

The sun was rising when we hit the ridge crest. Makalu, the world's fifth-highest peak, appeared as a massive molar in the cast. In the oblique sunlight, Nepal seemed an endless succession of parallel ridges and cloud-filled valleys, of steaming jungles and iced peaks. Tibet's horizon was a sheet of earth-colored velvet, the foreground a swirl of porcelain-white glaciers.

We passed the First Step, then sidled across a limestone shelf festooned with tattered ropes tied to old pitons, some of which I could pull out of the rock with my fingers. Sometimes a tricky free-climbing move had to be made to connect the footpath-width ramps the route followed. At one point I got off route and found myself poised on small, crumbling holds. In my muzzle, mittens, and Frankenstein boots, I had no feel for the rock. I looked between my legs at a huge drop leading to the glaciers, and I saw a pinkish dot about 500 feet down – the body of Michael Rheinberger, an Australian who had summited in 1994. Reaching the top was his life's dream, and his partner, Mark Whetu, a New Zealander, saw him hug the summit and weep with happiness. But Michael had exhausted himself and could only descend a couple of hundred feet before he weakened, forcing them to bivouac in the open. Mark's feet froze, but he continued down the next day; Michael, though, had lost the strength to move, and he remained. Some say he fell down the cliff when he tried to move; others say the wind blew his body there; still others say that a climber had lowered his body off with a rope, so travelers to the summit would not disturb him when they passed.

At the Second Step we encountered the Chinese ladder, flanked left and right by wide fissures that split the wall. Here I wondered if Mallory and

Irvine had overcome this obstacle, with their heavy steel oxygen tanks, hobnail boots, and wool tweed jackets. Only the Chinese in 1960 were known for certain to have climbed this cliff. The official Communist-Party book of their ascent says it took three hours to overcome it and that they climbed 'with the power of Mao Ze Dong Thought'.

Even though I was using bottled oxygen, I'd been gasping desperately for the past hour. Scaling the ladder nearly made me faint. At the top of the step I checked the pressure gauge on my bottle. It registered zero. No wonder I felt so wasted. How long it had been empty I didn't know. I switched onto another bottle, added the spent one to a cluster of abandoned orange torpedoes, and joined the ranks of the world's highest litterbugs.

After an easier quarter-mile of ridge we caught up to Bob, the Frenchman, and three Sherpas. They had set off an hour earlier that morning.

'Hi, Greg,' said Bob.

'Hi, Bob,' said Greg.

It was then that Bob fell off Mount Everest.

I still don't understand what stopped him from taking the big dive. When I got to him, he was lying on a steeply tilted, coffee-table-size slab of rock, on his back, head pointed down-mountain. Seeing his legs and arms waving about reminded me of the character known as K, in Kafka's book *Metamorphosis*, who turns into a beetle and who, at one point when he tries to walk like a man, falls over and lies on his back wriggling around pathetically. I considered taking a photo – Bob looked really funny – but I thought better of it.

'Help!'

'Don't move an inch!'

Bob was out of reach, and I was damned if I was going to risk reaching over the cliff to offer a hand and getting catapulted over the North Face. I needed a rope but didn't have one. He was sliding off the rock, and his face was turning red as blood flowed to his head, his eyes seemed to plead for fast action. I was about to remove my harness to toss an end of that to him, when I looked at my feet and saw an old hank of rope.

This 'seek and ye shall find' discovery didn't give me religion, but it may have if I were in Bob's position. I hacked the rope out of the ice, tied a loop, and cast it to him. He grabbed it. Then Ang Babu arrived, dug out more rope, and tossed it down. When we hauled Bob up, I asked him what caused his fall.

'I was daydreaming,' he answered.

The summit, which I reached at 9.45 a.m., proved to be a busy spot. For the seven of us up there, there were hands to shake, radio broadcasts to make, and photos to take. Cameras were exchanged in a confusing number of permutations to ensure that everyone had their photo taken with everyone else. The apex of the mountain bristled with a forest of metal poles decorated with fluttering red, yellow, and blue prayer flags. One object up there, a scientific instrument, appropriately resembled a traffic light. I remembered that in 1990 on K2 I had hallucinated the figure of a person while I was alone; on Everest that day, not seeing a person constituted a hallucination.

Bob spun his lariat and then left with the mob. I spent a few minutes on top alone. Quiet at last. Just the flapping of prayer flags and the beat and heave of my heart and lungs. No clouds. A curving horizon. Somewhere out there in the great southern distance the monsoon was rolling toward the Himalaya, pushing aside the jet-stream winds like a cosmic bulldozer to create the freakish spell of calm that surrounded Everest. I pocketed a few small, ancient rocks from a scree patch thirty feet below the top, and then I headed down too.

There were sixty-seven ascents of Everest from Tibet that spring. No climbers or Sherpas died on the Tibetan side, though one young Sherpa fell to his death in Nepal. Record-keepers tell me that mine was the 736th ascent of the mountain. Not exactly an exclusive club, but it felt good to have stood up there.

The Green Arch
by John Long

Climbers know John Long (born 1953) for his gung-ho ascents in Yosemite during the '70s and '80s, and for his instructional rock-climbing books and videos. Readers know him for his anthologies of various writers' work, and for his own stories about climbing and other adventures. Here Long writes about his youth, when ambition boiled down to one directive: Climb the hardest routes before someone else does.

We came from nowhere towns like Upland, Cucamonga, Ontario and Montclair. None of us had done anything more distinguished than chase down a fly ball or spend a couple of nights in juvenile hall, but we saw rock climbing as a means to change all that. *The Lonely Challenge, The White Spider, Straight Up* – we'd read them all, could recite entire passages by heart. It is impossible to imagine a group more fired up by the romance and glory of the whole climbing business than we were. There was just one minor problem: there were no genuine mountains in Southern California. But there were plenty of rocks. Good ones, too.

Every Saturday morning during the spring of 1972, about a dozen of us would jump into a medley of the finest junkers two hundred dollars could buy and blast for the little mountain hamlet of Idyllwild, home of Tahquitz Rock. The last twenty-six miles to Idyllwild follows a twisting road, steep and perilous in spots. More than one exhausted Volkswagen bus or wheezing old Rambler got pushed a little too hard, blew up and was abandoned, the plates stripped off and the driver, leaden with rope and pack, thumbing on toward Mecca. We *had* to get to a certain greasy spoon by eight o'clock, when our little group, the Stonemasters, would meet, discuss an itinerary, wolf down some food and storm off to the crags with all the subtlety of a spring hailstorm.

The air was charged because we were on a roll, our faith and gusto growing with each new route we bagged. The talk within the climbing community was that we were crazy, or liars, or both; and this sat well with us. We were loud-mouthed eighteen-year-old punks, and proud of it.

Tahquitz was one of America's hot climbing spots, with a pageant of pivotal ascents reaching back to when technical climbing first came to the States. America's first 5.8 (The Mechanic's Route) and 5.9 (The Open Book) routes were bagged at Tahquitz, as was the notion and the deed of the 'first free ascent', a route first done with aid but later climbed without it (The Piton Pooper, 5.7, *circa* 1946). John Mendenhall, Chuck Wilts, Mark Powell, Royal Robbins, Tom Frost, T. M. Herbert, Yvon Chouinard, Bob Kamps and many others had all learned the ropes there.

The Stonemasters arrived about the same time that the previous generation of local hardcores – a high-blown group consisting of would-be photographers and assistant professors – was being overtaken by house payments and squealing brats. They hated every one of us. We were all ninety cents away from having a buck, ragged as roaches, eating the holes out of doughnuts – and we cared nothing for their endorsement. We'd grappled up many of their tougher climbs, not with grace, but with pure gumption and fire, and the limelight was panning our way.

The old guard was confounded that we of so little talent and experience should get so far. When it became common knowledge that we were taking a bead on the hallowed Valhalla (one of the first 5.11 routes in America) – often tried, but as yet unrepeated – they showed their teeth. If we so much as dreamed of climbing Valhalla, we'd have to wake up and apologize. The gauntlet was thus thrown down: if they wouldn't hand over the standard, we'd rip it from their hands. When, after another month, we all had climbed Valhalla, some of us several times, the old boys were stunned and saw themselves elbowed out of the opera house by kids who could merely scream. And none could scream louder than Tobin Sorenson, the most conspicuous proponent of a madman to ever lace up Varappes.

Climbing had never seen the likes of Tobin, and probably never will again. He had the body of a welterweight, a lick of sandy brown hair and the faraway gaze of the born maniac; yet he lived with all the precocity and innocence of a child. He would never cuss or show the slightest hostility. Around girls he was so shy he'd flush and stammer. But out on the sharp end of the rope he was a fiend in human form. Over the previous summer he'd logged an unprecedented string of gigantic falls that should have ended his career, and his life, ten times over. Yet he shook each fall off and clawed straight back onto the route for another go, and usually got it. He became a world-class climber very quickly, because someone that well formed and savagely motivated will gain the top in no time – if he doesn't kill himself first. Still, when we started bagging new routes and first free ascents, Tobin continued defying the gods with his electrifying peelers. The exploits of his short life deserve a book. Two books.

One Saturday morning five or six of us hunkered down in our little restaurant in Idyllwild. Tahquitz was our oyster. We'd pried it open with a piton and for months had gorged at will; but the fare was running thin. Since we had ticked off one after another of the old aid routes, our options had dwindled to only the most grim or preposterous ones. But, during the previous week, Ricky Accomazzo had scoped out the Green Arch, an elegant arc on Tahquitz's southern shoulder. When Ricky mentioned he thought there was an outside chance that this pearl of an aid climb might go free, Tobin looked as though the Hound of the Baskervilles had just heard the word 'bone', and we nearly had to lash him to the booth so we could finish our oatmeal.

Since the Green Arch was Ricky's idea, he got the first go at it by rights. Tobin balked, so we tied him off to a stunted pine and Ricky started up. After fifty feet of dicey wall climbing, he gained the arch, which soared vertically above for another eighty feet before curving right and disappearing in a field of big knobs and pockets. If we could only get to those knobs, the remaining three hundred feet would go easily and the

Green Arch would fall. But the lower corner and the arch above looked bleak. The crack in the back of the arch was too thin to accept even fingertips, and both sides of the corner were blank and marble-smooth. Yet by pasting half his rump on one side of the puny corner, and splaying his feet out on the opposite side, Ricky stuck to the rock – barely – both his butt cheek and his boots steadily oozing off the steep, greasy wall. It was exhausting duty just staying put, and moving up was accomplished in a grueling, precarious sequence of quarter-inch moves. Amazingly, Ricky jackknifed about halfway up the arch before his calves pumped out. He lowered off a bunk piton and I took a shot.

After an hour of the hardest climbing I'd ever done, I reached a rest hold just below the point where the arch arched out right to melt into that field of knobs. Twenty feet to pay dirt. But that twenty feet didn't look promising.

There were some sucker knobs just above the arch, but those ran out after about twenty-five feet and would leave a climber in the bleakest no-man's-land, with nowhere to go, no chance to climb back right onto the route, no chance to get any protection, and no chance to retreat. We'd have to stick to the arch.

Finally, I underclung about ten feet out the arch, whacked in a suspect knifeblade, clipped the rope in – and fell off. I lowered to the ground, slumped back, and didn't rise for ten minutes. I had matching and weeping strawberries on both ass cheeks, and my ankles were all rubbery and tweaked from splaying them out on the far wall.

Tobin, unchained from the pine, tied into the lead rope and stormed up the corner like a man fleeing Satan on foot. He battled up to the rest hold, drew a few quick breaths, underclung out to that creaky, buckled, driven-straight-up-into-an-expando-flake knifeblade, and immediately cranked himself over the arch and started heaving up that line of sucker knobs.

'No!' I screamed up. 'Those knobs don't go anywhere!' But it was too late.

Understand that Tobin was a born-again Christian, that he'd smuggled Bibles into Bulgaria risking twenty-five years on a Balkan rock-pile, that he'd studied God at a fundamentalist university, and that none of this altered the indisputable fact that he was perfectly mad. Out on the sharp end he not only ignored all consequences, but actually loathed them, doing all kinds of crazy, incomprehensible things to mock them. (The following year, out at Joshua Tree, Tobin followed a difficult, overhanging crack with the rope noosed around his neck.) Most horrifying was his disastrous capacity to simply charge at a climb pell-mell. On straightforward routes, no one was better. But when patience and cunning were required, no one was worse. Climbing, as it were, with blinders on, Tobin would sometimes claw his way into the most grievous jams. When he'd dead-end and have to stop, with nowhere to go and looking at a Homeric peeler, the full impact of his folly would hit him like a wrecking ball. He would suddenly panic, wail, weep openly, and do the most ludicrous things. And sure enough, about twenty-five feet above the arch those sucker knobs ran out, and Tobin had nowhere to go.

He was, in fact, looking at a fifty-foot fall – *if* that blade I'd bashed under the roof held. But I *knew* it would not. At best, it might sufficiently break his fall for the next lower piece to stop him. That piece was ten feet below the shitty blade, at the rest hold, so Tobin was looking at a seventy-footer, a tad more with rope stretch.

As Tobin wobbled far overhead, who should lumber up to our little group but his very father, a minister, a quiet, retiring, imperturbable gentleman who hacked and huffed from his long march up to the cliff side. After hearing so much about climbing from Tobin, he'd finally come to see his son in action. He couldn't have shown up at a worse time. It was like a page from a B-movie script – us cringing and digging in, waiting for the bomb to drop; the good pastor, wheezing through his moustaches, sweat-soaked and confused, squinting up at the fruit of his loins; and Tobin, knees knocking like castanets, sobbing pitifully and looking to plunge off at any second.

There is always something you can do, even in the grimmest situations, if only you keep your nerve. But Tobin was gone, totally gone, so mastered by terror that he seemed willing to die to be rid of it. He glanced down. His face was a study. Suddenly he screamed, 'Watch me! I'm gonna jump.' We didn't immediately understand what he meant.

'Jump off?' Richard yelled.

'Yes!' Tobin wailed.

'NO!' we all screamed in unison.

'You can do it, son!' the pastor put in.

Pop was just trying to put a good face on it, God bless him, but his was the worst possible advice because there was no way Tobin could do it. Or anybody could do it. There were no holds! But inspired by his father's urging, Tobin reached out for those knobs so very far to his right, now lunging, now hopelessly pawing the air like a falling man clasps for the cargo net.

And then he was off. The blade shot out and Tobin shot off into the grandest fall I've ever seen a climber take and walk away from – a spectacular, cartwheeling whistler. His arms flailed like a rag doll's, and his blood-curdling scream could have frozen brandy. He finally jolted onto the rope, hanging upside down and moaning softly. We slowly lowered him off and he lay motionless on the ground and nobody moved or spoke or even breathed. You could have heard a pine needle hit the deck. Tobin was peppered with abrasions and had a lump the size of a pot roast over one eye. He lay dead still for a moment longer, then wobbled to his feet and shuddered like an old cur crawling from a creek.

'I'll get it next time,' he grumbled.

'There ain't gonna be no next time!' said Richard.

There was, but it came four years later. In one of the most famous leads of that era, Ricky flashed the entire arch on his first try. Tobin and I followed.

Tobin would go on to solo the north face of the Matterhorn, the Walker Spur and the Shroud on the Grandes Jorasses (all in Levi's), would make the first alpine ascent of the Harlin Direct on the Eiger, the first ascent of the Super Couloir on the Dru, would repeat the hardest free climbs and big walls in Yosemite, and sink his teeth into the Himalaya. He was arguably the world's most versatile climber during the late 1970s. But nothing had really changed: he always climbed as if time were too short for him, pumping all the disquietude, anxiety, and nervous waste of a normal year into each route.

I've seen a bit of the world since those early days at Tahquitz, have done my share of crazy things, and have seen humanity with all the bark on, primal and raw. But I've never since experienced the electricity of watching Tobin out there on the very quick of the long plank, clawing for the promised land. He finally found it in 1980, attempting a solo ascent of Mount Alberta's north face. It was a tragedy, of course. Yet I sometimes wonder if God Himself could no longer bear the strain of watching Tobin wobbling and lunging way out there on the sharp end of the rope, and finally just drew him into the fold.

from Addicted to Danger: A Memoir
by Jim Wickwire and
Dorothy Bullitt

Jim Wickwire (born 1940) in 1978 was a member of the first American team to summit K2. He climbs in part because he likes the risk — though he of all men knows what's at stake. A 1981 accident on the approach to Mt. McKinley's fearsome Wickersham Wall forced Wickwire and his young partner to accept the unacceptable.

We moved down the Peters Glacier slowly, a sled between us loaded heavy with supplies. Twenty feet of rope linked us – too close, we knew, but required by the rough, undulating surface beneath our feet. A glacier is not a fixed, solid thing. It flows like a river, with currents, some parts smooth, others rough. Where it changes direction, or where the angle of its slope steepens, the surface will split, creating cracks as deep as a hundred feet. A thin layer of snow can make them invisible.

Chris walked in front. I walked behind, righting the sled each time it flipped. The afternoon sun beat down on us, softening the snow, casting long shadows. Moments after we had decided to head toward smoother ground, Chris broke through the crust and plunged headfirst into a crevasse. I was concentrating on the sled and did not see him fall. Just as I sensed trouble, the rope yanked me into the air, then down into an icy void. 'This is it,' I thought. 'I'm about to die.'

In an instant, the sled and I slammed on top of Chris. Stunned but still conscious after the impact, I checked myself for injuries. My left shoulder felt numb and I could not raise my arm. (I later learned my shoulder had broken.) Suppressing an urge to panic, I glanced around and considered what I should do. Balanced awkwardly with one foot on the sled, the other against a slight bulge in the ice, I tried my best to reassure Chris as I took off my pack and squeezed it into an eighteen-inch space between the walls. Then, using my pack for support, I shoved the sled off Chris into an area just below us, where it lodged.

All I could see of my companion were his legs, still in snowshoes, dangling behind his large black pack, which had compressed to half its normal width between the crevasse walls. Suspended facedown, parallel to the crevasse bottom far below, he yelled, 'I can't move, Wick, you've got to get me out!' Trapped under the pack, Chris's entire upper body was immobilized. When I noticed his left hand, twisted back, caught between his pack and the wall, I grabbed it and asked if he could feel the pressure. 'No,' he barked, 'I can't feel anything! You've got to get me out, Wick!' I assured him, 'I will, Chris, I promise.' I tried lifting him by his pack, but hard as I pulled, he would not budge. Within a few minutes I realized I could do nothing more for him until I got myself out of the crevasse.

The tapered walls were as slick as a skating rink. The distant slit of daylight looked a hundred feet away. To make it to the surface, I needed to put on my crampons – steel spikes attached to each boot to prevent slipping. Luckily, they were on the back of my pack. In a space so tight I could maneuver only by facing the wall, I awkwardly pulled off my snowshoes and strapped the crampons on. Then I retied our rope to the back of Chris's pack, clipped a three-foot aluminum picket and a pair of jumars – mechanical devices to move up and down a rope – to my waist sling, and prepared to climb out. When I tried kicking the front two points of a crampon into the wall, they bounced off. I tried using my ice hammer, but without room to swing my arm, I barely made a scratch. How could I get out if I couldn't penetrate the ice? I began to panic. 'Calm down,' I told myself, 'think of something that will work.'

I tried chipping out a little indentation, narrower than a finger width, and placed the front points of my crampon on the tiny ledge. I edged myself up, placing my back against the opposite wall as a counterforce. The front points held my weight. Using my good arm to wield the hammer, I slowly worked my way up the cold, glassy walls, chiseling a ladder of little ledges as I went. Three chips and a step up, again and again. I concentrated harder than I ever had before. The whole time Chris kept yelling from beneath his pack, 'You've got to get me out, Wick! You've got to get me out!' Between puffs and grunts I continued to reassure him, 'It'll be okay, I'll get you out.' And I felt sure I could.

Despite my impatience to reach the surface, I never let the distance between indentations exceed six inches. I knew that if I fell back down, I would probably get wedged, like Chris, between the walls or be hurt worse than I already was. This was my only chance. Near the top, where the shaft widened to about three feet, I twisted my upper torso, drove the ice hammer into the lip of the crevasse at my back, and pressed my feet against the opposite wall. With one rapid movement, I levered my body over the lip and onto the surface of the glacier. It had taken an hour to ascend what turned out to be a twenty-five-foot shaft.

Nearly exhausted, relieved to be alive, I lay on the snow and gasped for breath. Raising my head to look around, I was startled by the quiet and the brightness of the sun on the broad, tilted glacier. Though I was tempted to rest a little longer, a sense of urgency made me struggle to my feet. I knew I must work fast. If I didn't get Chris out before nightfall, he would die from the cold.

From the crevasse edge, I took up the slack in the rope and pulled with all my might. He did not budge. I tried again – nothing. And again – still no movement. I would need to go back down. I tied the rope to the picket, which I pounded into the hard snow. Then I attached the rope to the jumars (with nylon slings for my feet), which allowed me to descend swiftly but safely into the crevasse.

It took me about five minutes to return to Chris. Hanging a few inches above him, I tried to hoist his pack with my hands and one good arm, but nothing budged. In the hope that changing the rope's position would make a difference, I tied it to each of the pack's accessible cross straps and pulled. But still the pack did not move. I tried to reassure Chris, but when I drove my ice hammer into the pack, all I did was move the top a few inches; then it settled back into place. I attempted to use the power of my legs to lift the pack by stepping upward in the slings. Nothing was working.

I thought that if I could open Chris's pack and empty its contents, enough pressure would be released to let him move, but when I tried tearing its tough fabric open with my ice hammer I could only make ineffectual punctures. The pack, like a block of wood in a vise, was simply too compressed. Lacking equipment with which to construct a pulley system, I could not dislodge Chris. So, after two hours of continuous effort, I stopped. 'Sorry, this isn't working,' I conceded. 'I'm going back up to try to get someone, *anyone* on the radio.'

After hauling up my pack, I retraced our tracks to a nearby knoll, where I desperately radioed for help: 'This is an emergency. Can anyone hear me? If you can, I need your help.' I repeated the message again and again, but no one answered; I never really expected a reply. In this valley, so far away from anyone who might have come, our line-of-sight radio was useless. We had set out to climb Mt. McKinley by a remote, untraveled route, and this was the price we paid. No one would come to help. We were alone.

I went back down with little hope of freeing my friend and repeated the rescue maneuvers I feared would fail. Chris's incessant pleas subsided as he gradually realized I could *not* get him out. Having planned to climb Mt. Everest with me the following year, he said, 'Climb it for me, Wick. Remember me when you're on the summit.' A classical trumpeter, Chris asked me to take his mouthpiece there. 'I don't know about me,' I replied, 'but someone will. I promise.' We spoke of his imminent death, but I could not believe that so young and vibrant a man was actually about to die right in front of me.

After asking me to relay messages to his family and closest friends, Chris entreated me to help him die with dignity. However, I could think of no way to ease his suffering or speed his death. I asked him whether he wanted his body left in the crevasse or brought out. He said his father could decide. At about 9.30, six hours after we fell into the crevasse, Chris conceded, 'There's nothing more you can do, Wick. You should go up.' I told him I loved him and said a tearful good-bye. As I began my ascent, Chris said simply, 'Take care of yourself, Jim.'

Back on the surface, physically spent, emotionally exhausted, and racked with guilt, I pulled on a parka and collapsed into my half-sleeping-bag and bivouac sack – an uninsulated nylon bag used in emergencies for protection against the wind. Lying at the edge of the crevasse, I listened to my friend grow delirious from the searing cold. He talked to himself, moaned, and, at around eleven, sang what sounded like a school song. At 2 a.m. I heard him for the last time. Chris Kerrebrock was twenty-five. I was forty.

from The Price of Adventure
by Hamish MacInnes

The Scotsman Hamish MacInnes (born 1930) helped pioneer bold rock and alpine routes in Great Britain and the Alps. When things went wrong, he and his mates relied upon grit to get through — as in this 1958 epic on the Bonatti Pillar of the Petit Dru. It featured the young Chris Bonington and the irascible Don Whillans as well as MacInnes himself.

My own tangle with the Petit Dru was in 1958. My climbing companion was Chris Bonington. We had first met up in 1953 in Scotland where we had launched assaults on hitherto unclimbed gullies and faces and later in 1957 had made a short-lived attempt on the Eiger North Wall, a route then unclimbed by a British party.

Our quixotic sortie on the flanks of the Eiger had only served to whet my appetite for Alpine firsts, but had had the opposite effect on Chris. He wanted to get an established route or two under his belt, not waste his time chasing dazzling possibilities and great last problems. So when we took up residence in a tumbledown goat herder's hut at Montenvers the following season there was a constant running argument between us, me holding out objectives like the Shroud on the Grandes Jorasses, Chris muttering about suicide routes and Highland idiots. As the weather was desperate, with heavy early-season snow, much of the great debate was academic anyway. So we sat there reasonably amicably tucking into army compo rations left over from Chris's last tour of duty with his tank crew in Germany. My contribution to the catering was for some reason twenty-five pounds of figs and a gallon of molasses, an unfortunate choice for the general atmosphere of the hut and one necessitating frequent nocturnal dashes to the shrubbery.

We eventually settled on a compromise. When the weather lifted I agreed to go on a training climb before we ventured on more serious objectives. We made the ascent profitable by de-pegging the route, that is to say, extracting all but the essential pitons, thereby making it a more enjoyable ascent for those who were to follow and bringing our ironmongery reserves up to scratch. Such is the logic of the impecunious.

Now, with a known climb under our waist loops, it was my turn, and I suggested a new line to Chris on the Pointe de Lépiney.

'Just the thing for you, Chris, bugger-all snow and lovely warm smooth granite.'

'I'll believe it when I see it,' he muttered.

Our stepping stone for this enterprise was the Envers des Aiguilles Hut, perched crazily on the south side of the Charmoz like a fairy castle, though perhaps squarer in profile. It still boasted a beautiful princess in the form of the custodian's daughter, the only person in residence. No doubt dutifully remembering the 'Auld Alliance' she took me under her wing, much to Chris's chagrin.

Our new route lived up to Chris's worst fears. Our attempt turned out to be a fiasco. We soon discovered that the reason it hadn't been climbed was because it bristled with overhangs. On one of these, after we had a frigid bivouac, Chris fell. He didn't injure himself, and consequently went back at it again with the determination of a Jack Russell terrier. He got up, only to find other overhangs sprouting above, even more menacing than the one just vanquished. After a meeting of the partnership we decided to retreat with what dignity we could muster, and I had the bright idea of descending a couloir which seemed to be the shortest distance between two points – our present position and the glacier a thousand feet below.

In an hour we were in the innards of a horrendous chimney with water beating on our heads. I had gone down first and was hanging from a peg which I had inserted with difficulty. When Chris joined me to share the only mini-foothold, we found that the abseil rope had jammed. Showing great fortitude Chris went up the rope using the painstaking technique of prusiking, using a special sliding knot which locks when weight is put on it.

The final sting in the tail of this Aiguille route was a rimaye at least ten feet wide. That's a gap between snowfield and rock face. When I abseiled down, Chris was ensconced on a mantelshelf-sized ledge above this intimidating slot like an eaglet contemplating its first flight. As the rope was long enough, I continued past him, kicking out from the last nose of rock on an overhang, and just managed to reach the snow on the far lip of the gap. It was a hairy business.

Bedraggled, we slunk down, pride hurt and bodies aching with this abortive encounter. The two young knights who peacocked about the hut on the way up now stole furtively past the door in case the shapely gardienne should spot us. Finally, to make bad worse we lost our way among the crevasses of the Mer de Glace in the dark, and what normally takes half an hour took us three.

We had now been joined in our hut by two young Austrians, after whom our abode would eventually be known as the Chalet Austria. Walter Philip was twenty-one, tall and dark with panther-lithe movements; Richard Blach, three years younger, was quiet and slightly built. Despite their youth they had done some impressive climbs in the Eastern Alps. Chris and I immediately struck up a friendship with them and we pooled our gastronomic resources. The diet of the two Austrians was almost as monotonous as ours. They had arrived with rucksacks bristling with salami and very little else. As they feared for the lifespan of their protein cylinders, I suggested they use the Mer de Glace as a refrigerator. With due solemnity they lowered the salami into the depths of a crevasse, not before I had made an exchange for some figs and molasses, and the nocturnal atmosphere deteriorated accordingly.

At last the sun struggled out and Chris and I reached an honourable solution as to our major objective. I proposed what was still regarded as probably the most serious rock climb in the Alps at the time, the Bonatti Pillar of the Petit Dru. First climbed by Walter Bonatti, who had done it in a breathtaking solo lasting five days in 1953, the South-West Pillar had been climbed four times since, but none of the parties had been British. I knew it would tempt Chris.

'The Pillar's right up your alley,' I encouraged. 'Rock most of the way and good rock at that.'

It was agreed and Walter and Richard would make it a foursome. The previous year Walter had made a fast ascent of the West Face of the Petit Dru, a 3000-foot sweep of smooth featureless granite which borders on the Pillar, and so he knew the way down, always a reassuring factor should the weather take a turn for the worse.

We were, however, at a loss where to obtain a description of the Bonatti Pillar and descended to Chamonix to recruit Donald Snell, a local sport-shop owner, to obtain this for us. We succeeded. After steak and chips at the Bar Nationale we hiked back up the cog railway to Montenvers and our shack.

This (1958) was before the days of routine helicopter monitoring, where parties are often checked each evening from the air to see if they are all right. An accident on such a climb as the Bonatti Pillar was too awful for us to contemplate, but we made a simple arrangement with the stationmaster at Montenvers next day as we left with laden sacks. We would give him a torch signal to record our progress on the climb. 'Every night at nine o'clock, André.'

There was a great feeling of relief in leaving the penned-in area of Montenvers where hundreds of multi-coloured tourists gaze at the mountains and cluster round the large pay-and-look telescopes.

We crossed the dirty slug of the Mer de Glace and climbed the steep moraine on the far bank – a hazardous business as it was then a cliff of scree. The normal bivouac for the start of both the West Face and the Bonatti route is the Rognon du Dru, a pleasantly located rock 'dwelling' comprising an overhang which, if the wind is from the right quarter, and it doesn't rain or snow, offers one-star comfort for uncomplaining alpinists.

Just before dusk we saw two figures approaching with large rucksacks. As they came closer we could see that one was almost as broad as he was tall. Like me he wore a flat cap. We immediately recognised him as Don Whillans, one of the foremost climbers of his generation and probably the greatest British alpinist ever. It was Don who had made the first British ascent of the West Face with Joe Brown. His companion now was Paul Ross, one of the English Lake District's star climbers. They had long French loaves fingering from their packs.

'How do', Don spoke. It was a gruff but neutral-sounding greeting, neither friendly nor aggressive. He gave his home-rolled fag a drag and studied us with his small beady eyes, obviously weighing us up.

'Hello, Don,' Chris responded. 'Heading for the Bonatti?'

'That's right, Chris.' Don looked steadily at me. 'I hear that you have a description of the Bonatti, Hamish.' It sounded as if I had just filched some classified documents. 'I was in at Snell's,' he added, explaining how he had gleaned this intelligence.

'Not much of a description, Don,' I returned. 'You know Bonatti is as tight with his route descriptions as a Yorkshireman with brass!'

'Aye. Well, we'll be seeing you.' Don gave another draw on his cigarette. 'It looks as if this doss is fully booked so we'll mosey up higher to see if we can find somewhere to bivy.'

We set the alarm for 2 a.m. and settled down for what sleep we could get. But that early reveille, shared by bakers and alpinists, proved to be cloudy, so we turned over and Chris soon announced with snores that he was at peace with the world.

By 5.30 a.m. the weather looked better and I gave him a shake.

'Wake up, fella, time to move.' The Austrians were already up and Walter was champing at the bit.

'Could be a good day, Walter,' I greeted, 'even though we'll be keeping office hours.'

'Ja, Hammish, we will have much fun.'

I was later to reflect on this observation.

As we entered the jaws of the couloir we could see two small figures above. Don and Paul were already roped up, but when we reached the rimaye between the lower snowfield and the rocky start to the couloir, Walter suggested that we should climb unroped to save time. We agreed, which proved to be a somewhat foolhardy decision. For, preparing to make the long stride from the snow to gain the rock, Walter fell when the lip of unstable snow which he was standing on collapsed. He instinctively threw himself backwards thereby avoiding a rapid and chilly descent into the hole. Undeterred, he jumped across and raced up the rock on the other side as if he was in four-wheel drive. There was a lot of grit and stones on the smooth granite which made it very treacherous.

In a short time we had caught up with Don and Paul and it was the classic hare and tortoise fable. Don was leading and Walter clambered past him as if he was in the fast lane, with a brief 'Good Morning'.

When Walter was just above the stoic Mancunian, he slipped and fell on top of Don, who only with considerable effort arrested Walter's fall. It was a close thing and I thought Don was most restrained. The MacInnes, Bonington, Philip, Blach combine belatedly decided to rope up!

So we emerged at the wall of the Flammes de Pierre which effectively blocks off the top of the couloir. I had been pushed into the lead for the previous few hours on the false assumption that I could cut endless steps in the hard ice. The top of the couloir was steep snow and ice and as there was only one pair of crampons in our party, steps were essential.

From the cold dark depths of the couloir, we could see the Pillar above wrapped in a golden brown with sunshine. We were elated, just as Druids must have felt when addressing the dawn.

In a slot in the rock at the very base of the Pillar, we found a walking stick, as if it had been placed in a hallstand. We never did find out who left it there. Here was the sun, its warm rays probing our bodies and rejuvenating us. But there was work to do, 2,000 feet of it, some of the most intimidating rock climbing in the Alps. Don now came into his own and for me it was the start of a long association from which my respect for him as a master alpinist grew.

'Aye, well,' he drawled, 'I think you, Walter, and your mate Richard should go in front and Paul and I can follow behind and give you a spell if you get tired.'

'Zat is all right by us,' Walter responded eagerly.

'Fine. Paul and I can do the sack-hauling up the pitches and Hamish and you, Chris, can take up the rear de-pegging.'

'Suits me, Don, I've got the 'Message'.' I brandished my large piton hammer made in a Clydeside shipyard.

In minutes the Austrians had vanished like inspired chamois. The climbing was a kaleidoscope of overhangs, cracks, dièdres, slabs and walls, all at crazy angles. None was easy and we realised that this was climbing of a high order. It had taken us five hours to get up the couloir, which was normal, but now on warm rock we were keen to make fast

time. We soon concertinaed, however. It was becoming harder and
Walter had trouble getting over a large overhang. He did this using an
étrier, a short rope ladder, which he clipped into the pegs and wedges in
a crack. Don, who was watching this exhibition of gravity defiance, told
Paul that he'd start sack-hauling here and he tackled the pitch with
deliberation. He climbed it by holding on to the pegs but instead of
continuing up the line which the Austrians had taken, which is the
normal route, he climbed directly up a groove, a new variation which was
desperately hard. When he was above, Don hauled up all our rucksacks
and Paul joined him at his stance. When it was Chris's turn to lead this
pitch, he had a struggle, but he didn't ask for a top rope, which he could
easily have had from Paul. Chris admitted to me later that it was one of
the hardest pitches he had ever led. I agreed that it was desperate and I
had the security of a top rope when it was my turn, thankful as I thrutched
upwards that I hadn't had to lead it.

Above, the climb became very exposed and the void below our
climbing boots seemed to have a magnetic quality as if trying to pull us
into the depths of the couloir. I could see Don above. He had let Paul lead
and somehow both ropes had got threaded through the karabiners with
the result that Paul couldn't now haul the rucksacks. Don had two of
these on his shoulders and was climbing an overhanging pitch free, with
his fingers hooked through the loops of the wedges. We heard him yell
for the rope to be taken in, for there was slack, probably caused by friction
through the runners. A peg he was holding on to with two fingers of his
left hand was slowly coming out, but with a burst of energy he grabbed a
small wooden wedge above and succeeded in fighting his way to the
stance. He said later that this pitch had caused him more exertion than
the rest of the climb put together.

A couple of hundred feet above, there was a pendulum move across the
wall from a flake. Actually, it was a tension traverse where we swung
across a vertical smooth wall holding on to a short rope secured to a piton
above; an exhilarating experience when there's 2,000 feet of fresh air
beneath boots that don't have anything to stand on.

After a short steep chimney we found ourselves on a luxurious ledge
and as it was now late in the afternoon we decided to call it a day. Walter

and Richard had gone up some eighty feet to a further small platform, which they informed us was quite adequate for their humble needs.

We consulted our abbreviated bible, Bonatti's description, and discovered that we had made good progress. It was obviously the wise decision to take advantage of this horizontal haven in such blank verticality. Directly above, the rock rose in one mighty sweep as high as the Empire State Building.

One of the fascinating aspects Himalayan and Alpine climbing have in common with hitting your head against a wall is that it's wonderful when you stop. Not that you hate the process of actually climbing, but when you settle down for the night in some airy bivy, you have time to reflect and collect yourself, and, if it's a good evening, soak in the view. At such times one almost feels like a bird – like Tennyson's eagle, clasping the crags, lord of all you survey. It was such a night on our bivy ledge on the South-West Pillar. The lights of Chamonix twinkled like a fairground, and across the valley above tourist-deserted Montenvers, the Grepon and Charmoz stood to attention in the twilight. My thoughts took me back to when I was a young lad traversing those peaks solo.

Actually, I was following the famous French guide, Lionel Terray, who allowed me to tag along behind him and his current client. In this way I gained alpine experience and he kept a fatherly eye on me.

That particular excursion, however, had a drastic ending. We had reached the top of the Charmoz and I was following them down in a series of abseils, when the sling I was abseiling from snapped. It had held for both of them. I fell about forty feet, fortunately stopping on a small ledge. Lionel, who was a few hundred feet lower, saw me fall and was with me in ten minutes.

I had injured both feet and my knees had jack-knifed into my eye sockets with the impact, so that I couldn't see. Lionel was obviously going to require help to get me down and after ascertaining that I could descend on a rope, decided to get me below the main difficulties and then go for help. He couldn't abandon his client though, who was looking anxious, no doubt concerned at being left on his own.

With Lionel telling me where hand and footholds were, I moved down stiffly and painfully. I could face in all right, but couldn't put weight on my heels. I could just see through a red film; but we both realised that I would have to be carried back to Montenvers. I couldn't walk on level ground. Lionel spotted the guide Raymond Lambert on the Grepon and shouted to him to come and assist. In some twenty minutes Raymond and an aspirant guide joined us. In such distinguished company I had made steady progress back down to Montenvers.

My ruminations were cut short by the need to make our 9 p.m. signal to our friendly stationmaster. In a few minutes answering flashes winked up at us. It was comforting to know that down there, across the Mer de Glace, someone cared and took the trouble to keep in touch.

Don and Paul also had their stove roaring and the aroma of soup and compo wafted luxuriously around the Pillar. It was so peaceful. I can still recall thinking that when there was a hideous cacophony of falling rocks; they were below, piling into the couloir, sending up showers of sparks. They took ages to sweep down the rock and ice of this bowling alley and presently the appetising smell of soup was replaced by the pungent smell of brimstone, a smell to me associated with death and destruction.

'Just as well that bloody lot didn't roll this morning,' Don remarked drily, 'there wouldn't have been much of us left.'

All was quiet again, even more so after that shattering interlude. Then a high-pitched whine, like a ricochet from a sniper's bullet, cut through the silence. It had that confident, predestined note, which we all felt meant it was destined for us. I was the prime target. The rock bit into my scalp like a blow from a stone axe, catapulting me forward under its impact so that I was left hanging from my belay. Momentarily I was stunned. Instinctively my hands went to my head and I could feel warm blood oozing between my fingers. I can't remember a great deal of what happened next, but I gather that Chris, who had a wound dressing in his rucksack, pressed it over the gash to stem the bleeding and tied it under my chin.

Seating arrangements were changed and we all huddled back against the wall of the Pillar, out of range of any other stray missiles. I was poised above Chris in a shallow groove and several times during the night I slumped unconscious on top of him. It was cold and I for one was in no state to think of tomorrow, but the others did. There was no question of retreat, the couloir was just too dangerous and it would have been difficult to abseil down the Pillar in any case, due to the traverses we made on the ascent.

In the morning we unfolded like newly exhumed zombies, our joints cold and stiff.

Chris asked, 'How are you feeling, Hamish?'

'Not a bundle of fun, Chris, but I'll get by.' I must have looked a mess, for Richard, who was above, sharing a perch with Walter, turned pale when he first looked down.

We had a brew and Chris suggested that Don should rope up with me as he was the strongest member of the party.

'I'll take out the pegs with Paul, Don.'

'Aye, all right.' Don looked thoughtful. 'That may be the best policy. You think you'll make it, Mac?'

'I'll have a go,' I said, trying to muster confidence. 'Not many alternatives, are there?'

The Austrians had already started and the ring of pegs being driven home echoed from the rock. Walter was fighting his way up a line of grooves which scored the otherwise smooth face of the Pillar. It was climbing of a high order and Walter demonstrated his talent for pegging by inserting each new peg at the absolute limit of his reach, and he was tall. Sometimes it was possible to get finger jams and if it hadn't been for my nocturnal mishap I could even have enjoyed it. As it was, from time to time I could feel the Dru and my surroundings slipping away from me as I lapsed into wonderful unconsciousness where, for a minute or so, all was peaceful. Don played me like a sluggish fish, not giving me an inch of slack and exerting a persistent and welcome tension, and on the hardest sections literally hauling me up.

I looked up to where Walter and Richard were spreadeagled on the smooth red wall. For the last half-hour Walter had been requesting more and more pegs.

'That's the bloody lot,' Don yelled up as he tied on the last six pitons which Chris had extracted below – a strenuous and frustrating task.

'You watch my rope, Hamish, if you can, and I'll take a mosey round the corner to the right, there must be a bloody easier way than up there.'

In a couple of minutes he came into view again, a small broad figure with his large rucksack making him look like a hunchback gorilla.

'It's this way,' he jerked a thumb, a wide grin on his face, 'up the biggest overhang in the three kingdoms.'

When I went round to join him I saw this was no exaggeration. A great roof hung over the face up which ran a crack punctuated with wooden wedges in various degrees of decay. My heart seemed to stop, for I realised that I just didn't have the reserves to climb it.

Walter was recalled, de-pegging the long pitch as he abseiled. He had put a tremendous amount of work into attempting that terrifying red wall, all to no avail.

I secured myself to a small chockstone in a daze and craned my neck backwards to where Don was now swinging from the wedges. It seemed as easy for him as climbing stairs. I had to give up watching after a time, for it hurt my head. Presently the others joined me on my small ledge.

'What's it like above?' Chris shouted up.

'A bit steep, send up some more pegs.'

'It's getting late,' Chris yelled back. 'It's almost seven o'clock and it'll soon be dark.'

I could see Don looking at his watch.

'I'll come down,' he returned. 'We can bivy on the ledges where we spent most of the afternoon.'

He pulled the two ropes up through the pegs and lowered them, where they hung out beyond us in space. When he abseiled he had to swing in and Walter fielded him and pulled him on to our ledge.

We climbed down to the wider ledges, feeling despondent that we had made so little progress that day. Don had virtually pulled me up every pitch and I was feeling a burden to the party. But it was a matter of carrying on and not giving up, and I only hoped I would feel stronger in the morning. Chris signalled to the stationmaster, just the usual signal – we were continuing.

It was a night which didn't seem to end.

I huddled in a crack above the others with a peg belay behind me because I didn't want to descend any more than I had to, and Paul sent up my dinner, two bangers, on the rope. Anyhow, I suppose in some ways

I fared better on my perch than Chris. He shared Don's bivy bag and as Don was a chain smoker and Chris a non-smoker, one puffed and the other coughed all night. We hadn't had anything to drink since the previous morning and our throats felt swollen and sore. The cold was insidious, seeking out every chink and gap in our bivy sacks and, as we were hidden from the morning sun, it took ages to sort out the frozen ropes and to thaw our boots. Breakfast was an oatmeal block which looked and tasted like plastic wood.

Don suggested to Walter that he should lead.

'I'm going to have to help Hamish up this.' He pointed a gloved finger in the direction of the roof. 'It's a bit strenuous.'

I watched Walter climb. He seemed to have tremendous drive and literally threw himself at a climbing problem; usually he got up – but not always. He later told me of his attempt on the North Face of the Cima de Laveredo, when he fell from the second pitch and plunged the total length of the rope, a fall of 300 feet. At the full extension of the nylon he just touched the scree at the base of the climb and escaped with minor injuries. I felt envious as I watched him snap off icicles to suck as he climbed the overhang.

It seemed to take me ages to get up that pitch. Don couldn't give much assistance and from time to time I passed out. It was strange coming to again to find myself swinging from a rope threaded through pegs and wedges – a reversal of the normal nightmare situation, here reality was the nightmare. Chris coming up just behind was a comfort, he described me as 'hanging like a corpse from a gibbet'.

Above the roof was another, but not so overhanging. I was part way up, thanks to Don's persistent tension on the rope, when the sun hit me. It was now the time of day when more sensible people were sitting down to lunch and there was considerable power in those life-giving rays. Before I reached Don's ledge the heat was beginning to get to me and Chris, who was still wearing his duvet jacket, found it almost unbearable. It seemed amazing in so short a span of time to suffer such extremes of temperature.

Paul was behind Chris de-pegging the overhangs. I sat recuperating while Don made a brew using ice he had found in a crack, his dixie piled up with this frozen aggregate, for it had a high gravel content. I heard a call from below and peered over the edge. It was Chris. He had reached a peg on a hard blank pitch and was feeling shattered with the combination of cold, heat and dehydration. He asked for a top rope. In a couple of minutes he had tied on to this and joined us on the ledge, his eyes lighting up when he saw the brew – even if it was only a gritty mouthful each.

It was a strange situation. There was now standing room only, as the ledge was the area of a kitchen chair and with three of us on it everything had to be done by numbers. Walter and Richard were still ahead, and from what Don told us they were having trouble route finding.

Five minutes later we heard a cry from above. It was Walter. He had found the right line and was almost at the Shoulder, he said. The top of the Bonatti Pillar was close at hand, hallelujah!

I remember finding the last pitch of the climb desperately strenuous. With each new rope length my energy had ebbed. I felt completely done in, with a dull diesel-like throb in my head, realising that I couldn't go much further. Don kept saying that each pitch was the last – the very last and definitely the last. At least he kept me moving. Lines from Hassan ran through my mind – 'Always a little further: it may be beyond that last blue mountain barred with snow.'

Not that the ultimate pitch was particularly hard. I simply seemed to have used up all my steam.

During the day we hadn't noticed that the weather was getting progressively worse. Now leaden clouds were seeping in from the south and the wind had a razor's edge to it. It didn't need a prophet to tell us that we were in for bad weather.

The snow started to fall steadily and heavily and soon everything was blotted out. I remember seeing the Grandes Jorasses being swallowed in a white froth of cloud. We bivouacked on the broken rocks close to the summit. Don knew the route over the top of the mountain, but he felt that this would be too dangerous in the present weather. Walter, on the other hand, had gone down directly from where we were when he completed the West Face route the previous year, and felt that he could find the way. But not today, or rather that evening, for it was essential to get into our bivouac sacks to avoid being frozen. In ten minutes we were tied to our pegs, tethered like cowed dogs.

It was an even worse bivy than the previous night: bitterly cold, and the fine driven snow seemed to find every cranny and tear in our bags so that we were first soaked, then frozen as if set in casting resin. Our only food was one packet of soup divided by six. There was not a great deal to be cheerful about; no joy in having climbed the route, only a numbed realisation that we had got up, but what was now much more important was to get down, and fast, for we knew that we couldn't survive long in such conditions.

We witnessed dawn through storm clouds. It was still snowing and everything was plastered: a world of white and metallic-looking ice. The ropes were again frozen solid and our plastic bivy bags, now the worse for wear, cracked like celluloid when we tried to fold them.

Walter led the descent of the West Face, abseiling into a white nothingness on slippery ropes. The wind was so strong now that we could barely communicate. We had gone down about four rope lengths when Don, who had an acute instinct for danger, called a halt.

'Walter,' he shouted, 'I think you're wrong. This is too dicey for the descent route.' Indeed it was becoming desperately steep.

The Austrians, snow-covered figures on a minuscule ledge, were another rope length down.

'I think you are correct, Don. We will try further to the right.'

But they had trouble joining us again, and when they came alongside I could see that Richard was in a bad way, suffering from exhaustion and exposure. Don and Chris had already set off on the proper descent line.

Now, for some strange reason I was feeling stronger, possibly because I was descending, which required less effort, and I was probably more used to these abominable conditions with my Scottish background of blizzard and flood than our Austrian friends.

I tried to help Richard as best I could, while Paul and Walter were preparing the abseil belays. Walter had fallen when coming up from the low point of his descent and appeared in a nervous state. Now he launched himself on the next abseil. I could see, as if in slow motion, what was about to happen but my brain wasn't working fast enough to prevent it. He had looped a sling round a sharp spike of rock so that there was no slack, and his abseil rope was threaded through this so that when he put his weight on the doubled rope the tight sling was under great strain. It snapped when he was a few feet down, but luckily Richard, who had him on a top rope, prevented a very nasty accident.

I heard a call from Don below. 'The Flammes de Pierre, Chris. We're on the right route now.'

I breathed a sigh of relief. With my revival I could now grasp the seriousness of our situation, but in fact the worst was behind us. Both Walter and Richard, who had got into such a physical and mental state, possibly through lack of food, now responded like a pair of huskies that had scented home base.

Abseil followed abseil, and with the lower altitude the wind dropped and we came out of the snow clouds. It was still miserable, but we could see the broad couloir below and shortly afterwards the hut.

We decided not to stay at the Charpoua Hut that night, but carried on in the gathering dusk to Montenvers where we ate and ate until we finally staggered off to our sleeping bags at the Chalet Austria. Above, a great storm raged in the Aiguille, but we didn't give a damn.

It was the end of my holiday for I had to return to Britain nursing a fractured skull; an injury which with its legacy of headaches and blackouts was to remind me of our Dru epic and forever make me grateful to Don, without whose help I may have remained on a lonely ledge on the Bonatti.

A Short Walk with Whillans
by Tom Patey

Tom Patey (1932–70) was a leading Scottish climber, with all that implies: boldness, irreverence, competitiveness and a perverse liking for cold, dark, horrendously difficult climbs. He's the climber many of his readers would most like to have known: sunny, sweet-natured, wildly amusing with a whip-smart prose style. Here, Patey teams up with the superbly misanthropic Don Whillans for history's most entertaining attempt on the Eiger's North Face.

Did you spot that great long streak of blood on the road over from Chamonix? Twenty yards long, I'd say.'

The speaker was Don Whillans. We were seated in the little inn at Alpiglen and Don's aggressive profile was framed against an awe-inspiring backdrop of the Eiger-Norwand. I reflected that the conversation had become attuned to the environment.

'Probably some unfortunate animal,' I ventured without much conviction.

Whillans' eyes narrowed. 'Human blood,' he said. 'Remember, lass?' (appealing to his wife Audrey), 'I told you to stop the car for a better look. Really turned her stomach, it did. Just when she was getting over the funeral.'

I felt an urge to inquire whose funeral they had attended. There had been several. Every time we went up on the Montenvers train we passed a corpse going down. I let the question go. It seemed irrelevant, possibly even irreverent.

'Ay, it's a good life,' he mused, 'providing you don't weaken.'

'What happens if you do?'

'They bury you,' he growled, and finished his pint.

Don has that rarest of gifts, the ability to condense a whole paragraph into a single, terse, uncompromising sentence. But there are also occasions when he can become almost lyrical in a macabre sort of way. It depends on the environment.

We occupied a window table in the inn. There were several other tables, and hunched round each of these were groups of shadowy men draped in black cagoules – lean-jawed, grim, uncommunicative characters who spoke in guttural monosyllables and gazed steadfastly towards the window. You only had to glimpse their earnest faces to realise that these men were Eiger Candidates – martyrs for the 'Mordwand.'

'Look at that big black bastard up there,' Whillans chuckled dryly, gesturing with his thumb. 'Just waiting to get its claws into you. And think of all the young lads who've sat just where you're sitting now, and come back all tied up in sacks. It makes you think.'

It certainly did. I was beginning to wish I had stayed at Chamonix, funerals or no funerals.

'Take that young blonde over there,' he pointed towards the sturdy Aryan barmaid, who had just replenished his glass. 'I wonder how many dead men she's danced with? All the same,' he concluded after a minute's reflection, ''t wouldn't be a bad way to spend your last night.'

I licked my lips nervously. Don's philosophic discourses are not for the faint-hearted.

One of the Eiger Candidates detached himself from a neighbouring group and approached us with obvious intent. He was red haired, small and compact and he looked like a Neanderthal man. This likeness derived from his hunched shoulders, and the way he craned his head forwards like a man who had been struck repeatedly on the crown by a heavy hammer, and through time developed a protective over-growth of skull. His name proved to be Eckhart, and he was a German. Most of them still are.

The odd thing about him was his laugh. It had an uncanny hollow quality. He laughed quite a lot without generating a great deal of warmth, and he wore a twisted grin which seemed to be permanently frozen onto his face. Even Whillans was moved.

'You – going – up?' he inquired.

'Nein,' said Eckhart. 'Nix gutt! . . . You wait here little time, I think . . . Now there is much vatter.' He turned up his coat collar ruefully and laughed. 'Many, many stein fall . . . All day, all night . . . Stein, stein.' He tapped his head significantly and laughed uproariously. 'Two nights we wait at Tod Bivouac.' He repeated the name as if relishing its sinister undertones. ('It means Dead Man,' I said to Whillans in a hushed whisper.) 'Always it is nix gutt . . . Vatter, stein . . . Stein, vatter . . . so we go down. It is very funny.'

We nodded sympathetically. It was all a huge joke.

'Our two Kameraden, they go on. They are saying at the telescopes, one man he has fallen fifty metres. Me? I do not believe this.' (Loud and prolonged laughter from the company.)

'You have looked through the telescope?' I inquired anxiously.

'Nein,' he grinned, 'Not necessary . . . tonight they gain summit . . . tomorrow they descend. And now we will have another beer.'

Eckhart was nineteen. He had already accounted for the North Face of the Matterhorn as a training climb and he intended to camp at the foot of the Eigerwand until the right conditions prevailed. If necessary, he could wait until October. Like most of his countrymen he was nothing if not thorough, and finding his bivouac-tent did not measure up to his expectations he had hitchhiked all the way back to Munich to secure another one. As a result of this, he had missed the settled spell of weather that had allowed several rivals to complete the route, including the second successful British team, Baillie and Haston, and also the lone Swiss climber, Darbellay, who had thus made the first solo ascent.

'Made of the right stuff, that youngster,' observed Don.

'If you ask me I think he was trying to scare us off,' I suggested. 'Psychological warfare that's all it is.'

'Wait till we get on the face tomorrow,' said Whillans. 'We'll hear your piece then.'

Shortly after noon the next day we left Audrey behind at Alpiglen, and the two of us set off up the green meadows which girdle the foot of the

Eigerwand. Before leaving, Don had disposed of his Last Will and Testament. 'You've got the car-key, lass, and you know where to find the house-key. That's all you need to know. Ta, for now.'

Audrey smiled wanly. She had my profound sympathy.

The heat was oppressive, the atmosphere heavy with menace. How many Munich Bergsteigers had trod this very turf on their upward path never to return to their native Klettergarten? I was humming Wagner's Valkyrie theme music as we reached the lowest rocks of the Face.

Then a most unexpected thing happened. From an alcove in the wall emerged a very ordinary Swiss tourist, followed by his very ordinary wife, five small children and a poodle dog. I stopped humming immediately. I had read of tearful farewells with wives and sweethearts calling plaintively, but this was ridiculous. What an undignified send-off! The five children accompanied us up the first snow slope scrambling happily in our wake, and prodding our rucksacks with inquisitive fingers. 'Go away,' said Whillans irritably, but ineffectively. We were quite relieved when, ultimately, they were recalled to base and we stopped playing Pied Pipers. The dog held on a bit longer until some well directed stones sent it on its way. 'Charming, I must say,' remarked Don. I wondered whether Hermann Buhl would have given up on the spot – a most irregular start to an Eiger Epic and probably a bad omen.

We started climbing up the left side of the shattered Pillar, a variant of the normal route which had been perfected by Don in the course of several earlier attempts. He was well on his way to becoming the Grand Old Man of Grindelwald, though not through any fault of his own. This was his fourth attempt at the climb and on every previous occasion he had been turned back by bad weather or by having to rescue his rivals. As a result of this he must have spent more hours on the Face than any other British climber.

Don's preparations for the Eiger – meticulous in every other respect – had not included unnecessary physical exertion. While I dragged my weary muscles from Breuil to Zermatt via the Matterhorn he whiled away the days at Chamonix sun bathing at the Plage until opening time. At the Bar Nationale he nightly sank five or six pints of 'heavy', smoked forty cigarettes, persuaded other layabouts to feed the juke box with their last few francs and amassed a considerable reputation as an exponent of 'Baby Foot', the table football game which is the national sport of France. One day the heat had been sufficiently intense to cause a rush of blood to the head because he had walked four miles up to the Montenvers following the railway track, and had acquired such enormous blisters that he had to make the return journey by train. He was nevertheless just as fit as he wanted to be, or indeed needed to be.

First impressions of the Eigerwand belied its evil reputation. This was good climbing rock with excellent friction and lots of small incuts. We climbed unroped, making height rapidly. In fact I was just starting to enjoy myself, when I found the boot. . . .

'Somebody's left a boot here,' I shouted to Don.

He pricked up his ears. 'Look and see if there's a foot in it,' he said.

I had picked it up: I put it down again hurriedly.

'Ha! Here's something else – a torn rucksack,' he hissed. 'And here's his waterbottle – squashed flat.'

I had lost my newfound enthusiasm and decided to ignore future foreign bodies. (I even ignored the pun.)

'You might as well start getting used to them now,' advised Whillans. 'This is where they usually glance off, before they hit the bottom.'

He's a cheery character I thought to myself. To Don, a spade is just a spade – a simple trenching tool used by gravediggers.

At the top of the Pillar we donned our safety helmets. 'One thing to remember on the Eiger,' said Don, 'never look up, or you may need a plastic surgeon.'

His advice seemed superfluous that evening, as we did not hear a single ricochet. We climbed on up, past the Second Pillar and roped up for the traverse across to the Difficult Crack. At this late hour the Crack was streaming with water so we decided to bivouac while we were still dry. There was an excellent bivouac cave near the foot of the crack.

'I'll have one of your cigarettes,' said Don. 'I've only brought Gauloises.' This was a statement of fact, not a question. There is something about

Don's proverbial bluntness that arouses one's admiration. Of such stuff are generals made. We had a short discussion about bivouacking, but eventually I had to agree with his arguments and occupy the outer berth. It would be less likely to induce claustrophobia, or so I gathered.

I was even more aware of the sudden fall in temperature. My ultrawarm Terray duvet failed by a single critical inch to meet the convertible bivy-rucksack which I had borrowed from Joe Brown. It had been designed, so the manufacturers announced, to Joe's personal specifications, and, as far as I could judge, to his personal dimensions as well.

Insidiously and from nowhere it seemed, a mighty thunderstorm built up in the valley less than a mile away. Flashes of lightning lit up the whole Face and grey tentacles of mist crept out of the dusk threatening to envelop our lofty eyrie.

'The girl in the Tourist Office said that a ridge of high pressure occupying the whole of central Europe would last for at least another three days.'

'Charming,' growled Whillans. 'I could give you a better forecast without raising my head.'

'We should be singing Bavarian drinking songs to keep our spirits up,' I suggested. 'How about some Austrian yodelling?'

'They're too fond of dipping in glacier streams . . . that's what does it,' he muttered sleepily.

'Does what?'

'Makes them yodel. All the same, these bloody Austrians.'

● ● ●

The day dawned clear. For once it seemed that a miracle had happened and a major thunderstorm had cleared the Eiger, without lodging on the Face. Don remained inscrutable and cautious as ever. Although we were sheltered from any prevailing wind we would have no advance warning of the weather, as our horizons were limited by the Face itself.

There was still a trickle of water coming down the Difficult Crack as Don launched himself stiffly at the first obstacle. Because of our uncertainty about the weather and an argument about who should make breakfast, we had started late. It was 6.30 a.m. and we would have to hurry. He made a bad start by clipping both strands of the double rope to each of the three pitons he found in position. The rope jammed continuously and this was even more disconcerting for me, when I followed carrying both rucksacks. Hanging down the middle of the pitch was an old frayed rope, said to have been abandoned by Mlle Loulou Boulaz, and this kept getting entangled with the ice-axes. By the time I had joined Don at this stance I was breathing heavily and more than usually irritated. We used the excuse to unrope and get back into normal rhythm before tackling the Hinterstoisser. It was easy to find the route hereabouts: you merely followed the pitons. They were planted everywhere with rotting rope loops (apparently used for *abseils*) attached to most of them. It is a significant insight into human psychology that nobody ever stops to remove superfluous pegs on the Eiger. If nothing else they help to alleviate the sense of utter isolation that fills this vast Face, but they also act as constant reminders of man's ultimate destiny and the pageant of history written into the rock. Other reminders were there in plenty – gloves, socks, ropes, crampons and boots. None of them appeared to have been abandoned with the owners' consent.

The Hinterstoisser Traverse, despite the illustrations of pre-war heroes traversing 'a la Dulfer', is nothing to get excited about. With two fixed ropes of unknown vintage as an emergency handrail, you can walk across it in three minutes. Stripped of scaffolding, it would probably qualify as Severe by contemporary British standards. The fixed ropes continued without a break as far as the Swallow's Nest – another bivouac site hallowed by tradition. Thus far I could well have been climbing the Italian Ridge of the Matterhorn.

We skirted the first ice-field on the right, scrambling up easy rubble where we had expected to find black ice. It was certainly abnormally warm, but if the weather held we had definite grounds for assuming that we could complete the climb in one day – our original intention. The Ice Hose which breaches the rocky barrier between the First and Second Ice-fields no longer merited the name because the ice had all gone. It seemed to offer an easy alley but Don preferred to stick to known alternatives and advanced upon an improbable looking wall some distance across to the left. By the time I had confirmed our position on Hiebeler's route description, he had completed the pitch and was shouting for me to come on. He was well into his stride, but still did not seem to share my optimism.

His doubts were well-founded. Ten minutes later, we were crossing the waterworn slabs leading on to the Second Ice-field when we saw the first falling stones. To be exact we did not see the stones, but merely the puff of smoke each one left behind at the point of impact. They did not come bouncing down the cliff with a noisy clatter as stones usually do. In fact they were only audible after they had gone past – wrouff! – a nasty sort of sound half-way between a suck and a blow.

'It's the small ones that make that sort of noise,' explained Whillans. 'Wait till you hear the really big ones!'

The blueprint for a successful Eiger ascent seems to involve being at the right place at the right time. According to our calculations the Face should have been immune to stonefall at this hour of the morning.

Unfortunately the Eiger makes its own rules. An enormous black cloud had taken shape out of what ought to have been a clear blue sky, and had come to rest on the summit ice-field. It reminded me of a gigantic black vulture spreading its wings before dropping like lightning on unsuspecting prey.

Down there at the foot of the Second Ice-field, it was suddenly very cold and lonely. Away across to the left was the Ramp; a possible hideaway to sit out the storm. It seemed little more than a stone's throw, but I knew as well as Don did, that we had almost 1,500 feet of steep snow-ice to cross before we could get any sort of shelter from stones.

There was no question of finding adequate cover in the immediate vicinity. On either side of us steep ice slopes, peppered with fallen debris, dropped away into the void. Simultaneously with Whillans' arrival at the stance, the first flash of lightning struck the White Spider.

'That settles it,' said he, clipping the spare rope through my belay karabiner.

'What's going on?' I demanded, finding it hard to credit that such a crucial decision could be reached on the spur of the moment.

'I'm going down,' he said. 'That's what's going on.'

'Wait a minute! Let's discuss the whole situation calmly.' I stretched out one hand to flick the ash off my cigarette. Then a most unusual thing happened. There was a higher pitched 'wrouff' than usual and the end of my cigarette disappeared! It was the sort of subtle touch that Hollywood film directors dream about.

'I see what you mean,' I said. 'I'm going down too.'

I cannot recall coming off a climb so quickly. As a result of a long acquaintance Don knew the location of every *abseil* point and this enabled us to bypass the complete section of the climb which includes the Hinterstoisser Traverse and the Chimney leading up to the Swallow's Nest. To do this, you merely *rappel* directly downwards from the last *abseil* point above the Swallow's Nest and so reach a key piton at the top of the wall overlooking the start of the Hinterstoisser Traverse. From here a straightforward *rappel* of 140 feet goes vertically down the wall to the large ledge at the start of the Traverse. If Hinterstoisser had realised that he would probably not now have a Traverse named after him, and the Eigerwand would not enjoy one half its present notoriety. The idea of 'a Point of No Return' always captures the imagination, and, until very recent times, it was still the fashion to abandon a fixed rope at the Hinterstoisser in order to safeguard a possible retreat.

The unrelenting bombardment, which had kept us hopping from one *abseil* to the next like demented fleas, began to slacken off as we came into the lee of the 'Rote Fluh'. The weather had obviously broken down completely and it was raining heavily. We followed separate ways down the easy lower section of the Face, sending down volleys of loose scree in front of us. Every now and again we heard strange noises, like a series of muffled yelps, but since we appeared to have the mountain to ourselves, this did not provoke comment. Whillans had just disappeared round a nearby corner when I heard a loud ejaculation.

'God Almighty,' he said (or words to that effect). 'Japs! Come and see for yourself!'

Sure enough, there they were. Two identical little men in identical climbing uniforms, sitting side by side underneath an overhang. They had been crouching there for an hour, waiting for the bombardment to slacken. I estimated that we must have scored several near misses.

'You – Japs?' grunted Don. It seemed an unnecessary question.

'Yes, yes,' they grinned happily, displaying a full set of teeth. 'We are Japanese.'

'Going – up,' queried Whillans. He pointed meaningfully at the grey holocaust sweeping down from the White Spider.

'Yes, yes,' they chorused in unison. 'Up. Always upwards. First Japanese Ascent.'

'You-may-be-going-up-Mate,' said Whillans, giving every syllable unnecessary emphasis, 'but-a-lot-'igher-than-you-think!'

They did not know what to make of this, so they wrung his hand several times, and thanked him profusely for the advice.

''Appy little pair!' said Don. 'I don't imagine we'll ever see them again.'

He was mistaken. They came back seven days later after several feet of new snow had fallen. They had survived a full-scale Eiger blizzard and had reached our highest point on the Second Ice-field. If they did not receive a medal for valour they had certainly earned one. They were the forerunners of the climbing elite of Japan, whose members now climb Mount Everest for the purpose of skiing back down again.

We got back to the Alpiglen in time for late lunch. The telescope stood forlorn and deserted in the rain. The Eiger had retired into its misty oblivion, as Don Whillans retired to his favourite corner seat by the window.

from Summit Fever
by Andrew Greig

Scottish poet and novelist Andrew Greig (born 1951) joined a 1984 expedition to Mustagh Tower in the Karakoram; he brought to the team no climbing experience and a healthy fear of heights, crevasses and crumbling ice towers. His book about the trip is by turns funny, uplifting and sad; this account of his training climbs in Glencoe, Scotland, is all three.

As we head north on icy roads in mid-January, Mal enthuses about the conditions. A substantial fall of snow, a slight thaw, now freezing hard. 'Glencoe will be crawling with climbers this weekend.' I'm less enthusiastic; if anyone will be crawling this weekend, it'll be me. The van heater is broken so I huddle deep in my split-new climbing gear, watching our headlights skew out across deepening snow. We don't speak much, each absorbed in our own thoughts.

I'm keyed up, anxious yet oddly elated. To shut out the cold I mentally run through everything Mal had shown me about the basic mechanics of snow and ice climbing, in the warmth of his flat a day before. It had been quite bewildering – the knots, the principles of belaying, the extraordinary array of ironmongery, the pegs, pins, channels, screws, plates, nuts, krabs, slings . . . An evocative litany but especially confusing when everything seemed to have several alternative names. This was starting truly from scratch.

I try to review it all logically. First, the harness. I smile to myself in the dark. With our harnesses belted on and the full armoury of the modern climber dangling from them, we'd looked like a cross between gladiators and bondage freaks. Then the rope; I tried to picture again the basic figure-of-eight knot used for securing the rope through the harness loops.

Then the basic sequence of events for climbing. The leader climbs up, more or less protected by his second, who's on a hopefully secure stance at the other end of the rope. When the leader reaches a secure position somewhere near the rope's full extent, he in turn protects the second who climbs up after him. Simple and reasonably safe. At least, I hoped so.

We'd rehearsed it on the passage stairs. We stood roped together at the bottom of the stairs. Mal tied a 'sling' – a loop of incredibly strong tape – through the bannister and clipped it to my harness with an oval metal snaplink, the karabiner or 'krab'. This secured my belay stance. Then he took the rope near where it came from his harness, threaded it through a friction device, a descendeur, and clipped that to my harness. Then with a 'see you at the top, youth' he solemnly walked up the stairs while I paid out the rope through the descendeur. About 20 feet up he stopped and pointed out that if he fell now, he'd fall 40 feet in total before the line between us came tight. 'So I put in a 'runner'.' He looped another sling round a bannister rail, then clipped a krab to it, with the rope running freely through the krab. If he fell now, he'd only go down twice the distance he was above the runner till he was brought up short by the tight rope between us being looped through the karabiner.

I thought about it a couple of times till the logic of it sank in. Yes, it made sense. The runner was there to limit the extent of the leader's fall.

It was at this point a woman came bustling up the stairs and gave us a very strange look.

With the merest blush, Mal continued on up, putting in a couple more runners till he got to the top. There he tied himself securely to the rail. 'On belay!' The cry floated down the spiral staircase. I unclipped the descendeur, tried to remember the appropriate call. 'Take in slack!' I shouted. He took in the rope till it came tight between us. I waited as he put his descendeur onto the rope. 'Climb when you're ready!' With some difficulty I unclipped myself from my belay stance, shouted 'Climbing!' and set off up after him.

Some 20 feet up I was going great guns, then was suddenly brought up short with a jerk. I couldn't go any further. 'Try taking out my runner,' Mal called down. Of course, the first runner was preventing me from continuing above it. I unclipped the krab, untied the sling and continued.

At the top, we shook hands most movingly.

And that seemed to be the basic principle and practice of belay climbing. I hoped I'd remembered the calls correctly. I mumbled them over a few times in the freezing van. The rest of the gear – the pitons in various shapes and guises, the screws and nuts – were for use when there was nothing convenient to loop a sling over to set up a belay stance or a runner. We'd gone around wedging them into cracks in Mal's fireplace. It had all been wonderfully ludicrous, but next time it'll be for real. How did I get into this?

After Callander the glimmering countryside grows wilder and more desolate. Long slopes suddenly swoop upwards, the snow deepens as we skirt the wilderness of Rannoch Moor and wind down towards Glencoe. As we near the infamous Clachaig Inn I think back on the last time I was here, sixteen years ago. High on adrenalin, youth and Pale Ale at 2s. 3d. a pint, I'd stood in a corner in full hippie regalia – the gold cloak, quilted tea cosy for a hat, peacock feathers, the strawberry tunic, oh my God – and thrashed out Incredible String Band songs into a small bar dense with steam, smoke and climbers so large and hairy it was hard to tell where beards ended and sweaters began. Climbers must be exceptionally tolerant, and such was the confidence of youth and the mood of the times that I got off with it, even had a few drinks bought me. Then at closing time walked out with a nurse from Glasgow into the black night to try yet again to lose my virginity, mind intoxicated with Pale Ale, adventure and the great sensed bulk of the mountains . . .

Now I can't even recognize the interior. The clientele are much the same, only now they look younger and smaller. A motley crew: Straggly hair, gaiters, training shoes, bare feet, old jeans, blue fibre-pile salopettes, bright red Gore-Tex jackets, moving from table to table talking gossip or snow conditions, arm wrestling, playing pool. A number of girls too, some looking decorative and bored, others decidedly capable.

Mal's clearly well known and respected here. A constant stream of people come up to our table. Climbers' talk. 'Tower Ridge . . . still seconding all the time . . . solid for its grade . . . knew he was going to lob, so . . . Whitesnake . . . the crux after the chockstone . . . wiped out in Peru . . .' It's all new to me, exotic and bewildering, but I sense some interesting interactions behind these casual exchanges. Allegiances and rivalries, the seeking and withholding of information, put-downs and half-acknowledged challenges. How much a casual remark such as 'I thought it a soft touch at Grade 5' can imply! It suggests that for the speaker the climb was easy, that he is familiar with *real* Grade 5s, it inquires after the listener's capability and casts aspersions on his friend who first climbed and rated the route. Just how good are you, anyway? 'I found it hard enough last time,' Mal might reply mildly. This counterstroke makes it clear that he has climbed it, and more than once, that he doesn't need to pretend a hard climb was easy to bolster his reputation . . . .

In fact, it's just like the literary world. Competition and cooperation; jostling over places in an invisible league table; ideological, personal and geographical divisions. The Aberdeen crowd here to show the others what real climbing is, the hard men up from the North of England to make their point, the Central Scotland boys protecting their patch . . . yes, very familiar.

'Who are you?' one youth asks me, uneasy he can't place Mal's new partner. 'I'm a guitar player.' Pause. 'What are you doing up here, then?' 'Learning a few new chords.' He looks baffled, scowls and retreats. Mal grins and agrees that though climbing itself may be a pure activity, there's nothing pure and disinterested about the social side of it. Everyone seems extraordinarily vague about what they're going for tomorrow.

Tony Brindle and his climbing partner Terry Dailey walk in the door. Tony's one of the lead climbers for Mustagh, the only one I've met other than Malcolm. Handshakes all round, it's good to see a familiar face. I'd seen him last at Mal and Liz's wedding, carried off to do a Dashing White Sergeant by two tall girls and grinning wildly. Even sober as now, he's still bouncy and hyper-enthusiastic. As he chatters away about past and future routes it suddenly strikes me who he reminds me of: Davy Jones of the Monkees. Small, looks as if butter wouldn't melt, innocent brown eyes, hair in a neat fringe, something about Tony makes one want to pat him on the head. He's twenty-three and looks about fifteen. I think he both resents and plays up to it. It's hard to imagine that he's recognized by his peers as having quite exceptional stamina and self-reliance. There must be steel somewhere behind that baby face. Who or what put it there?

'So where are you taking Mal tomorrow?' he asks me, for the benefit of Mal who's locked in conversation about this season's big challenges on 'the Ben', i.e. Ben Nevis.

'Oh, I don't know, we'll just poke around,' I reply in the prescribed vague manner. 'Maybe warm up with Smith's Gully and see what he's up to. Then we'll take a look at something more serious.' Now we have a few attentive ears at the next table. Mal twitches slightly but can't get out of his conversation.

Tony grins, replies in his Lancashire accent, 'Yeah, he's a bit lazy is Duff. The old fella's buggered. Still, he'll second anything you lead.'

'Thought I'd maybe give him a couple of leads if he's shaping up . . .'

Mal is saved from further roasting by the arrival of more friends I recognize from the wedding. A big boozy night that was; the climbers there all gravitated towards the corner of the room and spent the night talking about the only relevant subject at such occasions – climbing. They're obsessed, but it's an interesting obsession, for the first couple of hours at least.

And so that first night at the Clachaig rolls on. Red faces, swollen knuckles, diminishing pints, growing excitement and anticipation as hopes and plans build for tomorrow. At least they don't train on orange juice and early nights. Their regime seems to be one of alcohol, nicotine, late nights and systematic abuse, both verbal and bodily. Suits me.

I stand outside our chalet door for a few minutes before going to bed. The air is clear and cold, smelling unmistakably of snow. Clouds move across a three-quarter moon and sweep enormous shadows over the glimmering slopes across the glen. Passing voices ring hard in the frost. Orion is rising, the wind whispers over the snow, distant echoing water. I feel uplifted and self-forgetting before the irresistible forces of moon, shadow, mountains, snow. This alone was worth coming here for. I shake my head and go inside. See what tomorrow brings. Hope I'm up to it. I've been training two months for this.

The wind's gusting spindrift into our faces, but my new gear keeps me surprisingly warm as we plod up through soft, deep snow into Lost Valley. We go over ice-axe braking and the placing of 'deadmen', which are in effect snow anchors. Then the fun's over. Time to do some climbing.

My heart thuds wildly as we gear up, I have to force myself to breathe slowly and deep. Concentrate. I buckle on the harness, tie in the rope, get the knot right on the second attempt. Then strap the crampons onto my cumbersome rigid-soled double boots. The crampons are like heavy-duty running spikes, with two additional fangs projecting out in front. Then I sort out my two ice axes. Both have sharply inclined picks with teeth notched towards the tip; the head of one ends with a hammer for knocking in and removing pitons, while the head of the other ends in an adze for cutting steps. Apparently this is largely redundant, as the combination of front-pointed crampons and inclined picks make step-cutting unnecessary in most situations.

I feel absurd and overburdened, like a deep-sea diver in a paddling pool, as I follow Mal up the steepening slope. It's not steep enough – he says – to merit belaying. I keep my gaze determinedly at my feet. Slip, flurry, recover. Continue. Untangle these stupid axes. Stop tripping over the crampons. Up and across, don't like traverses, getting pretty high now. Don't look, watch your feet, time for doing, not thinking. How clear the sounds are: scrape of crampons on rock, scrunch of boots in snow, jingling harness, echoing wind, a faint mewing cry . . .

We look up and spot a figure waving awkwardly further up John Gray's Buttress. 'Looks like he's got gripped,' says Mal. 'Kick yourself a ledge and wait here.' I feel a moment's pleasant superiority over the incompetent up ahead, then a surge of fellow feeling. Mal tries to persuade him to climb down, but the shake of the head is vehement even from here. I look down. Safe enough really, but just the same . . . Mal climbs further up, secures a belay. In crabbed, awkward movements the man picks his way down. When he finally passes me, he's white-faced and embarrassed. 'Snow's tricky in patches,' he mutters apologetically. I agree politely.

A shout from Mal. He's waving me up towards a ledge on the left beside a steep drop into a narrow gully, then adds something I can't catch. By the time I reach the ledge, he's disappeared. The rope runs over the edge into the gully, then drops out of sight. I wait. And wait. And wait.

Thirty minutes later there's still no sign of him and the view downhill is beginning to impinge on me, nagging like a toothache. I shout tentatively, feeling foolish. No answer. Adrenalin wears off and muscles stiffen. Now what? Don't think. Wait. Odd feeling alone up here . . .

He finally appears below me, plodding up the hill looking puffed and not very pleased. 'Dropped my glove belaying that wazzock, it slid right to the bottom of the gully.' I ask what had happened to the man he'd rescued. 'Gripped,' he says shortly and indicates our next line. A traverse right across a distinctly steep snow slope. He sets off. Looks like I'm not going to be belayed. I've had a lot of time to get nervous and don't like the look of it, but follow on gingerly, thinking about avalanche, about falling . . .

I reach his stance, a narrow ledge beside a boulder, panting hard. Nerves, mostly. 'Right, better clip in now, Andy.'

I put him on belay through the descendeur as we rehearsed on his stairway a lifetime ago. He checks my gear, goes over the call sequence and disappears round the corner. One day all of this will seem normal. I peer round to see where he's making for and find myself looking down the throat of an apparently sheer snow chute. I look away, feeling ill. How did we get so high? This fear is like seasickness, invading mind and body. Hands tighten, stomach lurches, legs feel weak, stare fixedly in front . . . 'gripped' is the right word for it. One grips and is gripped by an enormous fist of fear. I can't do this. I'll have to cry off the Expedition. What a farce. Then angry at myself, at this instinctive fear and revulsion. A clinking sound drifts faintly back. He must be putting in a runner. Good man. Put in a dozen. Stare at the weave in my gloves, the powder snow caught in the cuff of the windsuit. All sharp and vivid, too clear. 'I'll put you in controlled freak-out situations,' Mal had said. 'You freak out and I'll control them.' He knows what he's doing. You trust him, don't you? Yes. So nothing to worry about, just don't make an ass of yourself . . .

The rope stops paying out. I start untangling myself, take off the descendeur and clip it to my harness. The slack's taken in, then tugs come down the line. If only we had to face just one moment of truth, not many. Here goes . . .

'Good enough, youth.'

I arrive at Mal's stance and subside, jittering with adrenalin. I've just learned that waiting is worst; climbing itself is too novel, too demanding and intense to leave much room for anxiety. Or for memory. Already the last twenty minutes are reduced to a floundering through whiteness, stinging knuckles caught between axe shaft and rock, a flurried impromptu tango when my crampons interlocked, a hurried pull-up, the surge of satisfaction when the pick thuds into frozen turf. All so clumsy and unfamiliar, but something in this lark, perfectly safe really . . .

Then I look down and that anxiety that is like drowning rushes up to my throat. We're poised out on the edge of space. Horrible. Unnatural. I shrink back into the slope. Mal points out matter-of-factly that the crampons can't grip properly this way. Clinging to the slope actually increases the likelihood of falling. I point out this may well be true and would make a sound Buddhist parable, but every instinct in my body shouts at me not to stand upright.

By now the weather's deteriorating fast; a greenish-grey sky and each gust fiercer than the last. And the pitch above us isn't filled in with snow and ice – Mal points it out, I shudder and try to sound regretful when he decides we've done enough for today. And oddly enough, I suddenly am. He belays my descent along a ridge and down the sheerest slope yet. Perhaps because down is the right direction, I enjoy it and even find the blinding spindrift exhilarating. Then turn outwards and step-plunge down, feeling positively elated. Great to be in the hills, feeling oneself so physically immediate, so simple . . . And there's something pleasing in the essence of winter climbing; a rope, axes, crampons, things to wedge in cracks, and with these one can go almost anywhere, in reasonable safety. Pointless maybe, but satisfying. And I like the way in which, quite unlike rock climbing, routes appear and disappear, may only exist for a few days every other year, are never the same twice.

In the valley we find an ice slab and mess around on that, reluctant to pack in for the day. Vertical and all of 12 feet high. My first fall of the day leaves me dangling helplessly from one axe wrist-loop, unable to go up or down, feet six inches off the ground, cursing a Duff helpless with laughter.

As we plod back, the wind redoubles. The combination of spindrift and fresh snow forms drifts in minutes. A couple of gusts simply knock us over. It's exhilarating. We do not know this is the beginning of the worst blizzard for years in the Highlands and that five climbers will be dead before it's through.

That evening in the Clachaig the sense of siege and drama mounted like the storm outside as one group after another staggered in, redfaced, dazed, plastered from head to foot, head torches making them look like negatives of miners. I floundered through chest-high drifts to our chalet, passed two tents reduced to mangled poles and shreds of material. And this on the sheltered floor of the valley. Rumours spread rapidly. All roads out blocked . . . sixteen head torches still on the hill . . . Mountain Rescue team on four calls at once . . . Hamish MacInnes stranded in his Land-Rover . . . someone's taken a fall, broken his collarbone . . . We drank on, increasingly aware of Tony and Terry's absence. They'd left at 5 a.m. to go to Ben Nevis. Mal was quite confident in them, but still kept glancing at his watch.

Finally, round 10.30, a small and a tall figure pushed wearily through the door. They looked as if they'd been tested in a wind tunnel, a mangle, a car wash, then hit repeatedly over the head for hours with a particularly substantial edition of Being and Nothingness. Which turned out to be pretty much the case as, drinks in hand, eyes still unfocused, they recounted their epic day. They'd succeeded in doing Vanishing Gully in appalling conditions ('Very vertical,' said Tony, eyes wide at the memory of it, 'very'), abseiled off Tower Ridge where their lowered ropes flew straight up in the air like snakes charmed by the banshee howl of the wind, and made it to the CIC hut, mostly on hands and knees. There, unbelievably, they were refused shelter because they were not members of the Scottish Mountaineering Club, so they had to continue. From the hut to the road, normally an hour's walk, had taken them six and a half hours of tumbling, rolling, swimming, crawling, through a world gone berserk. 'I once took two and a half hours on that walk,' Mal said, 'and the conditions were desperate. For Tony to take six and a half hours . . .' He shook his head. Terry was slumped back, pale now, staring into his pint, completely drained. Tony was starting to recover, and entertained us with the absurdity of nearly being wiped out crossing the golf course ('Thought we might set a new record'), finally being slammed up against the fence ('I thought I was going to come out the other side as mince!'), getting to the car and realizing they'd have to dig it out. Then they'd driven through the blizzard, abandoned it on the road, and battered their way through to the Clachaig on foot.

A definite epic, a tale worth surviving for the telling of it. And sitting in that besieged inn in the wilderness, packed with dripping, excited, exhausted climbers, thinking back on the day and listening to the stories go round, I began to see something of what brings them there. Anxiety, adrenalin, physical endeavour, the surge of exultation; a day locked into the mountains, evening in the company of fellow nutters – after this, any other way of spending the weekend would be simply dull.

And one doesn't have to be a top-level climber to feel this. At any level the rewards and apprehensions are the same. This is what makes them risk life and limb, scrape, borrow, hitch, neglect work, lovers, family, the future. The moment you commit yourself to the next pitch all those ghostly chains of everyday worries fall away. Lightness in the midst of fear; all that exists is the next move, the mountain, and your thudding heart.

Come closing time we are invited into the Snug bar among the late drinkers. Something of a ceilidh starts; guitars come out and the songs go round. And looking round I suddenly see how this was the original bar I'd walked into sixteen years before. The door must have been here, the fireplace there. I see again the dartboard, the Pale Ale, my Glasgow nurse, myself singing out my teenage years into the hubbub of men. The place is recognizable though overlaid with changes. Me too. For a moment I long to go back, to have that night again, though I know I carry it inside me. Then one of the women's voices, trained and beautiful, lifts in a haunting Gaelic lament, and in the moment's silence at the end we are all briefly bound together by the silken, invisible rope of her song.

Next morning I helped Tony and Terry dig out their car. As we slithered towards Glencoe Village the car radio spoke of 2,000 people trapped in Glenshee, marooned trains, three climbers found dead in the Cairngorms . . . Tony and Terry glance at each other, the slightest shake of the head. Nothing is said. It could have been them but it wasn't.

At the village I waved them goodbye and plodded to the monument to the Massacre of Glencoe. It's a simple pillar of stone on a hillock near the river. The inscription was unreadable, being plastered with spindrift. I thought of the sign in the Clachaig: NO HAWKERS NO CAMPBELLS. Life was precarious enough in those days, no need for mountaineering. Climbing has some of the adrenalin, the release, and the self-discovery of combat; the difference is you're not being asked to kill anyone, and you take no orders but your own. But war and climbing partake of the same odd quirk in our nature – only when our survival is at risk do we feel how precious it is to be alive. Tony and Terry's silence came not from callousness but an acceptance of the risks involved.

Mal spent most of the day in his sleeping bag, looking haggard and listening to Frank Sinatra on his Walkman. Apparently last night's session went on long and late. We ate and slept, marking time. Climbers came, gossipped, picked up their gear and left. Towards evening the snow came down again, thick and swirling.

We went over to the pub for one beer, had several, and found ourselves having a long and surprisingly personal talk about our lives. Our paths have been so different, yet there are parallels. It's hard to imagine now, but Mal worked in insurance in London for five years. 'Then one day I looked around me, a long, slow look at all the familiar faces reading the papers or looking out the window, and I saw they were only existing, not living. And if I carried on, I'd be like that in another five years. I thought, screw that for a lark. I handed in my notice to quit that day.' He stared down at his lager with his characteristic frown, part impatience, part perplexity. 'That's why I could relate to you from the beginning, because somewhere along the line you've chosen not to live like most people.'

I nodded, knowing the unlikely kinship he meant. The turning point in my life had not been as sudden and clear as his. My dissatisfaction with the life I was leading some years ago grew slowly and unnoticed like an overhanging cornice until finally I fell through. I kept on writing because there was nothing else.

And the unhappiness we spread around us on the way makes it all the more important that we do it well.

Climbing and writing seem poles apart, but we had both rearranged our lives round a supremely satisfying central activity that seems pointless to many – sometimes to ourselves. We were both now doing what we wanted. That was our basis for mutual respect. That night he called out in his sleep, 'It's too late now.' And then, 'Better put some more runners in, Andy.'

Next morning loose snow still ruled out serious climbing. We spent it working on setting up runners and belay stances, and abseiling. There's something absolutely unnatural in walking backwards off a cliff. I found it also – when you're sure of the rope and the belay – surprisingly enjoyable. Just lean back and walk down, paying out rope through the descendeur. Pleasingly ingenious.

I spent some time on placing aids. Hammering pitons (blades, leapers, bongs, angles, channels, pegs, the wonderfully named RURPS – Realized Ultimate Reality Pitons) into cracks; wedging nuts (wedges, wires) into fissures. 'I lost a couple of friends here last year,' Mal remarked conversationally, fumbling with something on his harness. I didn't know what to say, made some sympathetic sound. 'They're worth nearly twenty quid now,' he continued. I stared at him. I know this is an age that sets a price on everything, but this is ridiculous. 'And even this one is a bit knackered,' he said, and held out a strange object to me with just the faintest hint of a grin.

It looked like a piece of particularly nasty dental equipment, like an adjustable wrench with its jaws turned inside out. They were spring-loaded so one could pull them back, shove them into a crack and then let them expand to grip the walls.

'It's called a 'friend'. Not totally reliable, but very useful at times.'

We went through the belaying sequence on the floor of a quarry. I was cumbersome and ponderous as I stumbled along pretending there was a 1,000-foot drop on my right, placing runners along the rock on my left. When I shouted 'On belay!' my voice sounded absurd and lacking in conviction, like the first time you try to hail a taxi or call 'Waiter!'. Mal followed on round the corner, walking slowly, treating this charade with elaborate seriousness. He came to the first runner, removed the peg – then abruptly fell back. I instinctively pulled the rope back on the descendeur and he was held. He came on again, head down. When he arrived at my stance he looked up, shook his head. 'Whew, that was a bit thin, youth!' We laughed. It was a game. The whole activity is an absurd and sometimes delightful game.

He led through and we did a couple of pitches on genuine slopes. It's clever and simple, this whole procedure, each climber alternately protecting the other. I was still getting tangled up and several times hit myself on the helmet with an ice axe, but it was beginning to feel more natural. Finding out what crampons can do, working out different moves, reading the slope ahead. The last pitch was a scramble; the snow deep and powdery, no purchase in it, then loose and shallow over rocks. Spindrift blowing up into my face, balaclava slipping over my eyes. The left axe pulled through and I was off balance, hacking away wildly for purchase, slipping . . . an internal voice spoke very clearly, 'Slow down, look for it.' I spotted frozen turf, the inclined pick went in and held. Lovely. Pull up, across, come out on the top and find Mal sitting patient and immobile as a Buddha, wrapped in a cloak of spindrift.

We finished up by building a snowhouse. It was more of a beehive than a classic igloo, but the shelter it provided was impressive. Absolutely silent and windless inside. 'If those missing Army blokes have made one of these and stay in it, they'll be all right for days.'

Back in the gloaming, in high spirits, for tea and the latest disaster stories. A few casualties, but no fatalities in Glencoe. In the evening I borrowed a guitar and sang a few songs I'd written years before to go with my *Men on Ice*. Mal was very taken with them, insisted I put them on tape, and spent much of the rest of our time in Glencoe wandering about with the earphones on, bawling out the lyrics. When he was over in the pub I wrote some new verses to *Throw me down some more rope*, and a middle section. Mal was amazed on his return. 'How can you do that?' 'How can you solo Grade Five?' I replied. It was good to be reminded there were things I could do competently.

'We'll try a harder route tomorrow,' he said as I crawled into my bag. I lay thinking about that as he muttered over a new verse and the chorus, trying to memorize the words:

> *Halfway up 'Whitesnake' when the blizzard hits,*
> *Can't feel your nose or your toes, everything goes*
> *And nothing grips (except you);*
> *It's a funny desire, wanting to get higher,*
> *Sometimes you wish you'd stayed below,*
> *Sometimes you know that it's right,*
> *Sometimes you know that it's wrong,*
> *And sometimes you just Don't Know –*
> *Throw me down some more rope (throw me down)*
> *Throw me down some more rope (hey, youth!)*
> *Throw me down some more rope 'cos I'm falling,*
> *Yes I'm falling . . .*

We set out in the half-light. No cloud, no wind, blue sky filtering through. The high ridges slowly become three-dimensional as we plod up the road in silence, our senses sharp and clear as the air. A flock of sheep freshly out of a snowdrift are encrusted with icicles; as they move, a delicate tinkling like wind chimes sounds across the valley. A buzzard circles into high sunlight, drifting on invisible currents. Three crows beside a frozen stream tear at a dead rabbit. Glencoe goes about its immemorial business.

It was a long day that, on the north face of Aonach Dubh, but only fragments of it remain lodged in the memory, like slivers of ice caught in a windsuit's creases. I was too caught up with what was happening to record, too present to stand back, too scared to take photographs.

The first pitch up a narrowing snow-choked gully made the first day's efforts seem child's play. Relief and exhilaration on arriving at Mal's stance, then half an hour clinging to a stunted rowan tree, fighting off paralysis and panic, hating it. Sitting still is the worst. Time to take in where you are, time to think, time to fear. I look down – too far, too steep, too empty. I glance up – too high, too steep, too endless. Contemplating going on this Expedition is absurd. My body hates this. Don't look, don't think. Keep the rope going. Where's Mal got to? If you think this is bad, imagine the sense of exposure on Mustagh . . . Extraordinary clarity of lichen on this branch, the precise angle of this fork. . . .

It's a relief to be climbing again, traversing onto a buttress of steep rock, soft snow, patchy frozen turf. Gloves off, treating some of it as a rock climb, half-remembered techniques from childhood scrambling. Chunks of knuckle left on rocks, arms with all the resilience of blancmange. Concentrating hard, each movement dreamlike in its intensity. I call for tight rope and get it. Thanks, pal. Over a bulge, there he is . . .

Another anxious wait on belay, then another pitch. It's beginning to feel more natural. I cease tying myself up in Gordian knots of slings, rope, krabs and ice axe lines. Even relax enough to snatch a photo as Mal works his way up an angled cleft above me. After two hours fear starts to lose its urgency, and though I know this pitch is tricky by my standards I push up through soft snow, cross onto rock, find some lovely frozen turf and almost shout with satisfaction as the picks thud home. Hold an elephant, that would. Now pull up . . . Something in this lark, after all.

Until you pause and catch a glimpse of below.

An hour and two pitches later we come out on top of the ridge. I'm shattered, puffing like an old espresso machine, arm muscles like wet newspaper from working above my head all the time. In addition to the long approach plod, then the physical effort of climbing, I've put out enough energy to light up Glencoe village for a year. But the weather is menacing and the light starting to go, so Mal hurries on and I plod after. We pause on the summit of Aonach Dubh – briefer than a kiss is this final pay-off, that's the joke of it.

Mal points down No. 2 Gully. 'Follow me as fast as you can – but concentrate.' I sense a certain urgency in his voice, and follow him down in the half-light. It seems steep, but I haven't the energy to care. Step, plunge, axe, step, plunge . . . it becomes endless, unreal, hypnotic. I begin to stumble, stuff snow in my mouth to stay awake. Somewhere along the line a crampon disappears. No time to look for it, carry on . . . I seem to have been doing this forever, stepping down through the gathering dark. In the distance Mal swings right and up onto a buttress. Eventually I join him. 'Well done,' he says briefly. Must have been harder than it looked. It's getting very dim now. We start feeling our way down over rock, scree and snow towards the yellow lights in the valley.

Finally his urgency relaxes, the rest is straightforward. We sit for five minutes on Dinnertime Buttress, munching biscuits and looking over at the glimmering slopes across the glen. We say nothing, but it is many months since I felt so at peace. 'What was that route called?' 'We can decide that in the pub,' he replies casually. Understanding comes slowly. 'You mean you . . . we . . . ?' I splutter. He nods. 'I'd been saving that one up for a while.'

A new route for my first route. I'm outraged, flabbergasted, and not a little chuffed. Of course it wasn't hard – Grade 2 or 3 he reckons – and all I did was follow on, but the sense of delight and absurdity sustain me on the rest of the trudge back. 'Two Shakes' I say finally. 'Why?' 'Well, there was two tree belays on it, there's two parts to it – the gully and the buttress – and I'm lying about the amount of shaking I did!'

Finally, we push through the door of the Clachaig into a gust of warmth and light and laughter. Then the simple wonder of sitting down. We've been on the go for eleven hours. I slump back against the wall, totally blank.

'Tired, youth?' Mal asks.

I search for the right epithet.

'Massacred,' I say briefly, and with some effort raise the first pint of the night to my lips.

● ● ●

We left Glencoe two days later. I was relieved yet oddly regretful as the old blue van struggled out of the valley. Five days in this place had been a month of normal time. Grinding and slipping past abandoned cars, cottages up to their eyelids in snow, a snowblower moving across the wilderness of Rannoch Moor, followed by a tiny man in yellow oil-skins . . .

We were silent as we worked our way south toward civilization and its dubious benefits. What had happened to me here, what had I learned? The extent of my fear, for one thing. It hadn't miraculously evaporated over the intervening years, like teenage acne. I felt weakened by that fear, yet strengthened for having coped with it. Perhaps one can never overcome fear completely – after all, it is often a sane and appropriate response – what counts is that it doesn't overcome you.

Being a novice climber is like having a weak head for alcohol: people may laugh at you, but you get high more easily. It didn't take much to get my heart thumping, whereas Mal has to push it a long way to get his kicks. Both novice and expert have the same experience, despite the huge gulf in their capabilities. Both know fear, exhilaration, satisfaction, relief. Both have to persist through discomfort and utter fatigue. Both have to recognize their limits, then push a little further. And both experience the great simplification of one's life that is the reward of all risk activities . . . But I was thinking most of all about the two Army lads who were found dead today in the Cairngorms, and of the half-buried monument to the Massacre of Glencoe. Our 'massacre' by the elements is a self-imposed one, a piece of personal theatre. When it is over, all but a few get to their feet again and feel themselves, behind their fatigue, somehow stronger and more alive than before.

For those who do not rise again, there remains the unyielding pillar of stone, the inscription obliterated by drifting snow.

from Stories Off the Wall
by John Roskelley

John Roskelley (born 1948) was among the strongest American mountaineers of his generation, with pioneering ascents of the Great Trango Tower, Dhaulagiri, and Makalu. His forthright personal style earned him respect and generated controversy among climbers. That style marks the best of his writing, including this account of a 1979 ascent of the imposing Uli Biaho in the Karakoram.

Blocky and angular, like a chunk of black marble chipped and molded by Michelangelo, the six-foot-two marine sergeant embodied his corps' credo, 'The Few, The Proud, The Marines.' Even his United States Marine Corps fatigues, called 'baggies' by most recruits, fit him like a Hong Kong suit.

'You!' he commanded, 'get your feet down.' There was none of this 'Please' or 'Thank you.' And there didn't need to be.

I followed the direction in which his oversized meathook was pointing. There slumped America's premier rock climber, Ron Kauk, lying in his theater seat, legs crossed, feet over the back of the seat before him, waiting for the night's movie, *Warriors*, to begin.

Kauk, a Cochise look-alike with his shoulder-length, thick brown hair, kept in check with his trademark folded bandana, turned his head in slow motion and squinted at the sergeant with a glint in his dark eyes that said, 'Maybe I will, maybe I won't.' Then, at that same speed, he removed his feet and sat up. From my seat on the aisle, I could hear the sergeant's breath quicken, as if air were a precious commodity. His carotid arterial cords dilated to the width of a climbing rope and threatened to explode as he contemplated action. Then his eyes closed, reptile-like, as he searched his memory for another one so insolent. The sergeant hadn't seen this long-haired creep before. Not around the American Embassy compound, and certainly not in all the days he had been in charge of operating the embassy's movie theater in Islamabad. The sergeant disappeared.

Kauk went back to jostling and kidding two sixteen-year-old embassy-employee daughters sitting next to him, while I caught a full breath. That coal-black marine, with muscles in his face bigger than my biceps, had me on the edge of my seat. The lights dimmed to match my loss of enthusiasm, and *Warriors* began.

The credits were still unraveling unknown actors when Kauk again raised his feet to the back of the seat before him. He hadn't even lowered into a full theater seat slouch when a rock-hard quadriceps bumped my elbow. It was the marine.

'YOUUUU! COM'ERE!' the marine bellowed. 'NOWWWW!'

Kauk pointed to himself as if to say, 'Little ol' me?', stood up, then crab-legged to the aisle and into the waiting grip of his accuser. Acting as if Kauk were cholera-ridden, Kim Schmitz and I squeezed into our seats and let him pass unobstructed. Despite the ruckus of New York street gangs fighting on screen, boisterously loud music, and solid oak lobby doors, the Marine Corps sergeant's earsplitting dressing down of Kauk reached the audience.

'What are you going to do?' Schmitz asked.

It is circumstances such as the one then before me that separate a true expedition leader from your classic load-carrying, mountain-climbing grunt. Should I interfere? Negotiate? Order a team attack? After all, I was leader of the American Uli Biaho Expedition, and with that came certain responsibilities.

'Nothing,' I replied. 'He got his butt into it, let him get his own butt out.'

Schmitz grunted an affirmative. He recognized leadership when he heard it. Kauk, with a cowed appearance and, perhaps, temporary hearing loss, eventually retook his seat. His feet stayed glued to the floor.

The 1979 American Uli Biaho team of Kauk, Schmitz, Bill Forrest, and myself, a unit I hoped would mold into perfection by the sum of its four parts, arrived in Islamabad, Pakistan, as distinct individuals. Each of us had at least one thing in common – climbing – but life-styles, work ethics, and a generation gap were question marks in regard to compatibility.

I sought the best climbers for Uli Biaho. Two years earlier, five American alpinists, Dr. Jim Morrissey, Galen Rowell, Dennis Hennek, Schmitz, and myself, had been the first to climb to the summit of Great Trango Tower in the midst of the Karakoram Range. As I turned to belay Morrissey to the sun-baked summit, a sabertooth-shaped peak across the Trango Glacier jolted that spot in my brain reserved for nightmares, or those 'challenges' best kept to my dreams.

'Galen, what's that peak across the glacier?' I asked. Rowell, one of America's best mountain photographers and a walking, breathing, mountain encyclopedia, knows the name, height, known attempts, and successful summits of every peak visible on the horizon and beyond.

'Uli Biaho,' he replied. 'The French attempted a route in 1976, but so far it's unclimbed.'

I wasn't interested in avoiding any difficulties or following a path. I wanted the face before me, the East Face – vertical, ledgeless, yet shot with Yosemite-like crack systems. It would be a climb like El Capitan, but at altitudes up to 20,000 feet, with extreme mountain weather, zero possibility of rescue, a 4,000-foot unexplored route, and an insane, 4,000-foot approach through a 100-yard-wide glacial combat zone shot with climber-seeking missiles to Uli Biaho's rock base. Seemed reasonable to me.

Standing on the summit of Great Trango Tower after three days of struggle, Uli Biaho seemed another light-year ahead of my time. But a seed of hope fell on fertile soil – soil thick with experience, rich in desire, and at the right time in my life to foresee a destiny. Uli Biaho would feel my boots.

Uli Biaho demanded a team. T-E-A-M: A group of people organized for a particular purpose. Not a P-A-R-T-Y: A group of people out for fun and games.

Too many American expeditions organize a party and expect to put one together that works, functions, and performs. What drives me to pursue a peak or route may not drive another, equally motivated climber. Not only did I have to find three more compatible individuals to make a team of four, but each had to possess skills that, when added to those of the others, would lead to success.

I first heard of Kim Schmitz from my two-years-to-the-wiser sister, Pat. 'Miss Liberal University of Washington,' as I referred to her, dated Schmitz's best buddy, Jim Madsen. Schmitz and Madsen, both six-foot-plus, broad shouldered, and muscular, were stunning the California climbing locals in the late 1960s by setting speed records on Yosemite's big walls. Their team ended abruptly in 1969, when Madsen, on a false-alarm rescue, made the first free descent off the top of El Capitan. Another speed record of sorts. Schmitz overcame Madsen's untimely death and went on to set climbing standards in Yosemite Valley for another decade.

Schmitz was difficult to get to know in Yosemite, where he was a guru of sorts, but as Pat's little brother I did receive a nod or two as I endeavored to climb the 'classics.' In early September 1971, after earning my stripes on the Dihedral Wall on El Capitan and other big walls, I asked him if he wanted to climb the North American Wall.

'Nope,' Schmitz declined. 'I'm trying to do all my El Cap routes in two bivouacs or less.'

His point was made. My Dihedral Wall partner and I had taken six days to succeed. I wasn't quite up to the guru's legacy. It didn't matter. Mead Hargis, another superb climber living in the Valley, and I flashed the climb, considered the hardest rock climb in the world at the time, in a little over two bivouacs. Schmitz no longer just nodded a greeting.

Our first climb together was on Trango Tower in 1977. Schmitz and I teamed up in the streets of Rawalpindi and bonded on the trek along the Braldu River to Trango. His habit of quiet introspection was unnerving at times, as if talk was for those who had nothing to say. If I wanted to know how to take a 'Schmitzification,' one of his tactless attempts to sum up a usually ridiculous situation, I would search his eyes. His large cheekbones and strong Germanic chin could have been chiseled in stone, but Schmitz's turquoise blue eyes were as easy to read as the next weather pattern in the sky. Schmitz wanted Uli Biaho.

As good as Schmitz was on big walls, I still wanted one of the younger Yosemite big-wall rock specialists on the team. There was a gang of them, like the Lost Boys in *Peter Pan*, living and breathing rock climbing all year round in the Valley, pushing vertical limits only the birds thought were possible. Ron Kauk was the best of these free-spirited athletes that only an Olympic gymnastic coach could appreciate.

To perform high-angle gymnastics on rock takes a high strength-to-weight ratio. Kauk, at 150 pounds and five feet nine inches of Jimmy Dean lean, was perfectly proportioned, plus he had the flexibility of a Labrador retriever and the grace and balance of Rudolf Nureyev. But it takes more – a lot more – to be the best. It takes the big D – Desire – and Kauk had that too.

He bouldered for hours each day; worked out in the makeshift Camp IV gym of hanging ropes, tilted boards, and balance chains; and practiced on past horror routes, while attempting and succeeding on next-to-impossible cracks. Given another athletic direction in life, Kauk could have been an Olympic champion in any sport. As it was, he lived with other Camp IV 'regulars,' hunted for food, bummed a buck or two, and worked part-time when convenient.

Kauk reminded me of me, except that I didn't have the guts when I was a kid to walk away from society's burdens. He did. We're raised to accept direction from our parents and society based on what's 'good for you'. But Kauk didn't listen. Why be another generic graduate who regurgitates generic information? He wanted the clean Yosemite air, not L.A. smog; friends who understood the freedom of rock climbing, not social clubs and lettermen sweaters; time to excel, taste adventure, and be himself.

I liked Kauk instantly. To survive year after year in Camp IV takes ingenuity, intelligence, and an easygoing attitude. Kauk had it all, plus a personality that said, 'Relax, life's to enjoy, so let's have some fun.' There was one enigma. Would he be there on departure day? The granite in Yosemite in June is warm and beckoning, and there's always the chance that a day's stunt work for a movie crew might come along, enough work to let him live for another year in the Valley. Was his commitment there? Schmitz was worried. And, since I didn't know Kauk, except for a brief telephone conversation, that had me worried.

'Kauk doesn't take to responsibility,' Schmitz said. 'We've got to find someone who will put him on the plane and organize him.'

'I'll get on it,' I promised, despite the impossible task. 'Meanwhile it's your job to keep him pumped up.'

I studied the team. It had everything – strength, experience, depth, youth . . . Wait, there it was. Youth needs balance. I needed someone on the other end of the climbing spectrum. Schmitz and I would be in Nepal climbing Gaurishankar prior to making our way to Pakistan. Our two teammates would have to finish organizing the Uli Biaho Expedition in the States, then meet us in Rawalpindi. To get Kauk to Asia, on time, with expedition money and equipment, I needed someone with all our skills . . . plus maturity. That's a tall order in any sport. But in climbing? No way.

Then Bill Forrest came to mind. *The* Bill Forrest of Forrest Mountaineering, a profitable business. *The* Bill Forrest of the Black Canyon of the Gunnison. *The* Bill Forrest who may have introduced Fred Beckey to mountaineering. He'd been around long enough. Bill Forrest was my answer to pre-trip organization once I left the States, and the key to getting Kauk away from Yosemite, on the plane, and in Pakistan on 31 May. Forrest was the only mature climber I knew who was capable, and perhaps willing, enough to go with three yahoos like us. He said yes.

F-O-R-R-E-S-T. That's how I spelled relief. I intended to have most of the expedition financed and organized before leaving with Schmitz for Gaurishankar that spring, but two months of last-minute details had to be taken care of, including getting Kauk onto the plane. Quiet, sincere, efficient, and trustworthy, Forrest was the man for the job.

I first met Bill Forrest in 1976, after my ascent of Nanda Devi in India. I was in Denver, riding the fleeting summit of success by describing heroic deeds before audiences, when the opportunity to meet the Colorado climbing legend presented itself. Not only were Forrest's ascents recognized as innovative, but his company, Forrest Mountaineering, was profitable, progressive, and competing with Chouinard's Diamond C.

Forrest's middle name should have been Easy. If I needed help contacting a corporation – he paved the way; if Kauk didn't have the right sleeping bag – Forrest got him one from his store in Denver; if our funds didn't balance – Forrest anted up out of his own pocket. With his thoughtful disposition, a smile straight out of a Roy Rogers movie, and a quiet, down-home laugh, Forrest was as easy to get along with as a meandering brook. With a profitable business like Forrest Mountaineering to his credit, Forrest was obviously sharp enough to have been in a business suit and working on Wall Street. But Forrest is his own man, and is drawn to the climber's game. I was comfortable with Forrest within minutes of meeting him – and that said it all.

Four pieces to the puzzle. Would they fit? One of the great questions in mountaineering is teamwork. What brings one group of individuals together and tears another apart? Leadership? Organization? Compatibility? As we rendezvoused in Islamabad at the home of my friend Andy Koritko, chief security officer at the American Embassy, I couldn't find a flaw. Optimistic perhaps, but never had I felt better about a team.

• • •

After Kauk's run-in with the marine, I knew it was time to get the team out of Islamabad. Our life at the Koritkos had been a step into paradise. As head of embassy security, Andy Koritko opened the American Embassy's facilities to us, which meant cold Heinekens in a Moslem country, embassy parties, cheeseburgers, lounge chairs around the pool, and pretty bikini-clad teenyboppers who surrounded Kauk and teased him unmercifully. Kauk ignored their innuendos, flirtations, and young girl games, while Schmitz and I, sunbathing nearby, drooled over ourselves, hoping for just a moment of their time for the 'old' folks. And Forrest? Well, he just wanted to get started climbing.

After eight days of negotiations with Mr. Naseer-Ullah Awan, Pakistan's head of Mountaineering and Tourism, and representatives of Pakistan International Airways (PIA, or Perhaps It Arrives), the Uli Biaho team was set to fly to Skardu in far northern Baltistan.

'What are you saying?' I asked Kauk.

'I don't like it,' he replied. 'There's too much rockfall.'

Another squadron of rock missiles whined and bashed down the gully. Kauk and I squeezed closer together beneath a bomb-proof ice wall and waited for a reprieve.

'It's the time of day, Ron,' I argued. 'We'll start earlier tomorrow to avoid the rock. Give it a chance.'

I didn't like the 100-yard-wide, 4,000-foot-high gully either. It flushed all of Uli Biaho's East Face debris onto us like a sewer pipe, but it was our only path to the wall. If I wasn't careful, Kauk would spook and quit.

'Let's cache our loads here, drop to camp, and come back tomorrow,' I suggested, with more optimism than I actually felt. 'It'll look better in the cool of the morning.'

'Not for me,' he replied, stuffing his pack with personal gear I thought we would leave.

Schmitz and Forrest were eagerly awaiting our reconnaissance report. I emphasized the great ice-climbing, the protection behind the ice walls, and suggested an early-morning departure to avoid rockfall. Then Kauk spoke for the first time in hours.

'I'm not going on the route,' he said. His eyes darted from the gully to us, then back to the gully. Kauk's admission put him in unfamiliar territory. I didn't speak, fearing we would lose Kauk without giving him some time to think it over.

Schmitz did. 'And why not?'

'I don't like the rockfall,' Kauk replied.

'Why, you big baby,' Schmitz said, as if it were fact, rather than opinion. This started an all-out verbal war, Kauk screaming at Schmitz, while Schmitz, knowing he had Kauk's goat, replied evenly time after time, 'You're a big man in the Valley, but you're nothing here,' along with a variety of other Schmitzifications. Schmitz finally said, 'We wouldn't take you anyway.'

And with that, Kauk replied, as expected, 'Well, I'm going, and to hell with you.'

Schmitz looked over at me with a glance that said, 'And that's how you handle Ron Kauk, America's rock climbing prima donna.'

Forrest and I just shook our heads and continued packing – for four.

The fear within oneself too often creates mountains out of molehills. At the end of the day, Kauk let the little gremlins that feed on the unknown get the best of him again. 'It's too dangerous,' he said, after a long silent spell listening and watching the gully. 'I'm not going.'

We let it stand at that. He'd struggled with it all day and, despite Schmitz's attempt to restore Kauk's motivation with the 'old boy' method, it was his decision. I knew it had taken a lot of guts to get there.

Forrest, Schmitz, and I climbed to Kauk's and my cache before dawn the next morning. Loaded with upwards of seventy pounds each, we dashed across the gully to the better-protected, higher-walled right side. Skirting large, vertical ice walls and climbing smaller seracs, we made our way to the upper ice field below the face. Intensified by the mid-morning heat, rockfall ricocheted through the gully, warning us to avoid the bottleneck and seek safety along the granite walls.

Leaving Forrest to chop out a future bivouac spot, Schmitz and I donned our armor of helmets, slings, hammers, pitons, and sundry climbing gear, to test the wall's resistance. I led a quick 150 feet of ledges and cracks to a pedestal. Like the toe leather of an old shoe, the low-angled, weathered rock at the base of the wall was broken and worn, but as I climbed higher, the granite wall cleansed itself of rubble and decay and aimed for the sky in a single 4,000-foot sweep. Schmitz jumared to my stance, then led another long pitch through blocks and up short cracks.

Burdened under fifty pounds of hardware and gear as I cleaned the pitch, I leaned far to my right to surmount a block and felt a snap in my lower back, then pain.

'Time to head down, Kim,' I said, as I reached his belay. 'I pulled a muscle in my lower back and it won't be long before I can't walk.'

By 1.30 p.m., we were down climbing the low-angled sections of ice in the gully and setting rappels over the seracs, trying to avoid the continual rock and ice fall. While we were beneath a series of twenty-foot-high ice blocks, two gravity-fed, climber-crushing boulders cut loose above Schmitz. He faced them squarely, defiantly, pitched one way, then dodged another as they hurtled by. Without so much as a 'whew,' or a change in the patented Schmitz muted expression, he turned downslope and continued to descend as though avoiding a close encounter with death was on his daily job sheet.

On 20 June, I stayed below on the glacier, cocked sideways, distorted by spasms, and unable to move without stabbing lower-back pain. While I lay in my sleeping bag, Forrest and Schmitz, supported by a recharged, and suddenly enthusiastic, Kauk, carried group gear partway up the gully. The team was now positioned for the final push up the gully – but I was unable to move.

Doubt within one's mind: can there be a more difficult adversary? I lay quietly absorbing the pain, watching my teammates disappear down the glacier towards base camp for food and rest, sensing an end to my dream of climbing Uli Biaho.

I'd had back problems since falling through a second-story stairwell and landing squarely on my backside while working construction in 1968. Periodically, the injury would reoccur and I would be immobile for days. But this was a first while on an expedition. With weeks of effort ahead of us – carrying massive loads and contorting in any number of strained positions day and night – could I recuperate quickly enough to continue? Would I be a burden to the team? Should I even take the chance of reinjuring my back and ending the climb for the others?

Two days later, my teammates had not returned. Out of food, irritated with their complacency, and discouraged with my injury, I limped down the glacier towards base camp. As I descended, the pain and discomfort diminished with work, and my spirit, depressed by inaction, returned. Once again, self-inflicted doubt, the disease of discouragement, proved to be more disabling and harder to overcome than physical injury. The four of us were now ready to attempt the face.

'Kim,' I said, 'I want you and Bill to team up. Ron and I will take the lead the first day, while you guys haul. The next day's yours.'

I wanted to climb with Kauk. He was considered the best rock climber in the world. What better way for me, a self-proclaimed mountaineer, to improve my skills than to watch Kauk perform on Uli's untested walls. I was fast on rock, but with his more-recent years in the Valley, Kauk had added to his repertoire small timesavers and special techniques that I wanted to add to my climbing 'tools.' Furthermore, like a young puppy in a kennel with an older dog, Kauk had begun a friendly harassment of the easygoing Forrest, mostly as a time filler during dead periods of the expedition. Regardless of his intent, I didn't want his youthful exuberance to lead to a confrontation on the climb, as hunger and exhaustion fed stressed-out tempers, and the slightest added catalyst might stop the expedition in a rope length. On the other hand, Schmitz and Forrest were well matched, both in climbing and personality, and, most important, they got along.

Kauk and I leapfrogged four leads up two-inch to four-inch cracks the first day. At four o'clock, we descended to help Schmitz and Forrest haul our seven sixty-pound haul bags to our high point, a four-foot-wide ledge big enough for cooking and for two to sleep on. Kauk and I spent the night close by in our aluminum-framed hanging hammocks, called Porta-ledges. By morning, clear skies had given way to thick clouds and light snowfall.

'Oh, shit!' Kauk said, early on the morning of the 25th. 'Schmitz, you got kerosene in the pot.'

'It's in the water bottles we filled last night, too,' Forrest added, sniffing his container.

There was no more ice on the tiny ledge for more water. None of us wanted to drink kerosene-tainted water, so we dumped it out. It would be a dry day until evening, when we could melt ice at our next camp.

As Schmitz and Forrest began leading new pitches, Kauk and I repacked the haul bags, adjusted the weight of each evenly, then began the tedious, backbreaking work of hauling them up the wall. Isolated rock and ice falling from thousands of feet above spit and cracked on the wall around us. Yells from Schmitz and Forrest warned us of the biggest or closest impending missiles.

On the third day, Kauk and I led parallel crack systems, penduluming into alternate cracks to avoid running water. Forrest and Schmitz, having fine-tuned their haul system by trial and error, moved quickly enough to catch me cleaning one of Kauk's long, difficult pitches. At mid-afternoon,

I reached a seventy-degree, forty-foot-high ice field in the shape of a flying bat, the only obvious landmark we had pinpointed earlier on the featureless East Face from the glacier far below. Ice debris and small rocks showered the haul team, as Kauk led one more short, hundred-foot pitch above the ice field. Schmitz's raucous verbal abuse of Kauk's ancestry, and the real danger of cutting loose an executioner block onto Schmitz, brought Kauk back to my belay and our night's bivouac.

Fluid intake is the single most important factor in preventing health problems at high altitudes and while undertaking physically strenuous activity. Our lack of water the previous day almost proved disastrous.

Dehydrated, no one slept peacefully on Bat Ledge at 18,000 feet. Kauk and I hung in our hammocks above our teammates, who were sleeping on narrow ice platforms that had been excavated after hours of labor. Forrest, puffy in the face, lethargic, and nauseous, was obviously showing the early signs of high altitude disease.

While Forrest rested and hydrated at the bivouac site the next morning, Schmitz, Kauk, and I led and fixed 450 feet of rope. Schmitz led the crux, an overhanging gully stuffed with loose debris, that had Kauk and me cowering on the open wall, dodging death blocks, and wondering if Uli Biaho – or, for that matter, any peak – was worth the risk. At each belay, our conversation turned to Forrest. It was my responsibility, as leader, to see that everyone returned alive and well. If Forrest didn't improve by the next morning, Uli Biaho would take second place to safely evacuating Forrest to base camp.

I expected to begin evacuating Forrest on the morning of June 28, if there was no indication he had improved during the night. To continue to a higher altitude would sentence him to death if he was suffering from high altitude disease.

'How ya' feeling, Bill?' I asked, as I started the stove.

Bill opened his tightly drawn sleeping bag hood, then peered out over the Karakoram Range as if seeing it for the first time. 'A lot better,' he replied. 'Nausea's gone and I feel a lot stronger.'

He looked better. His edema, a characteristic sign of fluid retention that had all but closed his eyes the day before, was gone. Before me was the Bill Forrest I knew – enthusiastic, energetic, determined.

Decisions are never clear-cut. Just when I think I've got the situation under control and I've made my decision, a gray area appears. In this case, Forrest seemed to have recuperated.

But questions still remained. Would he worsen as we went higher, a typical scenario for high altitude–related diseases? Could a three-man team evacuate an unconscious Forrest from a higher elevation or a more difficult situation? Forrest helped us make the decision. 'I'll let you know if I begin to feel worse, but we can't give up now.'

'All right,' I agreed. 'But, Bill, you will have to jumar behind us and without a load. I don't want you working at all.'

As the morning sun heated our camp, we packed quickly, then began hauling our bags up the four fixed ropes above us. After days of working together, not a moment was lost to wasted effort, nor an extra calorie spent on needless work.

The obvious crack system and deep open book we had followed up the left side of the East Face for days ended abruptly as our route and the southeast corner met. We continued on a vertical granite desert of discontinuous cracks, elephant-ear flakes, and small roofs.

At the fifth roped pitch above Bat Ledge, Schmitz and Forrest stopped to set up our four hammocks under a four-foot-wide roof. Kauk and I, released from the slow, monotonous drudgery of hauling bags and carrying packs, enjoyed two more long leads of effortless direct aid up round-edged cracks. At the end of the second lead, the summit block, an ugly assortment of icy ramparts, impossible-looking overhangs, and deep chimneys, was visible far above, but in another space and time. The hardest climbing was obviously yet to come.

We stashed the hardware at our high point and descended to the eyrie built by Schmitz and Forrest, four brightly colored Porta-ledges stacked in cliff swallow–fashion on the slightly overhanging wall. Our view stretched from Paiyu Peak to the southwest to Masherbrum to the southeast, with the second-highest mountain on earth, K2, dominating the skyline to the northeast. In addition, innumerable other peaks, snakelike glaciers, and unexplored canyons highlighted the panorama and filled our senses.

The wisps of mare's tails that had sped westward throughout the day as we climbed were pursued by peak-eating cumulo-nimbus clouds, which trapped the day's heat like a billowy comforter. I lay sweating on my hammock and watched as each peak was gobbled up by the approaching storm. By 3 a.m., a cold front had arrived and wet snow had begun to fall, blanketing the cool rock and forming puddles of water in the low points of our hammocks.

The windless, mild-mannered storm drifted slowly through the Karakoram throughout the morning. Rather than risk hypothermia while exposed on the wall, we chose to spend the next day resting out of the weather in our bivouac. By mid-morning, the four of us had dug out our hammock covers and secured them in place. We now had some protection from snowfall, dripping wall water, small ice and rock debris, and the intensifying wind. Water, a precious and rare commodity on the wall below, trickled down the granite, along our anchors, and onto the hammock webbing, to eventually soak our sleeping bags, clothing, and everything attached to the wall.

I wrote in my diary, on 29 June:

> I'm sometimes confused as to what I'm doing here, looking out at miles of rock and glacier, walls of ice, [and] peaks of unsurpassed beauty. Sitting on small ledges, or standing in slings, checking anchors and ropes, double checking, trusting my life to three others. Beating my hands in cracks – cold, swollen, bleeding and sore. Deadly rockfall and continuous ice. Where will it end, and for what purpose do I keep at it? Have you ever heard the whir of instant death whisk by on wings of fear? Rocks can speak, but you must always manage to hear them from beginning to end. Never break their sentence. One of the reasons I climb so hard, is so I can get above anything that can fall.

'My sleeping bag!' Schmitz, a putzer first-class, one who seems to move himself and other things continuously without purpose, yelled in frustration.

I peered, orb-eyed, out the slit in my hammock cover, through the snowstorm, and down at Schmitz. Fifty feet below him, hung up on the only ledge for 2,000 feet, a short, narrow step with a rock hook, was his sleeping bag. A teasing breeze swung it back and forth along the wall, threatening to steal it forever from Schmitz. Moving faster than I thought possible, he set up a rappel line and dropped to his bag before the breeze grew to a wind. He stopped his infernal putzing after that.

We climbed higher on 30 June, but not by much. Wet clothes, cold temperatures, and thick clouds dampened our enthusiasm and made it difficult to quicken our pace. Kauk and I, haul-bag boys for the day, waited in the insufferable chill, dodging debris set loose by Schmitz and Forrest. The thin, iced cracks proved difficult. Eight hours and three hundred feet higher, they rappeled to our night's hanging bivouac.

Despite another storm approaching from Skardu, Kauk and I hauled gear to Schmitz's high point the following morning. He had led a partial pitch before abandoning the overhanging, iced-up crack system and descending to our bivouac. I continued from his last piton, zippering up the hairline crack with knife blades and tied-off ice screws. I was in a devil-take-all mood, the kind of attitude I needed to abandon my fears and charge forward regardless of the outcome.

Kauk exposed the team's melodramatic foolishness as it surfaced, with a macabre sense of humor straight from *The Far Side*. There were no sacred cows. The continual storms, dehydration, our cracked and bleeding hands, granola three times a day, iced-up cracks, sleepless nights, stuck haul bags, Schmitz's putzing, even Forrest's illness, were fodder for laughter. I knew when one of Kauk's poignant jokes had hit Schmitz: his eyes would begin to sparkle, then the lines in his usually somber expression would lighten, until, as hard as he tried not to, a smile cracked upon his lips. For a few hours, Uli Biaho was not so dangerous – death not so close.

Ron led one hundred feet to a bivouac site, a crackless, sloping bulge that looked safer than the prospects above. While Schmitz and Forrest drilled holes for bolt anchors, Ron and I fixed another three hundred feet of rope up an open book and gully system. We were now back on the East Face and six hundred feet below the summit ridge, a razor blade of rock crowned with house-sized ice mushrooms. A light snow fell as we rappeled to the worst hanging bivouac of the trip, cooked and rehydrated, and talked of the end in sight.

We went for the summit on 2 July. I awoke at 4 a.m., hydrated the crew, then set off up two fixed lines at 7.30 a.m. It was my lead from the top of the ropes. We were below a ninety-five-degree wall, forty feet wide, enclosed by vertical side walls. A crack broke the joint of each corner.

I tried the right corner along a rotten and loose flaked chimney. It was too dangerous. I retreated and traversed left along snow, ice, and rock behind a detached flake of granite, then up a body-wide squeeze chimney. Schmitz seconded the pitch, reached my anchors, then aided an easy sixty-foot crack to an overhang. My next lead was easy aid, and I was soon on a good ledge, followed closely by the team.

'Ron,' I said, 'the ugliness above is *your* bag. It's all yours.'

A skin-eating, five-and-a-half-inch crack, deep in the corner we had been following, leaned slightly over us. It was past noon when Kauk moved off the ledge and began engineering a path up the off-width crack with bong pitons stacked back to back, sideways, and any way that would hold his weight. Kauk couldn't seem to find any of his humor on this pitch. He ended it short below another leaning off-width five-inch crack.

Schmitz finished off the five-inch, A3 section, without a word. I jumared and cleaned the pitch to his belay. It was my turn to lead again.

I free-climbed over several chockstones, then aided a perfect one- to two-inch crack, until it flared to four inches. As soon as the four-inch crack widened, I changed cracks, aiding one that narrowed to three inches and smaller. My pitch had everything. After aiding a one-inch crack in a V-shaped corner, I chimneyed a crack the width of my helmet with no protection to an alcove beneath an ice block clogging the everwidening chimney.

It was 6 p.m. Kauk, and then Schmitz, reached my stance. We were a pitch below the ice-mushroomed ridge and a long way from the summit.

'Kim,' I said, 'we can't spend the night out. Let's fix the three worst pitches, go back down to our bivy, then try again for the top tomorrow.'

Schmitz reluctantly agreed. After not summiting on Gaurishankar, he wanted the summit of Uli at any cost and was willing to bivouac without gear to get it. Kauk, on the other hand, was not about to risk his neck beyond his norm for Uli Biaho. In fact, his discomfort had turned to anger. As far as Kauk was concerned, the icy ramparts above, the cold, and our late predicament were all preludes to disaster. I sensed an oncoming rebellion and, accordingly, made the decision to descend. Forrest, a pitch below, was as ready and willing to bivouac as Schmitz, but trusted my judgment. Guided by starlight, we arrived at our bivouac late in the evening.

Thoughts of defeat filled my mind as I tried to sleep. Each of us had to have them. The route had turned from a clean, open wall with perfect cracks to an ugly assortment of gigantic stacked blocks, webbed together with rock-hard gray ice and crowned with immense umbrella-like cornices. The summit, well protected by battlements of rock and ice, was hidden somewhere above these monstrous cornices. Conceivably, some feature on the ridge could stop us short of the summit. It had happened on one peak or another to all of us during our years in the mountains. Not knowing what was above us, we let defeat sneak its way into our thoughts, like the thick, rising mist, until exhaustion kept it at bay.

By 7 a.m. we were on the move, jumaring to our high point. As Kauk got into a bombproof belay, I surveyed the ice plug blocking the chimney above me. It was my kind of terrain – a mountaineer's terrain – rock flakes, snow hummocks, icy cracks, and overhangs, known appropriately to mountaineers as mixed alpine shit.

I nailed a flake on the right side of the chimney, then crab-legged left underneath the ice plug. Kauk, directly below me, became a target for all the falling debris displaced by my thrashing as I struggled to gain altitude.

The one-ton ice plug that blocked my way was loose. Using my ice hammer sparingly, I chimneyed between it and the rock wall, finally reaching high enough to chop its left side away enough to crawl on top. Once past the ice plug, I surmounted one more chockstone on the ridge before pussyfooting along a sugar snow ledge to the safety of a rock cavern. Kauk, freezing from the snow that had cascaded down upon him while he was sitting in the morning chill, cleaned the pitch slowly, bringing with him my crampons and camera.

I led off again, surmounting a seventy-five-degree snow bump to steep ice steps on the left side of the ridge. One hundred and forty feet from

Ron, I reached a sharp corner above a vertical, sixty-foot-wide chimney and set up my belay. Eighty feet above me on the crest of the knife-edged ridge, and leaning in my direction, was a mushroom of ice that resembled a great blue whale sounding from the deep, with its tail down-ridge and its nose against the summit wall. It must have weighed three hundred tons. There was daylight underneath its belly, and, as much as I hated the thought, that keyhole looked like the quickest route to the top.

Kauk, jumaring the rope, reached my side. He apparently didn't realize the danger of the ice perched above us, so I asked for a belay and began front-pointing up the sixty-degree ice slope. I hadn't gone far, when I swung my single ice hammer into the blue ice and a ten-pound block broke loose, but temporarily stayed put.

'Watch this block, Ron,' I warned, as I continued. 'It could go anytime.'

As if on cue, my rope caught on the block's edge and knocked it loose. I yelled. Ron ducked, but the block, as if seeking human flesh, hit him squarely on the arm.

He cradled the arm, leaned into the rock, and moaned.

'Is it broken, Ron?' I yelled down to him. So close were we climbing to the edge of control, I feared a disaster was now about to unfold.

'That's it,' he yelled back, obviously scared and angry. 'I'm going down.'

I could deal with an attitude problem, but a broken arm was something else altogether. Balanced on steep ice squarely beneath the whale-like ice mushroom, I was not in a position to sit tight and wait for Kauk to make a decision to climb. I gave him a few minutes to regain his composure, then asked him to finish belaying me to the keyhole beneath the ice mushroom. Robotically, he did so, angrily cussing away at his pain and our fragile predicament.

Then Schmitz arrived at Kauk's side. A discussion ensued.

'Whaddaya mean, you're going down,' Schmitz asked, in a tone he reserves for lower life. 'So you got hit. It's not broken. I was right, you're nothing but a big baby.'

And, so it was that Kauk came next, probably to get away from all the Schmitzifications pouring from Kim.

While Schmitz and Kauk yelled at each other below, I had them tie another rope to the first, allowing me to lead through the keyhole and up a seventy-degree ice slope to avoid belaying under the mushroom. Within a few minutes I had traversed back over them and onto the last summit ridge. Once Kauk had reached my side, I led a low-angled snow pitch, the first easy pitch on the climb, to the top of the gully and into the setting sun.

A short walk and an easy slope away was the snowcapped summit. One by one, each of us climbed to its broad top, soaked in the evening's warmth, cried a little, laughed a lot, and, for just a few brief moments, forgot about the cold, thirst, and danger below.

Fifteen minutes on the summit and it was time to go. For the next two and a half days, we rappeled, lowered haul bags, and retreated. There were unavoidable incidents, close calls, bad bivouacs, and flared tempers, but as one we reached the bottom and the horizontal world we're used to calling home.

I often ask myself what the key to success was on Uli Biaho. God knows, success like ours doesn't happen every expedition. It was the team.

Putting aside my leadership, our goal, the route, the weather, and the dozens of other elements that make up an expedition, the players are what make or break the game. Schmitz, Forrest, Kauk, and I came together, body and soul, for one brief moment in time – and succeeded. Another time, another place, or a different team member, and Uli Biaho would still be a dream, instead of a memory.

from We Aspired:
The Last Innocent Americans
by Pete Sinclair

Pete Sinclair's (born 1935) memoir of life as a climber and climbing ranger in the Tetons during the '60s shows some young men and women find purpose and identity in the mountains. The book's account of a major rescue on the Grand Teton also shows how those same mountains can punish the inexperienced, the foolish or the unfortunate.

The back room of the Jenny Lake ranger station had a stove because in the winter it was used as a patrol cabin. On stormy days or on rest days it was a good place to make tea and to talk. Leigh Ortenburger spent much of his research time there when he was in the valley, and since he was our historian, the back room became one of the two storytelling places in the valley. The Climbers' Campground was the other one.

Late in July 1962, there was a storytelling session going on with Leigh Ortenburger and Dave Dornan in the group. On a couple of occasions while climbing with Leigh, I had surpassed myself and had managed to do the crux moves of new routes we put up. This prompted Leigh to remark, 'It really isn't safe to go into the mountains with Sinclair; he's a madman.' Dave looked at me and said, 'You can do this stuff; you ought to.' What he meant by 'this stuff' was his current project, raising himself to Yosemite standards. He had accepted the Yosemite challenge. That is, he did not expect to become as good as Chouinard or Robbins but he wanted to be good enough to carry on a conversation with them.

Dave wanted me to work on No Escape Buttress with him. Mt. Moran's south buttresses presented Teton climbers with a chance to do something that resembled Yosemite wall climbing. The easternmost of these buttresses, No Escape Buttress, was the last and most difficult of these problems. This did not sound like the climb for a person who climbs well only to escape, but because Dornan wanted this climb, I had to try.

There were encouraging signs in the heavens as we rowed across Leigh Lake in a rotting plywood skiff, one rowing, one bailing. The clouds looming up on the Idaho side of the range were massive and black. Such clouds in the morning indicated that this was not to be an ordinary storm; we were sure to be stormed off the climb. The prospect pleased me. We'd do a couple of pitches and then go home. Maybe I'd be more ready next time.

Dornan was near the top of the first lead when the storm hit. He rappelled off and we ran for the lake. Crossing the lake in that storm was one of the dumbest things we'd done. Fortunately, the energy of the storm was released in impulses rather than as a sustained force. The wind and rain combined to beat the surface of the lake down instead of lifting it into breaking whitecaps, or we would have been swamped. Dave, chortling because he was no longer a rescuer, remarked that if there was anybody in the mountains, my day was not over. I wasn't much worried. This storm was severe enough that the most desperate vacationing climber, with one day left on his vacation and fifty weeks of being chained to a desk facing him, could not pretend that this was a passing summer shower. It was cold as well as violent. There was a smell of the Gulf of Alaska about it.

As Dave and I headed back to Jenny Lake, I looked forward to a few quiet days in the ranger station. The climbers would be out of the mountains, and the campers would be heading for motels or the desert. The back of the ranger station would be warm, full of climbers drinking tea. The guides would be in, looking at our photographs of the peaks, planning one more climb, swapping stories.

When we got back to the ranger station, things were less peaceful than I'd hoped. The big news was that Lyn, Sterling's wife, had rolled their Volkswagen bus. She wasn't hurt badly, but she and Ster had a good fright. A minor piece of news was that the other ranger on duty had been sent out to check on an overdue party of ten from the Appalachian Mountain Club. This was an annoyance but couldn't be thought of as serious. Ten people can't just vanish in a range as small as the Tetons.

People frequently get benighted in the Tetons in circumstances like those attending this climb: a large party composed of people of varying experience, climbing a route that is reputed to be easy but is seldom climbed. Those circumstances are practically guaranteed to produce a bivouac. Normally we at the ranger station would give the party plenty of time to extricate itself from the route and get back before we went looking for them. Often there would be another party in the same general area who had spotted the late party. From when and where they were seen, we could make a reasonable estimate of how long it would take them to get back. We'd set things in motion if the missing party exceeded our estimated time of return as well as their own. Even then we wouldn't scramble a full-scale search. Our first action would be to send out a ranger, two if there was to be technical climbing, and, if possible, combine the search with some other activity such as a patrol. We would also pass the word around to one or two key rescue types that a party was overdue. What that meant to them was that they'd be where they could be easily reached and maybe pass up the second beer until the word went about that everybody was out of the mountains.

Sometimes a worried family or concerned friends who were waiting in the valley would take exception to this stalling for time. But there was no other way to do it. If we did a full-scale search and rescue operation every time a party was overdue, the expense would have been enormous. In addition, that increased pressure on the party to get back in the time estimated might well result in more injuries and deaths.

In this case, we did not stall as long as we normally would have before sending someone out. There were more than one hundred people in the Appalachian Mountain Club encampment, with little else to do but worry about their overdue party. Also, the storm increased the possibility that the party could be stuck for some time, and the party was not well equipped for cold weather. Thus, very soon after we were notified, Ranger George Kelly was on his way into the mountains on a patrol. He would begin by organizing a search party from the Appalachian Mountain Club encampment.

It's not that we didn't worry. We were paid to worry. There are people who do it for nothing. It was not difficult to imagine the worst, even after one hundred repetitions of our imaginings turning out to be worse than the fact, but we had learned an orderly procedure to follow in these cases and kept our imaginings for entertainment. It happened that in this one case, the event was much worse than we had imagined.

The leader of the party, Ellis Blade, was himself not an Appie but a hired expedition leader. He was in his fifties and had years of mountaineering experience.

The rest of the party varied greatly in experience. Steven Smith, quite young but a good rock climber, was the assistant leader. The other good rock climber was sixty-five-year-old Lester Germer. Charles Joyce was a good recreational rock climber, respectful of the western mountains because his experience had been mainly on the cliff bands of the East. Janet Buckingham was experienced mainly as a hiker. Lydia and Griffith June, Charles Kellogg, and John Fenniman were in various stages of beginning to learn to rock climb. Mary Blade, Ellis's wife, was also along and was an experienced mountaineer. The route they were to climb was known as the Otterbody Route after the shape of a snowfield in the middle of the east face of the Grand Teton.

The party got off as planned at 4 a.m. Thursday morning, a good sign. There had only been a couple of minor problems for Ellis Blade in the days prior to setting out. He hadn't been able to generate much enthusiasm for conditioning climbs. The time to get the party into condition had been scheduled, but things hadn't quite worked out. Going into the wilderness to set up a new society is an American passion, but it takes a lot of energy just to eat, sleep, and talk in a situation like that. There are new people to meet and hierarchies, liaisons, and enmities to be established before the group can truly focus on its stated purpose.

The problem, other than the lack of conditioning, that Blade might have had on his mind that Thursday morning was that Smith, the young assistant leader, was suffering from an attack of nonconfidence. Smith did not like the looks of the weather. He had vomited the evening before. Blade was fifty-four and Steven Smith was twenty-one. Smith had not approached Blade directly about his worries and nausea but had confided them to Joyce, who did talk to Blade. If Blade's employers considered part of his responsibilities to be training the next generation of leaders, then it would have been up to Blade to establish a rapport with his young assistant. ('Lack of communication' was just coming into vogue as a new sin – to which persons in positions of authority are particularly prone – so it is astonishing how much communication and its lack became a theme in postevent analyses of these events. In retrospect, the whole sequence of events seems another case of the gods using tragedy for parody.) Blade did not establish a rapport with his young assistant. He had all he could do just to get his party up and off the mountain. It is also true that mountaineering in America was undergoing a growth in rock-climbing skills; hundreds of good young climbers were, within three years, learning to do moves on rock routes that older climbers had thought only feasible on campground boulders. Blade would be an unusual man if he did not feel his authority somewhat undercut by this new generation.

As for Smith, it's possible that he had a touch of the flu or had picked up a bug from the water. One or the other happened to me at least once a season in the Tetons and to all the guides and climbing rangers I knew, which may only be saying that we all have our moments of discouragement. The bugs were always there. They determined the kind of sickness we would get, not when we would get it.

Whatever caused Smith's lack of confidence, the events of the rest of the first day conspired to keep him low. The early start was the last thing to go well.

Four and a half hours later, at 8.30, they started up Teepe's Snowfield, two and a half hours behind according to Blade's schedule. Making such schedules is the curse of being the party leader.

As the snowfield got steeper, Janet Buckingham broke out of her steps in the snow, and although Smith held her easily, Janet's feet ineffectively flailed away at the snow. Anybody who has taught beginning climbers is familiar with the scene. The student or client literally loses contact with his or her feet and thrashes away hoping that a miracle will occur and one of them will stick. Perhaps Smith didn't know how to deal with the situation; perhaps he hadn't the chance. It was Blade, leaving his own rope, who talked her back into confidence in her steps again.

There is something else about beginners on snow which Blade may have been thinking about while restoring Janet to her feet. To a beginner, going up is four times easier than going down. Ascending, the snow is right there in front of your face and you can touch it with your hands. You go up by slamming your foot directly into the slope. Descending, there's only empty space in front of your hands and eyes. You go down, not by shifting your weight from one firmly planted foot to the other, as in going up, but by stepping off a firmly planted foot into air. Every step going up is reversible at any point in the move. Every downward step is irreversible, a nervous-making succession of total commitments. What would it be like to try to descend this snowfield with people having these difficulties ascending? The incident with Janet might have been soon forgotten by all involved except that disturbing incidents began to accumulate.

The lead rope of five made it to the top of the snowfield half an hour before noon. The second rope, Smith's, didn't join the lead rope at the top. They stopped on an outcropping about three rope lengths below for their lunch. This area was scarred by debris fallen from the cliff band and two snowfields above. This detail did not go unnoticed by Joyce, and he was the one who spotted the ice falling from above and gave a warning yell. One block carried away Fenniman's ice axe. Another glanced off Kellogg's foot. Joyce had two blocks to dodge and only managed to dodge one. He was hit hard and knocked into the air. Though briefly stunned, he was uninjured.

To this point, Joyce, though he was Smith's confidant, had been maintaining neutrality on the question of whether the climb was advisable or not. After being hit, he still wasn't as shaken as Smith, whose hands were trembling, but he was now of Smith's opinion that this was an ill-fated climb and they ought to go down.

While they were getting underway, Joyce said to Smith, 'Let's get out of here.' Smith, who told Joyce that his alertness had saved their lives, said, 'He'll kill us all,' again the kind of tossed-off remark that usually doesn't survive the moment.

As the entire party joined at the top of the snowfield, a storm hit. It was noon. This was not the familiar late afternoon thunderstorm but the first impulse of the big storm that drove Dave and me out of the mountains. The party took refuge in the moat between the top of the snowfield and the rock. Smith finally confronted Blade directly with his desire to retreat. Blade responded that the snowfield was hardening and had become dangerous. As the heavy rainfall and hail from the first huge cumulus cloud passed and the rain moderated, Blade gave the word for everyone to put on their packs and start moving up. Joyce sought out Smith.

'What's he doing? Is he nuts? We've got to go down. You're a leader. Tell him we've got to go down.' Smith could not. Eventually it would be Joyce himself who would take command and make the decision to go down, but that was to be two days hence.

The party traversed the top of the snowfield to the base of a rock couloir. Blade sent Germer ahead to scout the route, asking him to report 'how will it go?' In the aftermath, every turn of phrase appears significant. If Blade's real question was 'Ought we attempt it?' he asked it the wrong way. Germer did not interpret Blade's question as a request for advice but as a request for a technical report.

This couloir, carved in the seam of the East Face and the East Ridge of the Grand, joins the Otterbody Snowfield to Teepe's Snowfield. It is rather alarmingly free of the debris which packs the bottom of most Teton couloirs. It is too steep and too water-, ice-, and rock-washed to hold anything in it. Obviously the rock is not particularly sound, which is why a couloir developed. Griffith June saw the couloir first as a bowling alley and then found in his mind the inscription from the *Inferno*, 'Abandon hope, all ye who enter here.' Wet, cold, late, tired, with weather threatening and tension in the party growing, it could not have been a cheerful party who geared themselves up for rock climbing.

Germer returned with his report, which he recalled thus: 'I told him it looked easy. I know now he was asking for advice, and I gave him a rock-climbing opinion. It was easy rock climbing. I was not considering the safety of the party. The camp had chosen Blade as a leader, but I should have said something.'

Possibly there was something else at work here. The opening sentence in the description of the Otterbody Route in Ortenburger's *Climber's Guide to the Teton Range* (1956 edition) says this of the first ascent, 'Petzoldt ranks this as one of the easiest routes on the Grand Teton.' Twenty-seven years after the first ascent, an eastern cliff climber of Germer's stature would be reluctant to rate this climb as more technically difficult than the first ascent party found it to be, unless Blade had reason to think that he was seriously off route. What Germer was acknowledging with his 'I should have said something' was that of those who did say something or might have spoken, he was the only one whose view Blade would have had to seriously consider.

When Smith once again said that they ought to go down, Ellis Blade retorted, 'I've been on that glacier before in weather like this. It's as hard as ice. If we go down, someone will get killed.'

Smith pressed the point, 'We can't climb the mountain now.'

Blade's response was 'You keep your mouth shut.'

'Well, I'm assistant leader of this group,' said Smith, 'and I think my opinion should be considered.'

'Well, don't you forget that I am the leader and I know it is safer to go up.'

In the hours that followed, they all got soaked, Lydia June got a shock from a lightning strike, Smith avoided a rock avalanche only by leaping across the couloir into the arms of Griffith June, and Kellogg was hit by a rock that drove his crampons through his pack and into his back. Griffith June thought of leading a splinter group back, a serious responsibility. He had the authority within the AMC organization but not as a mountaineer, and they were very much in the mountains now. He did urge Blade to lead them back, but Blade replied that they were committed.

Blade climbed quickly and well then, getting the party three-fourths of the way up the couloir. Griffith June found a huge boulder two pitches from the top, big enough for them all to sit on. Joyce secured them with pitons, and all bivouacked there except Blade, who had reached the wide ledges and easy slabs at the top of the couloir. There was to be no reconsideration of Blade's decision. There were some complaints, perhaps fewer than there might have been had Mary Blade not been part of the group. A decision to go down would have been a decision to abandon Blade on the mountain.

Three inches of wet snow fell during the night. They had no down garments or dry clothes, some had no wool clothes, and they had run out of food. In the morning, Germer asked Smith what he thought. Germer didn't like the rotten rock and had been weakened by the bivouac. Smith replied that he didn't know the route. Once almost out of the gully, even Smith seems to have lost interest in going down.

It took all of the next day, Friday, to get the party up the remaining two pitches to the top of the couloir. Joyce and Fenniman climbed up to Blade. June slipped on the ice just below the point where the angle of the couloir eased. He tried repeatedly. He cut steps up, almost made it, and fell again, this time further and over an overhang. There was danger of his being strangled by the rope. Smith muscled him over to the bivouac pillar, where June collapsed exhausted.

Germer then went up and set up an intermediate belay position, where he stayed until all six remaining climbers were up the couloir. (This was during the time when Dornan and I were being driven from No Escape Buttress a few miles to the north.) Though fit enough, Germer was in his sixties and the effort was too much; he had used all reserves. His hands were claws; he clutched a piton in each and made it up the ice. Blade moved on but was called back. Germer announced he was dying.

Blade assessed the situation and came up with a new plan but not a new direction. He was like a man possessed of an ultimate truth. There can be an infinite number of situations, tactics, and explanations, but there can only be one conclusion. He, Joyce, and Smith would go up. They might find climbers at the top. If not, they'd go down the Owen Spalding Route and get help. There was twice as much more snow above them than they had climbed on Teepe's Snowfield. There was a cliff band to climb between the Otterbody Snowfield and the East Face Snowfield. There was the descent from the summit, which, in icy conditions, is no easy matter. Ellis Blade knew about all this but appears to have forgotten it. He appears to have been in that state of mind where it's impossible to think beyond the next move. Every plan he had made, all preparations for the future, had been thwarted by unforeseen circumstances. It's happened to most of us.

When George Kelly got to the Appalachian Mountain Club camp at the Petzoldt Caves, there was no word of the missing party. By the time he radioed this news down, we were back in the ranger station and instructed him to organize a search. We were getting a little nervous. The search was, to a certain extent, window dressing. Any place the AMC people could be allowed to search would be a place the missing party could get out of by themselves. What they could do was look at the mountain and listen. They did, and what they saw was three members of the party up on the Otterbody Snowfield.

The need for a plausible explanation for what was happening with that party was increasing by the moment, while the prospects for getting such an explanation were decreasing. At their rate, it would be two days before they got to the top. We were at first inclined to believe that these three could not be from the party we were seeking, but there wasn't anybody else on the east side of the mountain. They had to be three of the ten. There was no way to make sense of it. It was hard to believe that if there had been an injury or a fatality, someone couldn't have gotten out to tell us. If there had been some kind of horrible disaster and these were the only survivors, it would explain why we hadn't heard from them but not why they were going up. Only one thing was clear – we had to get serious about finding out what was going on.

There had been a short rescue the evening before involving a client of the guide service. The guide service had provided most of the manpower for the rescue. Barry Corbet was one of those on the rescue. He had been scheduled to take a party up the Grand on Saturday, so another guide had taken Barry's party up to the high camp at the Lower Saddle Friday morning while Barry slept late. Barry was on his way up to join his party when he met George Kelly and was pressed into service. As they followed the track of the party up the snowfield and into the couloir, the storm renewed itself. Barry was equipped and George wasn't. (They had gotten, as we later determined, within four hundred feet of Blade's group when they turned back.) Barry joined his party; George came back down.

Doug McLaren, district ranger and member of the rescue team when it was originally organized a decade earlier, was our supervisor. He organized and coordinated rescue activities. Doug ordered a pack team to move as much equipment as we could reasonably muster up to Garnet Canyon. Garnet Canyon is the cirque which is rimmed counterclockwise from north to south by Disappointment Peak, the Grand Teton, the Middle Teton, the South Teton, and Nez Perce. Doug, Sterling, Jim Greig, and I left in the advance party at 7 p.m. Rick Horn and Mike Ermath, the remaining strong climbers on the park team, were to follow with more equipment. All the available Exum guides and some friends had volunteered: Al Read, Fred Wright, Pete Lev, Jake Breitenbach, Dr. Roland Fleck, Bill Briggs, Dave Dornan, and Peter Koedt. These guides and volunteers would come up in the morning. Another guide, Herb Swedlund, was holding at the Petzoldt Caves, awaiting developments. A majority of the professional mountaineers in America were to carry out this operation.

The four of us got a little sleep at the end of the horse trail, about an hour below the encampment at the caves, and started up around 4 a.m. We arrived at the top of the snowfield at about 10:30. Here I made a mistake in route finding. The party had to be either on the cliff band between Teepe's Snowfield and the Otterbody Snowfield or at the top of the Otterbody just above the point where the three climbers had been spotted. There were two obvious routes up the cliff band. One was the couloir to the right of the cliff band, dark, wet, rotten; and the other was a nice sunlit rock line straight up from where we were.

I'd never been there before, but I'd been near there six weeks earlier looking at it from a col four hundred yards to our left at the southern edge of the snowfield. I had come to take a look because the climbing pressure on the standard routes was becoming such that I was interested in finding another easy route to the summit that we could recommend to those climbers who mainly just wanted to get to the top of the mountain. What I had seen in June was far from being the easiest route on the mountain. The sun reflected off the snow into the couloir to reveal a mass of contorted ice. Debris, both ice and rock, cascaded·out of it. It seemed the picture of unpredictability. The mountain seemed to be saying, 'Here I keep no pacts.' At the same time, I noted the comparative warmth and orderliness of a sunlit route up an open chimney just to the south of the icy corner. I decided that the sunny route was the route Petzoldt had gone up. Though it may have been easy for him, it didn't appear easy enough for the type of climber I had in mind. I descended from the col without bothering to traverse the snowfield to take a closer look.

Now the ice was gone and water poured down the couloir. My comrades were of the opinion that the route went up the couloir. I said that was impossible, anybody could see that was no place to be. My memory of my first look at the couloir was influencing my present perception of it. Thus, I persuaded them to follow me up the route I had seen to the south (which is in fact not the Otterbody Route but, ironically, the Smith Route).

Though my view prevailed, the discussion had planted enough doubt in my mind that I wanted to make sure the climbing went as easily as I had claimed it would. I strained to find the easiest possible line. I almost frantically scanned the rock for holds, while trying to climb with as nonchalant a motion as I could. The climbing, while easy, was not trivial, and at the point that the guidebook account of the Smith Route describes as 'the difficult overhanging portion,' the climbing became seriously nontrivial.

As we paused to deal with this appearance of fifth-class climbing on what was supposed to be a third- and fourth-class route, we heard voices coming unmistakably from the top of the couloir. We spent the next hour rappeling back down to the top of the snowfield.

We decided that only two of us would go up to investigate, partly because of the rockfall danger and partly because the voices we heard seemed to be singing! Sterling and I had traveled together, worked together, and climbed together. I wanted him to stay at the bottom with Doug because it looked like that was going to have to be the organization point. I could not imagine what the tremendous barrier was between where we were and where they were, but there must be something keeping them from descending. Sterling could practically read my mind, and I wanted him where he would be in a position to do something if things got complicated. Also, Jim was bigger and stronger than either of us, and there were at least seven of them up there someplace.

Angry because of my mistake, I climbed carelessly and managed to break my hammer soon after we got underway. I remember the climbing as being more difficult than does Jim. The last two pitches, bypassing the overhang and crossing the ice, could easily intimidate a party not in good form. It was not any one thing; it was an accumulation of aggravations.

Once the overhang was passed, the route went up the right-hand, or east, side of the ice at the top of the couloir. The party was across the ice on the slabs at the 'tail' of the Otterbody, about thirty feet above and half a rope length in distance. There were seven inches of snow on the ice, just heavy and wet enough to adhere to the ice while bearing our weight. We weren't able to protect the pitch in a manner which could stop a fall short of the overhang. We had neither ice pitons nor crampons. A rope from them above would be just the thing.

For the first time, we turned our attention fully to the party we'd come to rescue. They seemed calm. Did they have a climbing rope? They did. Would they toss us an end? They would. The young man, Fenniman, stiffly approached the lip of the ledge with a rope. He seemed a bit perplexed. We instructed him to give the coil a healthy swing and toss it down to us. He swung the coil back and then forward but failed to release it. He did the same thing again. And then again. And again. He was not swinging the coil to build up momentum but was swinging indecisively, almost as if he weren't sure he wanted us to cross over to them and disturb the calm which reigned there. The swinging motion became mechanical. He'd forgotten that he was not only to swing the coil but also release it. We hadn't told him that he had to do both, swing and release. We told him. The coil, released in the middle of the swing instead of at the end of it, dropped in front of his feet. Jim and I exchanged glances. Perhaps if he climbed down the slab to the next ledge towards us?

'I won't! I won't!' He spoke not directly to us but first to the air at our left and then to the rock at his feet.

'Stay where you are!' we said in one voice we just managed to keep from rising. We were in for it, no doubt about that; we'd really gotten into something very strange.

Jim 'went for it' and we made it across and joined them on their ledge. They undoubtedly had been badly frightened and were probably making an effort to recover their wits. Possibly they were embarrassed. It seemed to be an effort for most of them to acknowledge our presence. There was a polite smile, a curious, almost disinterested gaze, the sort of thing I'd experienced in New York subways. Mary Blade seemed positively cheerful. They'd been singing, she told us. She also told us that Lester had been having a difficult time. Lester wanted to know if we'd brought any strawberry jam. We hadn't. We should have. According to Lester that's what we were supposed to do, bring strawberry jam and tea. He was a little put out with us and seemed to doubt that we knew our business.

I was offended. My first thought was, 'Jesus Christ, Lester, if I knew what we were going to find up here, I would have brought the Tenth Mountain Division!' Lester's intimation that we didn't know what we were doing was not far off. What were we going to do?

I signaled to Jim. Under the pretext of moving to a better radio transmission site, we climbed up to the next ledge and walked behind a boulder to talk.

'What in hell are we going to do?' asked Jim.

Jim later told me that I calmly lit a cigarette and replied, 'We're all going to die, that's what we're going to do.'

I guess I had to say it to get it out of the way. I'm glad I did. Life doesn't provide many opportunities to deliver a line like that. Anyway, the notion that we might be there forever was not that far-fetched. The radio would not work, and we had managed to go off without taking an extra battery. I restrained myself from throwing the radio down the mountain and satisfied myself shouting into it, cursing, and shaking it.

Eventually, by moving about from rock to ledge to chimney and bouncing our voices off the walls on the East Ridge, we found a place where we could shout out of the couloir and have some words heard and, we hoped, understood by Ster and Doug. All we could tell them was to stay out of the couloir. What we wished to have been able to tell them was that we would be setting things up, up here, while they organized the equipment and men coming up from below. At some convenient moment, we would freeze all motion in the couloir while they set up belaying and lowering positions below us. Then we would have a bucket brigade of various techniques, fixed ropes, maybe a litter or two, rappels, belay, and so forth, depending on the terrain and the condition of each person being lowered. It was an elegant picture I had of how it should go, but it was not to be. Jim and I would just have to start moving the party down the mountain any way we could until we were back in communication with our teammates or until they could see what was needed, we could see that they could see what was needed, and we all could do what was needed.

We started. There was a ledge big enough for the whole party below us, but it was further than the two short pitches Jim and I could manage with the equipment available. Could Fenniman, the only one of the party who was reasonably ambulatory, help us? He'd have to. The fact that we had to use Fenniman in the shape he was in made us feel absurd. We played existentialist.

'Do you think this boulder will hold?'

'If it falls off we can go down the mountain and roll it back up.'

The system we decided on was for Jim to lower one to me, me to lower that one to Fenniman, and he to belay them to the ledge. I anchored Fenniman to a slab about thirty feet above the big ledge and gave him precise instructions, which I repeated several times. While doing so, my sense that things were absurd became a feeling that things were desperate. The entire operation had to funnel to and through this youngster just out of high school who was headed for Dartmouth. I'd once been a kid just out of high school headed for Dartmouth and couldn't imagine what I'd have been able to do if I had been in the position he was in. He had been here, crawling around in this couloir, for two nights and now nearly three days. We put him in what must have appeared to him as the most precarious position he'd been in during the entire nightmare. He was securely anchored, but he had only my word for that. It would not be surprising if he had come to doubt the word of people who claimed to know better than he the position he was in.

I felt that I wasn't talking to Fenniman but to a messenger the whole Fenniman had sent to hear me out. The messenger seemed reliable, even heroic. I felt that Fenniman would get the job done but had the odd thought in the midst of talking to him that I'd like to meet him some day. I thought he might untie himself from the anchor and step off the mountain. That had happened a few years before to a guide with a head injury on this same mountain, three ridges to the south. I moved the knot tying him to the mountain around behind him where it couldn't be reached accidentally as he tied and untied the people we sent down. I made my instructions simple, precise, and routine while attempting at the same time to speak to him as a peer. This stuff I'm telling you to do, this situation you're in, it's just routine for mountaineers like you and me.

It worked. He did it exactly as I instructed him, exactly the same way every time. It may be that when he swung that coil mechanically back and forth when we asked for the upper belay, some part of my mind had registered the potential in his precise movements and had seen that his 'I won't! I won't!' could be made 'I will! I will!' But in the end, it all came down to the fact that Fenniman was the only person who stood up when we arrived.

We first assumed that they could provide their own motive power and set their own pace of descent while we belayed them along a fixed rope. The least experienced of them would not have found the first pitch at all troublesome under normal circumstances, but they fell down on flat ledges, fell into a stream two feet wide and three inches deep, and spent thirty seconds trying to figure out how to step over an eight-inch rock. Sometimes you see this in a beginning rock-climbing class when the client is really frightened. There are ways to deal with it. But these people did not look frightened. What we were seeing on their faces and hearing in their voices wasn't fear but confusion, as if the problems of balance and motion were complicated math problems. We gave up trying to talk them through the moves. We were becoming exasperated at the ineffectiveness of our explanations and instructions and knew that our exasperation would only make things worse.

Tactfully at first, and then less so, we relieved them of their autonomy. Staggering, slithering, stumbling, as long as they kept moving, they could pick their own way down. If they stopped too long, a segment of time which became shorter as the sun got lower, a tug or a nudge and finally a steady, unrelenting pressure kept them moving.

After the first of them had gone down the snow-covered ice, it wasn't snow covered. All pretense of down climbing could be abandoned. They got soaked sliding down the ice and water, and I shivered for them. The wetter they got, the slower they moved. The wetter they got, the greater the need for speed.

Fenniman caught on. I overheard someone ask Fenniman to wait because he had lost a foothold. To which Fenniman replied insistently, 'They say you have to keep moving.'

Speed under these circumstances was relative. We, who were trying to imagine that we were in control of things, were tying, untying, handling the rope with one hand, gesticulating with the other, and talking and thinking at a furious rate. Those who were being controlled were rudely precipitated off a pitch, tied to an anchor, and then left to a shivering wait of a half hour or more before it was their turn to move again.

Once down to the big ledge, things seemed better. Perhaps the ledge above on which they had spent so many uncomfortable but relatively safe hours had been difficult to abandon. The feeling of us and them lessened. There was some conversation. We found out what we could about what had happened. I began to learn their names and to take account of them as separate people. I noted that the Junes seemed to be holding together. That does not always happen to couples under stress in the mountains. I wondered if Germer was recalling warm summer days rock climbing in the Shawangunks. Janet was the wettest, coldest, seemed most out of place, but I was impressed by her endurance. I wondered if Mary Blade were worrying about Ellis and, if she were, would she be most worried about his safety or the repercussions that seemed obviously destined to come to him. Kellogg seemed to be not too badly off but looked haggard, like a nice young man just recently embarked on a course of dissipation.

There was little time for these thoughts. Above all was the fact that we could make a mistake and kill one of them or not make a mistake and still have one of them die. Lester Germer was the obvious candidate, the one everybody was worried about, but there were others. And what of the missing three? We had to take Mary's word that they were in pretty good climbing shape, but what did 'pretty good' mean? The best we could do was to hope that they would be spotted by Barry, who was on the summit that day. The trouble was, Barry should be down by now. Perhaps Doug and Ster already had news?

I chafed at our slow pace. My mistake cost us about two hours, and that was going to make the difference between day and night in this gully, between warm sun and thirty-two-degree granite, between wet pitches and ice pitches, between a snow you could heel down and snow as hard as ice. My mistake might end up meaning the difference between life or death for one or more of these people. Once you parade yourself in the world as a rescuer and once you take charge of the party, everything that happens after that is on your head.

I tried not to let myself think about the fear, pain, and suffering of the victims, except as objective facts which had to be entered into the calculations along with everything else that had a bearing on getting off the mountain by the quickest, safest means available. A sympathetic understanding of their plight could help little. Whether the pain and fear was tolerable or intolerable, being dealt with well or ill, there was still only one solution, getting down. But in this case, the sheer numbers of suffering people made it difficult to maintain that attitude. Jim appeared to accept the slow pace better than I, but he too had his troubles holding off their suffering.

We made another effort to talk to Doug and Ster. Our message was that we did indeed need everything they had, but they had to stay out of the gully. It was frustrating for them, and for the guides that had arrived too, to watch the shadow of the Grand move out over the valley while we appeared not to be moving at all. The rockfall we were setting off was fairly convincing. The main thing we wanted to be happening down there was to have the snowfield all set up for lowering so that as each of the party arrived at the top of the snowfield, they could be lowered quickly from anchor to anchor.

Just before dark, Jim called down to me the news that two of the missing three were coming down from above. The significance of the fact that there were two, not three, took hold slowly. I could not imagine how the third could be rescued. If we stopped everything to bring a litter and eight climbers up through us, I was sure somebody would die of exposure, there would be rockfall both above and below, and there'd be nobody left to help us get these seven down. I also found myself fervently hoping that I wouldn't have to go back up the mountain.

When Blade got down to me, I interrogated him fairly fiercely about the condition of the third. It was Smith and he was dead. I was in danger of feeling relieved, and that made me ruder. Also, it was difficult to believe. 'Are you sure he's dead, because if you're not sure somebody has to go up. How did you check? How long did you wait before leaving him?' Blade told me that the body had started to get stiff. That soon? Well anyway, whether he was dead when they left him or not, he was certainly dead by now. Still, I'd given a man up for dead on secondhand information. I sized up Joyce. He was in better shape than anyone else. It was surprising to see a normal person who was apparently unaffected by this place. I asked him. 'Yeah, he's gone.'

I had taken Blade aside to question him. I could imagine what the impact of the news that this strong young man had died of exposure might do to the will to survive of the rest. Furthermore, if someone else was going to die it was unlikely that they'd do it quickly and allow us to go on. I had an image of being immobilized there in that gully helplessly watching a slow chain reaction of dying. I told Blade not to talk about it.

He moved across the ledge and gathered everybody there around and made a little speech about how we were trying to help them and they'd have to cooperate with us. I found that astonishing and a little amusing. Astonishing that he still was functioning as a leader and amusing as I tried to imagine how they could not cooperate with us. Then I had an awful insight. What, from their point of view, would we be doing differently from what we were doing if we were not trying to save them but trying to kill them? They were back in the dreaded couloir, were wet again, rocks were falling around them, there was no tea and jam. Whatever his mistakes, Blade was one of them and not one of their tormentors.

I was ashamed of my tough talk to Blade. I had my own mistakes to worry about.

Janet got soaked again. She lost her footing while being lowered, swung into a waterfall and was too stiff and cold to roll out of it without help. I began to feel that she might not make it, and I had to do something personally to give her heart. The barrier the rescuer maintains between himself and the victims makes stepping across it a more effective gesture.

I made her squeeze in behind a flake which would protect her a little from the cold evening westerly pouring down on us from the snowfields above. I made her take off her Levi's, lectured her about the fact that denim was the worst possible material to wear in the mountains, and wrung the water out of them as much as I could. They were new and stiff.

I imagined that she'd bought them down in Jackson, in honor of her visit to the West. I gave her some food I'd been saving for someone to whom it might make the difference, me, for example. Then I took my favorite sweater out of my pack and made her put it on. I tried levity. I told her that it was a twenty-five-dollar sweater and she'd better not get it dirty! She thought I was serious – so much for levity.

There were shouts from below. They were coming up, and we were to be careful about rocks. It was worth being a climber to feel what I felt then. For the feeling I had, you have to learn to do something which is dangerous, has a code, and requires performance to a certain standard. Then you have to get in a jam and have 'your mates,' as Hemming would have said, get you out of it only because you are one of them.

First to arrive were Pete Lev and Al Read. Lev was the picture of earnest strength. Read was the picture of a man in command of himself. Witty, quick to perceive the ludicrous as the ironic, he is a natural leader and an unobtrusive one. Lev is very compassionate and was taken aback by what he saw, including me and Jim. Pete and Al were looking at us as if we needed a cab to get us home. Suddenly it seemed possible that most of us might escape from this place. Suddenly the mountain seemed covered with people who knew what they were doing.

Swedlund was down there, Swedlund who would joke with the Devil. I couldn't wait to get down to hear him say something like, 'Sinclair, you're quaking like a dog passing peach pits.' Horn was down there, probably performing great feats of strength and daring while screaming, 'The world is contrived to drive us insane.'

The next pitch below ended in the middle of a slab which bulged out from the base of the couloir. Every rock that came down the couloir had to hit that slab. Jake was at that anchor. When I got to him, I was afraid for him, a fear that was familiar. Then I recalled the boulder that seemed to pursue us in the great ice gully on McKinley. He, however, was ebullient. For him, this was what it was all about. He remarked, 'How often do you get to have fun like this, up here in an interesting part of the mountain with practically all your climbing buddies?' He was good for the people we were rescuing, too. He told them, as he prepared to send them down the vertical slab below, 'We always arrange to have these rescues at night so you won't know what you're stepping off of.' He picked them up and kept them going. For one or more of them, it is likely that Jake made the difference.

The one I was most eagerly waiting to get to was Sterling because once I got to him and passed below, he would take my place.

I asked Pete and Al if they had set up the snowfield. They hadn't. It turned out that the guides Jake Breitenbach, Al Read, Pete Lev, Fred Wright, Dave Dornan, and Herb Swedlund; Mike Ermath and Rick Horn of the rescue team; and Dr. Walker from Jackson had arrived at the base of the couloir just minutes after Jim and I reached its top. Even if the radio had worked, the word that we needed masses of gear would have gone out too late. Again, the critical two hours I had lost. There went my hopes that things would soon speed up. It had taken Jim and me five hours to get the party down five pitches. It was to be another seven hours, 2 a.m., before the last victim would be lowered to the top of the snowfield. Just two more ropes would have cut that seven hours in half.

Al and Pete tactfully suggested that Jim and I go on down to the snowfield; they could handle matters up there. They received no heroic protests from us.

My last image of the gully is of Horn working on the pitch exiting the couloir. I was rappeling down a steep slab and Horn came racing up by me, foot over hand it seemed, to help someone who'd gotten hung up on a ledge. He was muttering to himself and lunged to the ledge just as I realized that he was climbing unroped. I asked him if he thought that was wise. He didn't, but there weren't any more ropes.

At the top of the snowfield, a huge platform was being cut, large enough to hold all the rescued and some of the rescuers. After telling him he looked good enough to kiss, I described the situation above as best I could to Sterling. I told him that it wasn't at all clear that they all were going to make it. Lester had expressed a wish to be left alone to die. I'd been tempted to let him and was glad it was out of my hands. Actually, the fact that Germer had the whole party dedicated to keeping him alive gave them a badly needed focus for survival. Lester Germer was, I believe, in some degree conscious of this because, as we later found out, he had spotted the rescue team coming up Teepe's Snowfield and had said nothing to his companions. Not knowing that help was near, they'd kept some sense that they alone were responsible for their survival.

Jim and I stood around on the snow platform until the first victim arrived. The system was in place. There was some debate about whether to set up a series of anchors down the snowfield a rope length apart or establish fewer super anchors to which we would just add ropes. I tried to join in the discussion and realized that I couldn't think very well and that it was no longer our show. Jim and I headed down.

We were without ice axes and crampons. The surface was so hard that we couldn't kick steps deeper than half an inch. The pitons we held in our hands to stop a slip weren't convincing. I couldn't judge the surface either by sight or touch. I had difficulty keeping my body balanced over the pitiful footholds we were kicking because there was no elasticity left in my legs. At any time I could have moved from a marginal hold to a place where I quickly needed a good hold and found that I was on water ice, and that would have been it. I'd be rocketing down the snowfield at fifty miles an hour, slowing only as I hit chunks of ice. And I said we wouldn't need crampons.

We paid little attention to the commotion above us except to remark that we hoped our mates didn't bomb us with one of the victims.

What was going on up there was a battle of life and death which was literal but which had become for Fenniman an allegorical battle of good and evil. We had placed Fenniman in an ambiguous position by enlisting his help in the rescue. From his position in-between he could see that there were two sides in this struggle, those being done to and those doing it to them. He had been trapped into complicity in inflicting suffering on his comrades. In his suffering and exhaustion it was difficult to see that his life was being saved, and he could undoubtedly sense that Jim and I were not certain that we weren't killing them. After helping us with the second pitch, he rejoined the ranks of those being done to. It had been twelve hours since we first started them down the couloir. Progress to safety at that rate was imperceptible. Toward the end, the mountainside was filled with shadowy beings with one eye (the head lamps we wore), pushing and pummeling, binding and unbinding them, forcing them into one terrifying experience after another. Finally, Fenniman's great heart rebelled. He decided that we were one-eyed demons trying to drag them into hell and the only way he could escape was to kill us. He was one of five tied into one rope, the entire rope to be lowered at once. He endured one lowering down to where Pete Lev had established the second anchor. He untied himself from his waist loop and went after Peter's axe, announcing his intention to kill 'them.' Peter was twice as strong as Fenniman, but Fenniman had the superhuman strength of the mad and wasn't worried about falling. Rick Horn tied off a fixed rope and swung down to help. Fenniman then went for Horn. Rick ducked a round-house swing, grabbed Fenniman from behind, and tied him into the rope and moved off. Fenniman then went for the party on the big ledge. Sterling pushed him down the glacier. He came again. Rick shouted at him, trying to explain that they were trying to help him. Fenniman reiterated that he was going to kill all the devils.

When he reached the ledge, Rick gave him a tremendous kick to the head, which failed to improve communication between them. Fenniman went down and started to come out of his waist loop. Rick lowered himself to Fenniman to tighten the loop, fearing that he had killed him. He began slapping him to bring him around, which worked but probably didn't do much to disabuse Fenniman of his interpretation of what the one-eyed devils were about. From then on, Fenniman was Rick's personal responsibility. When Fenniman saw that he wasn't going to be able to kill the devils, he fought passively, digging in his heels and refusing to be lowered. Rick finally couldn't take the punishment and sat on him, knocking him out. Fenniman was soon gasping from exhaustion, retching, and moaning, and the rescuers began to wonder if he was going to make it. Sterling and Rick together wrestled, rolled, and fought Fenniman to the bottom of the glacier. It took practically the entire rescue team to get him out of his wet clothes, into a sleeping bag, and bound into a litter. When he got warm, he woke up and calmly told them about the strange dream he had been having. Who was the bravest? Joyce, who never lost his selfpossession, or Fenniman in his great-hearted madness? Odysseus or Achilles?

Jim and I slowly returned to the mouth of Garnet Canyon. We stopped to doze on a flat rock in the boulder field below the snowfield until the cold pushed us on. We slept at the cache of equipment until we heard the helicopter come in to pick up Fenniman and Germer. The rest of the party stayed further up the canyon, at the AMC camp, to recover, which they all did fully and quickly, except Germer, who'd suffered frostbite. The job of getting all the gear off the mountain would now begin, but I was relieved of that duty because something had to be done about Smith.

Throughout the day, Sunday, Jim and I wandered leisurely out of the mountains to spend one night in a bed before going up for Smith. We didn't want to bring the body down. The chief ranger, Russ Dickenson, and the superintendent contacted Smith's parents and asked for permission to bury him on the mountain. I don't know how they found the words to ask them, and I don't know how the Smiths found the words to grant it, but they did. I felt awful about it, as if we were violating the code that Achilles violated in refusing to allow Priam to give Hector a proper burial. Achilles relented; we didn't.

On Monday, Rick, Jim, and I were transported to the Lower Saddle by helicopter. The weather looked lousy. Soon it started to snow. We stayed in the guide's hut, enjoying the luxury of lounging on several layers of sleeping pads and drinking tea. Rick told us about his adventures with Fenniman. He still hadn't quite recovered from that experience and didn't relish the task at hand. Our plan was to go up the Owen-Spalding Route, cross over the top of the mountain just south of the summit and descend the snowfield to the shoulder of the Otterbody where Smith's body lay, bury him, and descend on down the evacuation route. The snowstorm was not an auspicious beginning. This was turning out to be one of the worst climbing seasons in memory. Jake used to say that Owen-Spalding is both the easiest and the most difficult route he had climbed on the Grand. When it snows, the lesser angle of this route allows more ice to stick to the rock than a steeper route would hold. That worried me some, but that wasn't what was worrying Rick, much the strongest climber. Every hour or so Rick would inquire as discreetly as possible as to what we thought he would look like when we got to him. It dawned on Jim and me that this was to be Rick's first corpse, and we laid it on a little. We weren't unsympathetic, but we knew that nobody can help you through that experience. The best you can do is to gain what distance you can by finding what humor you can, not laughing at the death, but laughing at what your imagination is doing to you.

It snowed throughout Monday night and for much of Tuesday and then began to clear. We would leave for the summit before dawn on Wednesday. It was not an unpleasant prospect. We were well rested, we were in good physical condition, and we'd spent most of the past five days high in the mountains. Compared to what might have been had we been setting out to carry the body down the mountain, we were lucky.

The Owen-Spalding Route is on the shaded side of the mountain. It was bitterly cold Wednesday morning for midsummer, and the whole upper part of the mountain was completely iced over. It might have been November. Jim and I climbed slowly and cautiously, protecting every high-angle pitch, but Rick found that maddening. He very much wanted to get to the summit ridge, out of the cold, and into the sun. We could not prevail upon him to be careful, so we just let him go. He shot up the seven hundred feet of roped climbing below the summit ridge at the same rate he would have if there had been no ice. Yet Jim and I felt little danger. Rick was inspired; he didn't hesitate, and he slipped slightly only a couple of times. It happens sometimes when climbing that you know that everything you know is at your command and no wayward doubt or fear is going to intrude to break your concentration. It is inconceivable that you could fall. Rick had it at that time, and we let him go, insisting only that he had good protection when he belayed us up behind him.

Over the crest of the ridge we found a beautiful summer day in the mountains. Not hot of course because we were in fresh snow above thirteen thousand feet, but the sun opened our jackets and loosened our overtensed muscles. We called a halt for an early lunch. Rick was outraged; he wanted to get on with it.

'Come on, Rick,' said Jim, 'relax. It's beautiful here.' And it was. The partially mown hay fields made squares of light green between the darker green willows along the Snake and Gros Ventre rivers and the greenish-grey and light brown sagebrush flats of the valley. The snow was clean and too bright for unprotected eyes. We had passed from winter to summer in the space of a few moments and a few yards.

Rick agreed to stop but not to eat. We stripped off our clanking gear and lay back in the sun, Jim and I chatting idly, musing over the events of the past few days, beginning to formulate them into shreds of the story of our lives. Rick was silent and then said, 'I can smell him.' We roared with laughter. 'Rick, he's a thousand feet below us and frozen stiff!' In the face of our laughter, Rick's imagination relented and he smiled a little. We, in turn, agreed to get going and get it over with.

We moved at normal pace, picking out a route with caution in the couloirs we had to cross to reach the snowfield, and then descended with an occasional belay down the East Face Snowfield to the rock band which separates it from the Otterbody Snowfield. The body was on a ledge in the middle of the band. Some scrambling and a short rappel got us down to it. Near it was an empty matchbook; the matches lay scattered about. Each one had been tried; none had lit. We tried to imagine what it had been like there but weren't to find out until three years later when Jim Lipscomb published the account he had gotten from Joyce:

Joyce, recalling what followed, remembers looking into Smith's dazed eyes, realizing that he was far gone and saying, 'Steve will never be able to climb.'

'Of course he will,' said Blade. 'We have got to get him moving.' So Joyce reached deep into his pack and pulled out a can of pineapple, one he had hidden there before the climb began. The three shared the fruit. Smith could not move his fingers to hold the pineapple pieces. He opened his mouth and Joyce dropped them in, chunk by chunk. Then they drank the juice.

Again, Blade started to climb. Smith's eyes were blank, his skin colorless. Air rasped in his throat. Joyce, recognizing the symptoms of shock, called after Blade, 'Smith can't climb.'

'Let's not talk about it,' Blade said. Blade moved very slowly. Joyce, standing behind Smith and belaying Blade with one hand, reached down with the other to put his arm around Smith. But Smith threw his arms over his head to push Joyce off. Joyce tried again. Smith threw up his arms again, hitting Joyce in the face. A glove fell off Smith's hand, dropping 10 feet down the slope. Joyce retrieved it and tried to get it back on, but Smith's hand was stiffened into a claw and Joyce could not get the glove on it. Joyce called up to Blade, 'I think he's dying.'

'Don't talk like that,' said Blade. 'I don't want you to say anything like that again.'

Joyce watched. Blade was still climbing very slowly above them. Finally he called down, 'All right, come on up.'

Joyce answered, 'Smith's dead.'

Blade climbed down. 'This is terrible,' he said. He forced Smith's mouth open and blew air into his lungs.

'He's not coming back to life,' Joyce said.

The two tied Smith's body in its bright-red parka to the ledge. They began climbing upward again. 'It was the first time,' recalls Joyce, 'that we really moved fast.' A hundred feet of progress brought them to the top of the couloir. They now faced the East Ridge snowfield, still 1,000 feet below the summit. A foot of new snow rested on top of the old crust.

'This snow won't hold,' said Blade.

'Let's traverse, then,' said Joyce, 'over to those rocks.'

'The route is to the right,' Blade said.

'Well, don't just stand there, what do you want to do?' said Joyce. Blade cast about, unable to decide. Turn back now? What could that mean to Ellis Blade, the leader who had insisted that going up was the only safe way for the party to get down? Blade turned to Joyce, looking past him to the valley below.

Then Joyce took Blade by the shoulder 'We are going down, down, down!' Joyce said. 'And this time we are going all the way.' And the two men started down.

For three days Blade had led all the pitches, taking the most exposed and dangerous positions. In descending, the first man down a slope can be protected from above and normally the more experienced climber would take the second position. But Blade, no leader now, was moving down first, with Joyce belaying him.*

---

*Sports Illustrated, 21 June 1965, pp. 67, 68.

We took what personal effects we thought his family might like to have, tied a rope to the body, and maneuvered the body over the moat between the base of the cliff and the Otterbody Snowfield. Jim and I relented in our education of Rick and handled the body while Rick handled the ropes. Getting the body adequately protected was a problem. We selected a place near at hand where the snowpack was thickest and seemed least likely to bare the rock in a dry year. Rick was anchoring the body. From a stance a few feet above the body, I guided the rope to a position where the body would drop directly down a small chimney to the debris at the base of the cliff. Jim straddled the rope at the body with his knife out.

I had forgotten to bring a Bible. Jim said, 'Well, so long, Buddy,' made the sign of the cross over Steve Smith, and cut the rope. We covered the body first with small rocks, in case there were any carnivorous rodents up there, and then with larger rocks to keep it safe not only from rodents and insects but from the motions of the mountain itself as the snow waxed and waned and as the granite flesh of the mountain checked, cracked, and sloughed off in its slow journey towards the valley.

from High and Wild: A
Mountaineer's World
by Galen Rowell

Galen Rowell (born 1940) is best known for his splendid mountain photography, but he's a prolific climber and writer as well. This selection from his 1979 book High and Wild *reminds us that mountaineering's greatest joys include the pleasures of discovery and self-sufficiency in the wilderness.*

On a Friday evening in 1971 I drove two hundred miles east from Berkeley, California, on a road as familiar to me as my home street. It led to Yosemite Valley, where I had been climbing on weekends for a decade. As the winding road enters the national park, it parallels the Merced River through a deep gorge, and the canyon broadens into a flat valley surrounded by cliffs that rise to the stars.

Even to those who have been there hundreds of times, the first glimpse of Yosemite is overwhelming. As a child I imagined that the valley at night looked like a movie set. Moonlight reflected from the massive granite forms made them appear too stark and simple to be big; the valley seemed like a small model of itself. I felt I could almost reach out and touch the tops of cliffs three thousand feet overhead.

I stopped at Yosemite Lodge, where I met a group of climbers who gathered there every weekend. Within minutes I was invited to join friends on a route I had done many times before. Though I had intended to climb in Yosemite, I felt a sudden urge to change that plan and suggested an alternative – the south face of Bear Creek Spire in the John Muir Wilderness adjoining Yosemite National Park. No interest. I might as well have suggested Patagonia.

I sat and thought for a while about why I had lost enthusiasm for a Yosemite climb, and soon realized that I felt a need to escape the security Yosemite represented. It was home – familiar walls, faces, sounds, smells – and I was already part of an earlier generation, from a time when climbers knew the wonder of gazing at great cliffs still untouched by the hand of man. When I first climbed in Yosemite in 1957, none of the big walls had been ascended. Since that time, all of Yosemite's major cliffs had been climbed by at least one route; El Capitan now had eleven; the front face of Half Dome, four. The simple joys of exploration were on the wane; in their place was a trend to count and compare experiences with those of others who had climbed the same routes. I had no doubt that many Yosemite climbs demanded greater skill than the hardest routes of the highest ranges, but a big red flag went up when I saw climbers far more talented than myself unwilling to test in the nearby wilderness the skills acquired in this fair-weather womb. There was little I could do personally to reverse what I considered an unfortunate trend, except to bow out of it. I decided to go to Bear Creek Spire, alone. The decision to solo did not come from any high motive; quite simply, no one would go with me.

I slept fitfully in a crowded campground before driving at dawn towards Tioga Pass, on the park's eastern boundary. The pass, at almost 10,000 feet, was just below timberline; and though summer was nearly over, the meadows were still lush. My climb would begin in just this sort of terrain, but farther south, where not a single road crossed the rugged Sierra crest for two hundred miles. To reach my starting point I drove another hundred miles, first dropping thousands of feet to the desert floor of the Mono Basin, then along the base of the mountains until a deadend side road brought me back up to 10,400 feet.

Here I locked my ten-speed bicycle to a tree in the woods not far from the roadhead. My plan was to drive on to another trailhead farther south, walk eight miles in and 5,000 feet up to the base of Bear Creek Spire, climb it, traverse the north side to pick up my bicycle, and ride forty miles back to my car.

From where I cached my bike, I could see Bear Creek Spire about ten miles away, and before turning around to continue south, I took a long look at it. I had once wondered why this undistinguished 13,713-foot peak, which had been climbed from the west by a moderate scramble in 1923, was named a spire. The answer was clear when I first saw its south face from the ridge of another mountain. The face is a pointed blade of granite, which to the best of my knowledge had never been attempted.

I drove on into America's deepest valley, the Owens Valley, created by a massive fault block between the 14,000-foot summits of the High Sierra and the White Mountains twenty miles to the east. An earthquake greater than the one that almost destroyed San Francisco in 1906 dropped the valley twenty feet in 1872. I took a side road up Pine Creek to the largest tungsten mine in North America. Outwardly it looks like a normal mining operation in a mountain valley; actually, it is upside-down. Shafts climb from the tunnels up into the mountains, and one penetrates Bear Creek Spire, four air miles away.

I left my car and began hiking away from the creaks and whines of the milling operation. I soon came upon what looked like a natural marble quarry: glacial polish had combined with frost-heaving to segment white aplite into piles of burnished blocks that gleamed against the surrounding granite. By noon I left the last whitebark pines below and set out across a barren moraine composed of loose granite boulders. When I saw the vivid green of a tiny lake set amid the glacial debris, I knew that ice somewhere beneath the surface was still carving this landscape. Glacially scoured rock dust – 'glacier milk' – accounted for the water's tint.

My memory of how impressive the south face appeared from a distance had been tempered somewhat by a recent look at the contour map, which showed the wall to be about 800 feet high and not particularly steep. Now, at close range, my original impression returned; the face was fully 1,200 feet high, without a single large ledge. The situation gave me pause. It was two o'clock in the afternoon, and I was carrying only minimal equipment: a ³/₈-inch rope, one quart of water, some food, a short, half sleeping bag, and a handful of pitons and karabiners. I foresaw a demanding afternoon on the face under a hot sun, but nothing to make me seriously consider giving up the ascent.

The climbing began with deceptive ease. I didn't even rope up for several hundred feet, because cracks and handholds kept appearing in just the right places. A squeeze chimney at nearly 13,000 feet left me panting, however; and I used rope and pitons for safety on the steep face above. I made steady progress until I reached a small pedestal and discovered a smooth headwall above; I tried to free-climb it with the rope for safety, but failed. The only crack I could spot was separated from better terrain above by about eight feet of blank overhanging rock.

Dropping back to the top of the pedestal, I drank the last of my water and thought about Yosemite. My bright idea of a remote climb was losing its luster rapidly. I could picture my friends in the Valley, who had probably come down from their routes before the afternoon heat, and were now sitting in the restaurant with a drink or cavorting in Camp Four, the Yosemite climbers' camp. I, on the other hand, contemplated a cold night at 13,000 feet and an arduous descent in the morning.

After a brief rest, I clipped a sling into my highest piton and stood in it. The overhanging wall pushed me out, and after a futile effort to surmount it, I descended again. The sun was about to leave the face, and I knew that my best chance was to give it everything I had while the rock was still warm. This time I put the shortest possible loop into the piton so I could stand a bit higher than before. The headwall had a shallow vertical groove; and I worked, with my elbow pointed skyward, to secure an arm-lock between my inverted palm and shoulder. When I tried to move my free leg, I felt completely helpless, but I made one final attempt. Dangling from the overhang by the arm-lock, I pulled my foot away from the security of the loop and up onto the eye of the piton. The extra inches let me move the arm-lock higher. I was now out of balance, but very near a wide crack, and a desperate lunge took me high enough to jam a fist into the bottom of the crack.

Relief surged through me, as though a gun aimed at my head had just misfired. The danger was not entirely over, however; I knew that my adrenalin-stimulated strength would be short-lived. I continued up, fist-jamming thirty feet to a narrow ledge, and panted there for long minutes. The ledge traversed the steep headwall for a hundred feet and then connected with a chimney system. It was a lucky break; I wouldn't need to bivouac on the cliff if I could move efficiently in the minutes remaining before dark.

The day's harsh sunlight gave way to dusk, and in the indirect light I could see into the shadowy north faces of an endless sea of peaks. It was a more rugged Sierra vista than I had ever known in summer. At my feet were alpine flowers; this very contrast of life and barren rock had led John Muir to call the range 'the gentle wilderness'.

All along the ledge yellow hulsea and purple polemonium were still in bloom. Sierra bighorn sheep depend on them as an important part of their summer diet. In Muir's day, the flowers might have been nibbled down to the roots. Weathered horns and ancient Indian hunting blinds attest to the fact that the bighorn, now a threatened species, once ranged as high as the very tops of most mountains along the crest. I could imagine a ram profiled on the summit ramparts only a hundred feet above me as I hurried along the ledge below.

Having reached the chimney, I climbed steadily with the pack suspended below me, and within minutes I was standing on the summit in the last rays of the sun. I would have liked to linger, but it was late. I scrambled towards the shadows of the north side, heading down the broken face towards a tiny meadow with a stream. An hour later, in the dark, I bent down for my first drink in many hours.

I had planned to stop by the stream for only a minute, then descend in the moonlight to the forest below, but after eating a package of freeze-dried hash mixed with cold water, I realized that my legs didn't want to support my body any longer. Without standing up again, I crawled into my half-bag. Though extremely fatigued, I lay sleepless for hours, still carried along by the forced awareness the day had demanded. I felt lucky to have made the climb and to have gotten down safely. I no longer envied the climbers loafing around the Yosemite campground. I was content where I was, alone under the stars on a clear night.

I set off again before dawn, walking through Little Lakes Valley towards the roadhead. After a single day high in the mountains, the well-used trail and established campsites seemed like civilization. At sunrise I reached the trailhead where my bicycle was cached and soon reveled in a 6,000-foot downhill ride. From the floor of Owens Valley I had to climb again, struggling up a 3,000-foot grade in desert heat that was already intense. I stopped half a dozen times to plunge my upper body into mountain streams. At nine that morning, less than twenty-four hours after starting up the trail towards Bear Creek Spire, I reached my car, with barely enough energy left to lift the light ten-speed inside.

A solo climb such as the one I had just made is not a logical extension of Yosemite technique, which stresses extending limits of ability while protected by equipment. Nor is solo climbing simply the means to an end, for there are far easier ways to reach summits. It is a form of private, heightened awareness – something that anyone who has spent time alone under stress can understand. What makes it different and desirable is doing so by choice.

from Looking for Mo
by Daniel Duane

Many climbers spend a lot of time fighting the urge to quit – a climb, an expedition, climbing itself. Why not give up and go down? Daniel Duane (born 1967) offers answers of sorts in this episode from his 1998 novel. Here, two friends find themselves high on the 3,000-foot face of Yosemite's El Capitan.

A t midmorning, just below the monstrous roof that led to the final headwall, I climbed over a loose block the size of a truck engine. I felt sure it would break free and give me a Doctor Strangelove ride to the Valley floor. I looked down at my speck of a truck, at a few dot people in the meadow and at the sad choreography of all those black cranes tiny on the river, rising and swirling, floating off the earth as a group. Lifting over the dead meadows and tall trees, they rode a current along the Cathedral Spires, over those broken buttresses and on to the Valley rim. Bound for some place far south, they swirled and rose like a party of souls en route to a different world. Then I saw why: the smoke had obscured an approaching storm. A translucent gray curtain of rain washed through the fire haze down-valley, and a ten-mile rain-beard answered the smoke jumpers' prayers. It moved not in drops or showers but in sheets shadowing whole mountainsides. I was only thirty feet below that big roof, so I climbed towards it. Just as the veil of water was so close I could taste it, I pulled underneath. No ledge to stand on, so I stuffed three friends beneath the roof, clipped slings through them, and anchored dangling there. Soon, lines of rain poured silently past. With no pavement to puddle in and no puddle to slap, the perfect spheres fell steadily by and disappeared below. The completely soundless downpour had the ethereal softness of heavy snowfall, as though water and earth were of such different substance that their collision never accrued meaning.

Mo dragged himself up to me, soaked through. We hung squashed together in quiet cogitation and welling fear. Odd to see a storm from so near its source, to see water seep out of clouds closer overhead than the ground was below. Mo had an extra sweater that would keep me warm as long as I stayed dry. We pulled out those morbid Vietnam vintage body bags, which had a creepy plastic smell. Not much to do besides pull mine around me like a Ziploc over a chicken thigh and to feel harness straps dig into my legs, to mutter speculations about the future and yearn for security and human warmth. Make banal observations about the immense value of things like soft-boiled eggs and sushi and hot sake. We hung all the rest of that day, muttering in chorus, 'Rain, rain, go away, come again another day.' In a windless downpour, without shadows or sunbeams or a changing sky, dusk came on as had dawn, in an imperceptible and perfectly uniform lessening of light. No vanishing source or burning alpenglow, just a fading out of the world as though it were nothing more substantial than light. The stirrups and harnesses became nearly unbearable, and we took a long time rigging nylon sacks into hammocklike seats. When it was dark, we opened canned minestrone soup and ate it slowly. Then we shared a liter of Burgundy. Soon, it became too cold to do anything at all. You'd expose a bit of skin and lose a bit of heat.

The acres of wet stone overhead drained down the wall until the roof's edge became a waterfall's lip. Big ribbons twisted before our eyes. On the Cathedral Rocks we could make out spraying funnels of foaming runoff. For most of that third day, we'd had the secret peace of the tropical waterfall cave, watching the shimmer from behind. By midnight, surface tension drew the spiraling streams along our dry ceiling. An inch at a time, our little haven shrank. My fingers and toes got increasingly cold and I shivered steadily.

The next morning, our hands were puffed to twice their normal size and coated with dirt-filled sores. By the end of the following day, we'd eaten our last few cookies – the very end of our food. We just waited and suffered in a Gordian tangle of rope and nylon, bound up and sweating. As I tried to sleep once again, I wondered if I was going to die there. For some reason, it no longer seemed so awful – probably because I knew what I was doing there, and which story I was living, and I believed in it. I even felt a little blessed for having reached such a stellar perch once in my short life. The south wind built in the cold hours of that afternoon. First its whisperings sounded like forewarning voices, and then the gusts became louder sucks and rents. Sweat condensed inside the body bag, even inside my clothing. Water found its way along the ropes and into our harnesses. Just before dark, a gust bounced us like ships dragging anchors in a gale. We could no longer keep the water out at all. Drops came hard across my face. I dozed once, only to awaken hyperventilating from cold.

'Mo,' I said, thinking he couldn't possibly be asleep. 'Mo.' He didn't respond, so I pulled myself over and grabbed his shoulder.

He shook violently and his head snapped upright. 'What?' he said in a panic. 'What the hell?'

'You awake?' I asked.

'You can have my hat, or something. I'll be all right.'

During a long silence, the wind became a breathless panting.

'I'm a little spooked.'

Mo rubbed his face in the darkness. 'Me too, huh? Pass the water.' He honestly didn't sound worried.

A few lights came on below – a new firmament to replace the obscured one above. I could not stop shaking, and I worried that the ropes would freeze. My fingers were thick and slow in the cold and I was unable to make a fist. Sometime that night, I turned on my headlamp to look at the anchor holding us to the wall. The very material correlative of faith and chance, it was just a few bits of steel, a few lumps of blacksmithery now playing the starring role in the Ray and Mo Death Drama. I could feel my weight in tension against it and had an unobstructed view into the blackness below. I thought of vanishing into the night sky, living for a time in a dream of black flight – past realms of shadowed stone, eyries and caverns and perches, perhaps soaring down towards the red blur of a fire truck hiding in the pit, away from the flames. Decided I wouldn't mind a cup of Earl Grey on a bright San Francisco morning on Fiona's porch with surf running high after a night of love and nothing to do but breathe and say thanks and kiss in nostalgia about that silly first night together. I imagined her agreeing to hike with me in some distant national park, or just to see a movie in the heart of a large city. Maybe a foreign film with a nihilistic message about human suffering. I pictured how I'd become too distracted by her lovely earlobes to pay any attention to the film, and she'd be irritated with me, but also delighted, and we'd leave the film early to go home together.

Near daybreak, I heard something through the hissing of the wind and rain slapping against the body bag. A voice.

'Did you hear that?' Mo asked, lifting his head again from its fetal huddle.

I had. A voice. A megaphone somewhere far below.

'CLIMBERS ON THE SALATHÉ,' Yabber's unmistakable voice said, apparently meaning us. 'RAISE ONE ARM IF YOU NEED A RESCUE. RAISE TWO IF YOU DO NOT.'

We held each other's gaze a long time, and Mo said, 'I'll go down now, if you want.' I remembered the last time, when there hadn't even been a storm, and I remembered the finality with which Mo had poured out all those water bottles. This time I was cold and weak and losing focus. We had no food left, and while I wasn't hypothermic yet, I would be. I imagined Yabber looking up through the crosshairs of that telescope. Muttering to Raffi perhaps: 'Looks like Ray forgot his rain gear.' A sinking weakness and sorrow came over me at the thought of leaving, both for the ignominy and failure and because I'd begun to love the way the world yawned away from us. It was as if we'd finally found that dwarfing perspective we'd always yearned for, that diving board in the heart of space. In the growing light, I could see the cluster of rescue personnel in the meadow now – a tiny group of colored specks. Off west, a charcoal-gray sky dumped a thick cloudburst into the foothills. I guessed they'd lower a few guys off the summit on thousand-foot ropes, bring us up that way. Looking at Mo, grizzled and bundled, I thought, *This is not my life.*

This is somebody else's life. Someone much stronger and cooler. Mo looked at me in the coming light, and the rain on his face made a broad wash of tears.

The twenty-pound rack of hardware swung away from the wall in a gust, and ropes whipped into the sky like tentacles. If El Capitan was my ten-megaton Old Testament God, certainly I was humiliated and suffering before it. The dawn seemed very dark, and the air tasted like aluminum. Whenever the mist parted, we could see those men in the meadow, waiting to help us. By trading leads – taking turns at risk and groveling – we'd kept the whole thing a game played between only us. Now this third element – the elements themselves – forced our relative solitude upon us. Our water tasted of the plastic containers. Shreds of stormfog hung onto the Cathedral Spires like torn sails on broken masts. For a moment, a cloud descended over the Captain. We could see nothing beyond our disembodied rock drifting in the original mists: no sound, no sky, no earth, sun, shadow, or even darkness.

Mo and I looked at each other without speaking, each waiting for the other to give in. Clouds rose as if on elevators, and raindrops passed through space from unknown origins to unknown ends.

'CLIMBERS ON THE SALATHÉ, RAISE ONE ARM IF YOU NEED A RESCUE, TWO IF YOU DO NOT.'

What else could I do? I hated raising an arm, felt a petulant outrage at nothing in particular. Steam wisped off my ribs as I reached upwards.

Mo's eyebrows lifted. He looked at that one hand held in plain view of the men so far below.

Then Yabber called again. 'ONE ARM FOR A RESCUE,' he said, as if to make sure we'd heard him right. 'TWO IF NOT.'

I wiggled my cold toes in those resoled shoes, and with my free hand, I felt something in my pocket: those Jolly Ranchers. A few thousand calories, maybe. Little bits of sugar and sweetness and flavor and of Yabber's weird confidence. Mo was looking at me, waiting.

I raised the other arm.

Mo smiled wide and lifted both his arms into the air, too. We hung with wings spread for laughing flight, like stone angels adorning a grand natural cathedral.

The storm tasted like ocean, like fog and surf – washing us clean of sweat and blood and shit. As we ate through those Jolly Ranchers and got warmed by their little sucrose rushes, the meadow vanished and water blew sideways. I shook in hard spasms against my cutting harness, hyperventilating. Dripping loops of nylon tangled around my legs, and ropes slapped like guy lines in a sea gale. With sky and earth now immaterial in the storm, we might have been on an unformed planet whose waters had yet to gather and mountains had yet to rise. The gear glowed with electricity, and claps of thunder made the whole mountain tremble as if something much worse had happened, as if the wall had split in two or broken off. *Hail Mary, full of grace, the Lord is with thee, blessed art thou amongst women and blessed is the fruit of thy womb, Jesus, Holy Mary, mother of God, pray for us sinners, now and at the hour of our death, Amen.* For a while my mind ran to everything I'd miss – Evan's wedding and the soft pleasures of big cities and especially a love that might have been and which now, of course, seemed like guaranteed life-mate material. A gust took water straight up and blew Mo away from the wall as a sheet of electricity flashed like a door to another time. 'Check it out, bro,' Mo screeched in electrified blue flight. 'I'm flying!' My own windy bouncing felt too much like falling for laughter to come easy, and I repeated under my breath, *I don't want to die, I don't want to die, I don't want to die.*

I worked at keeping that corpse sack around my shoulders and over my head for the interminable hours of that night. Rain lashed against it like pellets, and my wet feet lost feeling. At one point, Mo tried again to offer me his rain jacket, and in the lunacy of the gesture I realized he'd been making offers like that as long as I'd known him. He never felt that he had anything to lose, and so could let go, could always be the giving one and assume the world would take him where it needed him. It had always seemed so wasteful to me, risking everything just to maintain a childish openness. But in the misery of that storm, I felt the meaning to which Mo'd surrendered himself, the conviction that only in giving did you find out how little you had, and only then did you learn how little you were. *Please let this storm go away, please just forget about little old us and go rain somewhere else. Oh, yeah, and the wind. Any time we could have that wind stopped would be perfectly fine perfectly fine perfectly fine . . . ARRUUUGA!*

ARRUUUGA! THIS IS NOT A TEST! – the whole storm and even the dark side of the earth either an unjust persecution of Mo Lehrman and Raymond Connelly (animated and labeled flesh pockets) personally, or just a case of tripping in nature's subway station and having the misfortune to fall in front of the Downtown Express. Which indeed it turned out to be, as my breath first became uncontrollably frantic with the shivers and then changed to an even calm. A warmth came to my skin from an unknown source. The passage of time and the passage of a life seemed less a tragedy than an acceptable, warm fact. Mo was already dreaming in that kind of sleep – exposed to the rain without moving much, mouth faintly blue and eyes not open, not fighting it. The bottom of Yosemite Valley seemed a lake of liquid stars, a heaven to fall down into, so I yielded to the long, warm exhaling – breathed out and out all my heat and air.

• • •

Mo nudged me awake at dawn the following day. I couldn't believe I'd only slept. The rain had stopped, and the Valley floor came and went beneath a shifting, swirling fleece of cloud. The air was poignant with the cool humidity of a world pausing to breathe. The clouds seemed less black, like sponges squeezed almost dry. A dream treat: no wind at all. Perfect stillness again.

'The proverbial abyss,' Mo said.

'Mm . . . more like the actual one.'

'Kind of scary, huh?'

'Yeah. Think we're going to live?'

'Oh, yeah.'

'Yeah?'

'Yeah.'

'Bacon, diet of the ancients?'

Layers of storm peeled off like smoke rings and drifted upwards, immersing us for a moment in fog and then vanishing into a thankful hole of blue in the sky.

Mo coughed slightly. 'We need to move.'

'Actually,' I replied, 'I've been thinking about our options myself, and down's out. So, I had a thought.'

'Yeah?'

'Well, what about going *up?*'

'Hey, I trust your judgment.'

The storm hadn't completely passed, but we did have to get going. Everything felt stiff and dangerous again as we unclipped from those bolts and shuffled towards motion. My hands were very tender as I unpeeled the corpse-cover and watched condensation steam off its black interiors, felt dampness in every inch of my body. A cool chill ran along my neck and spine. Arranging the sodden, triply heavy ropes to climb again, Mo demanded he get to lead out the giant roof to the overhang. After all that dangling and shivering, he wanted to climb. And then he was working his way under the roof, along a seam that ran to our right, clipping his stirrups into old pitons. Soon it became clear that the ropes were too wet to pull through the gear. Mo struggled with them a long time, halfway out that roof – thousands of feet above the ground. I could tell how exhausted he felt by the slow, deliberate nature of his movements.

He reached out behind his head and placed a piece on the first step of the roof itself. He clipped his stirrups to it, and let his weight come away from the wall. As he placed the next, I realized he didn't intend to run the rope through each piece of gear – facing the same predicament I had on the Hollow Flake, he risked a long fall in open sky. Mo's cheeks reddened as he pulled out enough rope to let him move forward. His suffering gave me no pleasure now. He swung and jerked slightly as he thrashed around, and his fingers didn't seem to be working right. Eventually, he found his rhythm and worked with an unhurried attention to detail. Soon he'd gained the roof's lip, and then he'd vanished from my sight – Nature's window cleaners, dangling in the wind-worlds of the upper atmosphere.

From somewhere above, I heard, 'Hm.'

'What?'

'Oh. . .'

'What?'

'Wow,' he said, entirely to himself. A while later he seemed to remember me and said, 'Yeah, nothing. Just pretty wild up here.'

Half an hour later, the call came down: 'I'm off.'

'Belay off.'

Then fifteen minutes later: 'Rope's fixed.'

'Thank you.'

Ten minutes later: 'Ready to haul.'

When he'd brought the haul line taut against the bag's weight, I unclipped it from the anchor. It bristled with crushed water bottles like cheap Mardi Gras decorations. The haul line ran from the bag, up under the roof, and straight out around the ten-foot lip. When I let go of the bag, it swung nearly twenty feet away from me in a single rush of speed. Then it swung back in, and out again. Eventually, it began to jerk upwards. Because he'd placed no gear, the lead rope likewise ran straight between Mo and me with no attachment to the wall between. So I had to swing just like the bag, to cut loose from the anchor and fly away from the wall as if on a rope over a river. Bile came to my mouth as I spun and whirled. The walls of the Valley whipped past my eyes as I tried to get my ascenders in motion on the rope, tried to concentrate on simple, meaningful data only.

As I turned the roof myself, onto the final headwall, the first sun in thirty-six hours hit that gently overhanging rampart of polished granite. Directly through the headwall ran a single crack – just enough to make ascent possible. On a gleaming shield in the sky, we had a view as if from the bottom of an airplane. Clouds hung like dancers after a ball, tired and aimless. One of the stoppers Mo had wedged in the crack refused to come out. I had to knock at it with the long, flat piece of metal we'd brought for the purpose. Then the stopper popped entirely out, and fell. It drifted down, and down, and then became too small for me to see. I fell asleep several times while hanging from the ropes, drifted to a far-off bonsai garden with Fiona beside me on a hand-carved cedar bench. I would have given a great deal for one last piece of candy.

'Mo, you got another Rancher?'

'Nada.'

It could all have been the ramparts of heaven with Michelangelo's God-plus-man drifting past and Venus in a clamshell (wool-lined, perhaps) or maybe just the whole clam, or even some oysters. Raw would have been fine, but barbecued with cheap barbecue sauce would have been better, or maybe with butter and garlic and a little thyme like you'd get with Fiona at a bar in a November storm hammering Tomales Bay's sheet metal to an elegant ripple. Maybe with a beer and clam chowder, too, on the kind of brooding, drizzly afternoon that makes a contemplative lovers' weekend in a car on remote highways seem the finest, most melancholy form of eco-philia.

'Hey, Japhy.' Mo dangled from the crack twenty feet overhead. He'd spoken softly.

'Mm?' Autumn, that was it. Autumn in the air.

'Whatcha doing?'

I hadn't moved in ten minutes. 'Nothing. Just thinking about Tomales Bay. You ever been up there?'

He thought awhile, shifted his weight around at his anchor. 'Yeah. It's pretty.'

My life strained against my leg loops and waist belt, gravity right there in the flesh. The rope thinned under my weight, and I stared at the strand before my eyes – an expression of fate and faith. No swallows anywhere. Damp, metallic air and broken clouds. 'They got oysters up there. Barbecued or raw. However you like them. I bet Fiona'd eat them barbecued.'

'Not raw?'

'I don't think so.'

'Why don't we finish the pitch, huh?'

I wouldn't have minded eating more than my share with maybe a little baked pheasant and winter vegetables followed by chocolate biscotti and liqueured coffee. Nor would I have minded forgetting that one fuck-up would send me falling for nearly *twenty seconds* before exploding in the talus.

'Hey, Mo. Think how long we'd fall right now, if we fell.' One one-thousand, two one-thousand, three one-thousand, four one-thousand *Hey, there's the ledge we slept on last night!* seven one-thousand eight one-thousand *And the place we got shit on!* ten one-thousand, eleven. . . .

He laughed a sudden shouting guffaw and hung his head back to look at the clouds. 'Pretty absurd for humans, huh?'

'Just dumb.'

'Yeah. Poor thinking.'

'Think we're having an actual experience?'

'You mean, like art where you could get hurt?'

The storm seemed to be swirling slowly, watching, deciding whether or not we'd had enough. The work had all the drama of replacing a carburetor – tie a knot, clip a biner, pull a rope, pull on rock, pull on gear, clip a biner or two and rearrange. Glinting fields of sculpted stone looked bright and freshly made, as if just brushed into form by a celestial putty knife. With only clouds above and below, the wall was like an asteroid in a galaxy of mist and light, a fairyland we'd snuck into through a hole in the sea. Amazing that the ordinary earth could be so far down and still connected to us. When the Valley floor became visible again, my itty-bitty pickup truck seemed smaller than a matchbox toy, just a dot of blue. People in the meadow were tiny flecks, like they must be to SEAL paratroopers toppling foreign emirates. I reached Mo, and I could see a dazed astonishment in his eyes. He didn't seem quite afraid, just open to the gravity and the religion. He was also very tired. He passed me the gear I'd need for the next lead, then lowered his head to nap while I got organized. His hands were bloody and almost entirely black with filth. He'd pulled his wool cap to just above his eyes.

'You looked in the mirror lately?' I asked.

'Why?'

'You look like awful.'

I could see the little platform of the spire straight below and, farther still, the sweeping Heart Ledge. Taking the next lead, with the galactic auditorium yawning at my back, I had chores to do. Look overhead at the crack, gauge its width and shape, select something appropriate from the mass of hardware at my side. Then reach up, fit the unit into the crack, jerk it snug. Clip a stirrup to it, work a foot into the stirrup, then, holding the unit close with both hands, haul my body up until my waist came even with the unit. Place my waist hook and sit.

When I pulled onto Long Ledge – our final resting place – I stumbled along that rock catwalk to the old anchor bolts. There, I found a plastic bag containing a note.

'Sorry,' the scrawled little letter read, 'we didn't know you were there.' Also inside were gifts whose value the givers could never have dreamed: a can of tuna, a box of Lemonhead candies, a joint, and four strike-anywhere matches. The bombers were definitely forgiven their heinous crime. When I'd hauled in the bag and Mo'd joined me on the ledge, I showed him the food.

Mo raised his eyebrows, seemed to think very hard about something. Then he nodded as if he'd reached a conclusion: 'It's a good thing those guys shit on us.'

'Probably saved our lives.'

'How bout that, huh?'

'Yeah, that was good shit.'

We were both delirious, so we got a gigantic kick out of that remark and laughed ourselves into hurting. Mo did the honors of opening the can of tuna, revealing our last supper. We ate slowly and carefully, and then we each licked out exactly one half of the residual vegetable oil. We even divvied up the Lemonheads. Our patch of earth had begun reeling away from its sun, so we pulled out wet sleeping bags and both tied many knots – even Mo – agreeing in advance, with a handshake, to touch none of them after that first hit of weed. Then we listened to the mute THC muse in the cooling afternoon light. That last sunset was like the dateline: tomorrow, life would begin again and our truce would weaken. But for now, the wall was just a planet-sized ship's prow cleaving through time. When night finally fell, the stars – free of smoke and mist – were dazzling and profligate. I dreamt my first dream in a week, and it was just love on white couches in sun-flooded seaside rooms with billowing curtains and fresh guacamole.

That last morning, we woke up filthy, swollen, sore, and witness to the first true autumn day of the year: the air still and cold, a faint snow dusting the meadows below, and the storm clouds vanished like Raffi's coverings pulled back from the soul. Those cranes were long gone – soaring somewhere before the southward marching storm. With the summit attainable even in our low-glycogen, high-lactic-acid state of dispassionate unconcern, we lingered to let things dry in the sun. My fingers were disastrous: every cuticle torn off, every finger hangnailed, joints rigid, gangrenous kielbasas absolutely unclenchable. I'd slept all night with them out of my bag. My whole body felt cramped, too, like a single pulled muscle with no point superior to any other, a sensory clarity devoid of anal or phallic cathexis, a body transfigured. The storm had cleared most of the fire smoke, and only smoldering little columns warbled lazily towards the sun. One swallow fell cheerfully past, dropping off the world above rather than surging up from the one below. Samtanarasa, and we certainly risked falling both materially back to splatter and figuratively back to suffer in the material plane. Homeostatic nirvana, meditating on nothing. It took Mo a long time to get over his weed-bleariness, and we sat on that ledge for hours. I felt close to Mo just then, to his endlessly cheerful strength and even to whatever part of him would now keep me outside. With my toes over the abyss and my body deeply still – inert, even – I suffered in blissful attunement and atonement and smoked the last little bit of that joint. Watched a hunting peregrine falcon soar by at a hundred miles per hour, like the starship *Enterprise* looking for Klingon sparrows to dismember midflight.

The skies were so clear that the world seemed for once a manageable universe, my own Pueblo sand-painting writ large. The way those first astronauts wept at our small blue planet's beauty, I saw at last a bonsai California. From this diamond in the spine of the state, the golden sky poured westward across California's Kansas, eddied among the hot and quiet coastal range, and gushed through redwood canyons to the kelpy sea, all from this center I'd defined by a jar on a hill – Sierra my soul's axis, and that home in the fog awaiting far beyond. Hot granite warmed inner ligaments and even bone marrow, and wet clothes steamed where we'd spread them out to dry. Ate a last Lemonhead. Saw a butterfly and a little grass in the cracks indicating the proximity of the top – botany, as encouraging as a shorebird would be to an ocean castaway. Eventually felt dry through and through, stood with shirt off on the ledge and walked up and down, feeling reborn. Saw clearly crystals in the granite that I'd always known were there but had needed four days of constant scrutiny and the spaciness of this complete yang deficit to truly appreciate – salt-and-pepper scatterings of feldspar, hornblende, and mica bonded at the earth's core, the billions of little parts making the whole, the whole maybe, just maybe, big enough to actually count. The body needs catatonic exhaustion from worthy means to feel free and pure, and a little ibuprofen is immensely helpful.

I woke from a nap to see Mo packing the haul bag. It was noon and we hadn't moved.

'Kinda hate to leave,' Mo said.

Mm.

'Also kind of dying to get out of here.'

Mm. Strange to be at last an agent of my own destiny, to become as a child up here, sucking my thumb. I'd craved this day for so long, had spent so many nights dreaming of it with this very man, and now it was so undeniably sad. I also noticed that Mo had left our traditional celebratory bottle of summit wine out of the haul bag, sitting on the ledge. I asked what was up.

'Just seems like we ought to leave it here, doesn't it?'

'Why?'

'I don't know. Just seems like we should leave something.'

I am a climber, I am an American, I am a stool-eating hog.

While none of it could be helped, I climbed slowly to savor the firm concretion of that bright white granite and the tacit commands Mo and I now barely had to voice to each other: *On belay? Yeah, you're on. Climbing.* A double rainbow splashed over the now-visible Sierra highcountry, over distant saw-toothed ridgelines shimmering with the early snow. As we climbed, the sun warmed the stone and I wanted to linger, to savor the joys of being connected by a rope, and of living with a clear mission and no history. It all seemed so familiar now, the known world. The filth and suffering would soon recede, and the larger world would remind us of other people we were and of all the things between us. I led a last body-width crack observed only by a blue moth. Felt weak and dispassionate. Certainly the need for vigilance lingered.

'Boy, let's not blow it now, huh?'

'No kidding. Check your belay.'

'Yeah.'

Mo let me lead the last pitch to the summit. He knew summits were my problem, not his. At around two o'clock I pulled lazily up the last crack Mo and I would ever climb together. Sank hands deep into the stone, fattened them out, shoved feet in the crack, and pulled up. Move after move. Then slapped a hand onto flat rock, and pulled over the top of the Big Stone.

Funny, too, because there were a few small pines and shrubs there, and the earth sloped gently up towards a forest. A red butterfly sat on a black boulder.

When Mo had followed, he stumbled away from the edge and mumbled something in surprise at a solitary crimson columbine dangling its ovaries like a bloody ballroom chandelier.

'Hm?'

'No top,' he said. The filthy, sodden cord lay between us, dead on the ground.

'No top?' I looked around again and realized that was exactly what had struck me. El Cap is really a cliff, not a tower, so it doesn't have a proper summit. It doesn't end in any special world of stone or light. It just left us sprawling in the dirt under a tree on a sunny afternoon while a beggar of a squirrel moved in on our empty cans. The dirt trail back to the meadow passed through bushes nearby.

'Amazing,' Mo said, delighted by this geographical peculiarity. He sat heavily on a slab, looked at the little white fir I'd tied us into, and laughed in the heat. 'I can't believe it.' He grinned in childlike joy from his new crow's feet to the upturned corners of his huge, friendly mouth. 'We're just back on the ground.' And of course it was true. No top, and no more journey.

Little Mother Up the Mörderberg
by H.G. Wells

H.G. Wells (1866–1946) wrote science fiction (War of the Worlds; The Invisible Man), ghost stories ('The Red Room'), history (The Outline of History) and a great deal of other work – including this story about a mountaineer and his mom.

made a kind of record at Arosa by falling down three separate crevasses on three successive days. That was before little Mother followed me out there. When she came, I could see at a glance she was tired and jaded and worried, and so instead of letting her fret about in the hotel and get into a wearing tangle of gossip, I packed her and two knapsacks up, and started off on a long, refreshing, easygoing walk northward, until a blister on her foot stranded us at the Magenruhe Hotel on the Sneejoch. She was for going on, blister or no blister – I never met pluck like Mother's in all my life – but I said, 'No. This is a mountaineering inn, and it suits me down to the ground – or if you prefer it, up to the sky. You shall sit in the veranda by the telescope, and I'll prance about among the peaks for a bit.'

'Don't have accidents,' she said.

'Can't promise that, little Mother,' I said; 'but I'll always remember I'm your only son.'

So I pranced . . .

I need hardly say that in a couple of days I was at loggerheads with all the mountaineers in that inn. They couldn't stand me. They didn't like my neck with its strong, fine Adam's apple – being mostly men with their heads *jammed* on – and they didn't like the way I bore myself and lifted my aviator's nose to the peaks. They didn't like my being a vegetarian and the way I evidently enjoyed it, and they didn't like the touch of color, orange and green, in my rough serge suit. They were all of the dingy school – the sort of men I call gentlemanly owls – shy, correct-minded creatures, mostly from Oxford, and as solemn over their climbing as a cat frying eggs. Sage they were, great head nodders, and 'I-wouldn't-venture-to-do-a-thing-like-that-ers.' They always did what the books and guides advised, and they classed themselves by their seasons; one was in his ninth season, and another in his tenth, and so on. I was a novice and had to sit with my mouth open for bits of humble pie.

My style that! Rather!

I would sit in the smoking room sucking away at a pipeful of hygienic herb tobacco – they said it smelled like burning garden rubbish – and waiting to put my spoke in and let a little light into their minds. They set aside their natural reticence altogether in their efforts to show how much they didn't like me.

'You chaps take these blessed mountains too seriously,' I said. 'They're larks, and you've got to lark with them.'

They just slued their eyes round at me.

'I don't find the solemn joy in fussing you do. The old-style mountaineers went up with alpenstocks and ladders and light hearts. That's my idea of mountaineering.'

'It isn't ours,' said one red-boiled hero of the peaks, all blisters and peeling skin, and he said it with an air of crushing me.

'It's the right idea,' I said serenely, and puffed at my herb tobacco.

'When you've had a bit of experience you'll know better,' said another, an oldish young man with a small gray beard.

'Experience never taught *me* anything,' I said.

'Apparently not,' said someone, and left me one down and me to play. I kept perfectly tranquil.

'I mean to do the Mörderberg before I go down,' I said quietly, and produced sensation.

'When are you going down?'

'Week or so,' I answered, unperturbed.

'It's not the climb a man ought to attempt in his first year,' said the peeling gentleman.

'You particularly ought not to try it,' said another.

'No guide will go with you.'

'Foolhardy idea.'

'Mere brag.'

'Like to see him do it.'

I just let them boil for a bit, and when they were back to the simmer I dropped in, pensively, with, 'Very likely I'll take that little Mother of mine. She's small, bless her, but she's as hard as nails.'

But they saw they were being drawn by my ill-concealed smile; and this time they contented themselves with a few grunts and gruntlike remarks, and then broke up into little conversations in undertones that pointedly excluded me. It had the effect of hardening my purpose. I'm a stiff man when I'm put on my mettle, and I determined that the little Mother *should* go up the Mörderberg, where half these solemn experts hadn't been, even if I had to be killed or orphaned in the attempt. So I spoke to her about it the next day. She was in a deck chair on the veranda, wrapped up in rugs and looking at the peaks.

'Comfy?' I said.

'Very,' she said.

'Getting rested?'

'It's so nice.'

I strolled to the rail of the veranda. 'See that peak there, Mummy?'

She nodded happily, with eyes half shut.

'That's the Mörderberg. You and me have got to be up there the day after tomorrow.'

Her eyes opened a bit. 'Wouldn't it be rather a climb, dearest?' she said.

'I'll manage that all right,' I said, and she smiled consentingly and closed her eyes.

'So long as you manage it,' she said.

I went down the valley that afternoon to Daxdam to get gear and guides and porters, and I spent the next day in glacier and rock practice above the hotel. That didn't add to my popularity. I made two little slips. One took me down a crevasse – I've an extraordinary knack of going down crevasses – and a party of three which was starting for the Kinderspitz spent an hour and a half fishing me out; and the other led to my dropping my ice axe on a little string of people going for the Humpi

Glacier. It didn't go within thirty inches of anyone, but you might have thought from the row they made that I had knocked out the collective brains of the party. Quite frightful language they used, and three ladies with them too!

The next day there was something very like an organized attempt to prevent our start. They brought out the landlord, they remonstrated with Mother, they did their best to blacken the character of my two guides. The landlord's brother had a first-class row with them.

'Two years ago,' he said, 'they lost their Herr!'

'No particular reason,' I said, 'why you shouldn't keep yours on, is it?'

That settled him. He wasn't up to a polyglot pun, and it stuck in his mind like a fishbone in the throat.

Then the peeling gentleman came along and tried to overhaul our equipment. 'Have you got this?' it was, and 'Have you got that?'

'Two things,' I said, looking at his nose pretty hard, 'we haven't forgotten. One's blue veils and the other Vaseline.'

I've still a bright little memory of the start. There was the pass a couple of hundred feet or so below the hotel, and the hotel – all name and windows – standing out in a great, desolate, rocky place against lumpy masses of streaky green rock, flecked here and there with patches of snow and dark shelves of rhododendron, and rising perhaps a thousand feet towards the western spur of the massif. Our path ran before us, meandering among the boulders down to stepping stones over a rivulet, and then upward on the other side of the stream towards the Magenruhe Glacier, where we had to go up the rocks to the left and then across the icefall to shelves on the precipitous face on the west side. It was dawn, the sun had still to rise, and everything looked very cold and blue and vast about us. Everyone in the hotel had turned out to bear a hand in the row – some of the *déshabillés* were disgraceful – and now they stood in a silent group watching us recede. The last word I caught was 'They'll have to come back.'

'We'll come back all right,' I answered. 'Never fear.'

And so we went our way, cool and deliberate, over the stream and up and up towards the steep snowfields and icy shoulder of the Mörderberg. I remember that we went in absolute silence for a time, and then how suddenly the landscape gladdened with sunrise, and in an instant, as if speech had thawed, all our tongues were babbling.

I had one or two things in the baggage that I hadn't cared for the people at the inn to see, and I had made no effort to explain why I had five porters with the load of two and a half. But when we came to the icefall I showed my hand a little, and unslung a stout twine hammock for the mater. We put her in this with a rug around her, and sewed her in with a few stitches; then we roped up in line, with me last but one and a guide front and rear, and Mummy in the middle carried by two of the porters. I stuck my alpenstock through two holes I had made in the shoulders of my jacket under my rucksack, T-shape to my body, so that when I went down a crevasse, as I did ever and again, I just stuck in its jaws and came up easy as the rope grew taut. And so, except for one or two bumps that made the mater chuckle, we got over without misadventure.

Then came the rock climb on the other side, requiring much judgment. We had to get from ledge to ledge as opportunity offered, and here the little Mother was a perfect godsend. We unpacked her after we had slung her over the big fissure – I forget what you call it – that always comes between glacier and rock – and whenever we came to a bit of ledge within eight feet of the one we were working along, the two guides took her and slung her up, she being so light, and then she was able to give a foot for the next man to hold by and hoist himself. She said we were all pulling her leg, and that made her and me laugh so much that the whole party had to wait for us.

It was pretty tiring altogether doing that bit of the climb – two hours we had of it before we got to the loose masses of rock on the top of the arête. 'It's worse going down,' said the elder guide.

I looked back for the first time, and I confess it did make me feel a bit giddy. There was the glacier looking quite petty, and with a black gash between itself and the rocks.

For a time it was pretty fair going up the rocky edge of the arête, and nothing happened of any importance, except that one of the porters took to grousing because he was hit on the shin by a stone I dislodged. 'Fortunes of war,' I said, but he didn't seem to see it, and when I just missed him with a second he broke out into a long, whining discourse in what I suppose he thought was German – *I* couldn't make head or tail of it.

'He says you might have killed him,' said the little Mother.

'They say,' I quoted. 'What say they? *Let* them say.'

I was for stopping and filling him up with a feed, but the elder guide wouldn't have it. We had already lost time, he said, and the traverse around the other face of the mountain would be more and more subject to avalanches as the sun got up. So we went on. As we went around the corner to the other face I turned towards the hotel – it was the meanest little oblong spot by now – and made a derisive gesture or so for the benefit of anyone at the telescope.

We did get one rock avalanche that reduced the hindmost guide to audible prayer, but nothing hit us except a few bits of snow. The rest of the fall was a couple of yards and more out from us. We were on rock just then and overhung; before and afterward we were edging along steps in an ice slope cut by the foremost guide, and touched up by the porters. The avalanche was much more impressive before it came in sight, banging and thundering overhead, and it made a tremendous uproar in the blue deeps beneath, but in actual transit it seemed a mean show – mostly of stones smaller than I am.

'All right?' said the guide.

'Toned up,' I answered.

'I suppose it *is* safe, dear?' asked the little Mother.

'Safe as Trafalgar Square,' I said. 'Hop along, Mummykins.'

Which she did with remarkable agility.

The traverse took us onto old snow at last, and here we could rest for lunch – and pretty glad we were both of lunch and rest. But here the trouble with the guides and porters thickened. They were already a little ruffled about my animating way with loose rocks, and now they kicked up a tremendous shindy because instead of the customary brandy we had brought non-alcoholic ginger cordial. Would they even try it? Not a bit of it! It was a queer little dispute, high up in that rarefied air, about food values and the advantages of making sandwiches with nuttar. They were an odd lot of men, invincibly set upon a vitiated and vitiating dietary. They wanted meat, they wanted alcohol, they wanted narcotics to smoke. You might have thought that men like these, living in almost direct contact with nature, would have liked 'nature' foods, such as plasmon, protose, plobose, digestine, and so forth. Not them! They just craved for corruption. When I spoke of drinking pure water one of the porters spat in a marked, symbolic manner over the precipice. From that point onward discontent prevailed.

We started again about half-past eleven, after a vain attempt on the part of the head guide to induce us to turn back. We had now come to what is generally the most difficult part of the Mörderberg ascent, the edge that leads up to the snowfield below the crest. But here we came suddenly into a draft of warm air blowing from the southwest, and everything, the guide said, was unusual. Usually the edge is a sheet of ice over rock. Today it was wet and soft, and one could kick steps in it and get one's toes into rock with the utmost ease.

'This is where Herr Tomlinson's party fell,' said one of the porters, after we'd committed ourselves to the edge for ten minutes or so.

'Some people could fall out of a four-post bed,' I said.

'It'll freeze hard again before we come back,' said the second guide, 'and us with nothing but *verdammt* ginger inside of us.'

'You keep your rope taut,' said I.

A friendly ledge came to the help of Mother in the nick of time, just as she was beginning to tire, and we sewed her up all but the feet in her hammock again, and roped her carefully. She bumped a bit, and at times she was just hanging over immensity and rotating slowly, with everybody else holding like grim death.

'My dear,' she said, the first time this happened, 'is it *right* for me to be doing this?'

'Quite right,' I said, 'but if you can get a foothold presently again – it's rather better style.'

'You're sure there's no danger, dear?'

'Not a scrap.'

'And I don't fatigue you?'

'You're a stimulant.'

'The view,' she said, 'is certainly becoming very beautiful.'

But presently the view blotted itself out, and we were in clouds and a thin drift of almost thawing snowflakes.

We reached the upper snowfield about half-past one, and the snow was extraordinarily soft. The elder guide went in up to his armpits.

'Frog it,' I said, and spread myself out flat, in a sort of swimming attitude. So we bored our way up to the crest and along it. We went in little spurts and then stopped for breath, and we dragged the little Mother after us in her hammock-bag. Sometimes the snow was so good we fairly skimmed the surface; sometimes it was so rotten we plunged right into it and splashed about. I went too near the snow cornice once and it broke under me, but the rope saved me, and we reached the summit about three o'clock without further misadventure. The summit was just bare rock with the usual cairn and pole. Nothing to make a fuss about. The drift of snow and cloudwisp had passed, the sun was blazing hot overhead, and we seemed to be surveying all Switzerland. The Magenruhe Hotel was at our toes, hidden, so to speak, by our chins. We squatted about the cairn, and the guides and porters were reduced to ginger and vegetarian ham sandwiches. I cut and scratched an inscription, saying I had climbed on simple food, and claiming a record.

Seen from the summit, the snowfields on the northeast side of the mountain looked extremely attractive, and I asked the head guide why that way up wasn't used. He said something in his peculiar German about precipices.

So far our ascent had been a fairly correct ascent in rather slow time. It was in the descent that that strain in me of almost unpremeditated originality had play. I wouldn't have the rope returning across the upper snowfield, because Mother's feet and hands were cold, and I wanted her to jump about a bit. And before I could do anything to prevent it she had slipped, tried to get up by rolling over *down* the slope instead of up, as she ought to have done, and was leading the way, rolling over and over and over down towards the guide's blessed precipices above the lower snowfield.

I didn't lose an instant in flinging myself after her, axe up, in glissading attitude. I'm not clear what I meant to do, but I fancy the idea was to get in front of her and put on the brake. I did not succeed, anyhow. In twenty seconds I had slipped, and was sitting down and going down out of my own control altogether.

Now, most great discoveries are the result of accident, and I maintain that in that instant Mother and I discovered two distinct and novel ways of coming down a mountain.

It is necessary that there should be first a snow slope above with a layer of softish, rotten snow on the top of ice, then a precipice, with a snow-covered talus sloping steeply at first and then less steeply, then more snow slopes and precipices according to taste, ending in a snowfield or a not too greatly fissured glacier, or a reasonable, not too rocky slope. Then it all becomes as easy as chuting the chutes.

Mother hit on the sideways method. She rolled. With the snow in the adhesive state it had got into, she had made the jolliest little snowball of herself in half a minute, and the nucleus of as clean and abundant a snow avalanche as anyone could wish. There was plenty of snow going in front of her, and that's the very essence of both our methods. You must fall on your snow, not your snow on you, or it smashes you. And you mustn't mix yourself up with loose stones.

I, on the other hand, went down feet first, and rather like a snowplow; slower than she did, and if, perhaps, with less charm, with more dignity. Also I saw more. But it was certainly a tremendous rush. And I gave a sort of gulp when Mummy bumped over the edge into the empty air and vanished.

It was like a toboggan ride gone mad down the slope until I took off from the edge of the precipice, and then it was like a dream.

I'd always thought falling must be horrible. It wasn't in the slightest degree. I might have hung with my clouds and lumps of snow about me for weeks, so great was my serenity. I had an impression then that I was as good as killed – and that it didn't matter. I wasn't afraid – that's nothing! – but I wasn't a bit uncomfortable. Whack! We'd hit something, and I expected to be flying to bits right and left. But we'd only got onto the snow slope below, at so steep an angle that it was merely breaking the fall, Down we went again. I didn't see much of the view after that because the snow was all around and over my head, but I kept feet foremost and in a kind of sitting posture, and then I slowed and then I quickened again and bumped rather, and then harder, and bumped and then bumped again and came to rest. This time I was altogether buried in snow, and twisted sideways with a lot of heavy snow on my right shoulder.

I sat for a bit enjoying the stillness – and then I wondered what had become of Mother, and set myself to get out of the snow about me. It wasn't so easy as you might think; the stuff was all in lumps and spaces like a gigantic sponge, and I lost my temper and struggled and swore a good deal, but at last I managed it. I crawled out and found myself on the edge of heaped masses of snow quite close to the upper part of the Magenruhe Glacier. And far away, right up the glacier and near the other side, was a little thing like a black beetle struggling in the heart of an immense split ball of snow.

I put my hands to my mouth and let out with my version of the yodel, and presently I saw her waving her hand.

It took me nearly twenty minutes to get to her. I knew my weakness, and I was very careful of every crevasse I came near. When I got up to her, her face was anxious.

'What have you done with the guides?' she asked.

'They've got too much to carry,' I said. 'They're coming down another way. Did you like it?'

'Not very much, dear,' she said; 'but I daresay I shall get used to these things. Which way do we go now?'

I decided we'd find a snow bridge across the bergschrund – that's the word I forgot just now – and so get onto the rocks on the east side of the glacier, and after that we had uneventful going right down to the hotel . . .

Our return evoked such a strain of hostility and envy as I have never met before or since. First they tried to make out we'd never been to the top at all, but Mother's little proud voice settled that sort of insult. And, besides, there was the evidence of the guides and porters following us down. When they asked about the guides, 'They're following your methods,' I said, 'and I suppose they'll get back here tomorrow morning somewhen.'

That didn't please them.

I claimed a record. They said my methods were illegitimate.

'If I see fit,' I said, 'to use an avalanche to get back by, what's that to you? You tell me me and Mother can't do the confounded mountain anyhow, and when we do you want to invent a lot of rules to disqualify us. You'll say next one mustn't glissade. I've made a record, and you know I've made a record, and you're about as sour as you can be. The fact of it is, you chaps don't know your own silly business. Here's a good, quick way of coming down a mountain, and you ought to know about it – '

'The chance that both of you are not killed was one in a thousand.'

'Nonsense! It's the proper way to come down for anyone who hasn't a hidebound mind. You chaps ought to practice falling great heights in snow. It's perfectly easy and perfectly safe, if only you know how to set about it.'

'Look here, young man,' said the oldish young man with the little gray beard, 'you don't seem to understand that you and that lady have been saved by a kind of miracle – '

'Theory!' I interrupted. 'I'm surprised you fellows ever come to Switzerland. If I were your kind I'd just invent theoretical mountains and play for points. However, you're tired, little Mummy. It's time you had some nice warm soup and tucked yourself up in bed. I shan't let you get up for six-and-thirty hours.'

But it's queer how people detest a little originality.

Queen of All She Surveys
by Maureen O'Neill

Like many mountaineers, Maureen O'Neill (born 1954) has lost friends to climbing accidents. Here she reviews her losses and ponders what we find in the mountains – including insight into what she calls 'the wilderness that is another person'.

My mother calls, and in her voice I can hear her wonder if she is the first to reach me: 'Have you heard? One of your climbing friends, Eve, died on Mt. Index this weekend. They think it was an avalanche. Her partner died, too; they fell roped together. Your sister just heard it on the six o'clock report and said to call. She said you climbed with her.' I tell her I know already, and she is relieved, then asks quietly, 'Do you think she suffered much?' My mother is from the East, and these Northwest mountains are foreign to her. I doubt she can even imagine the landscape against which a woman's body fell and shattered.

I can imagine it only too well. How many times have I scrutinized an ice-lined corridor such as the one Eve died in to see if it might *go* – lead magically, without dead ends, to the summit. I can feel the angle of snow so steep it seems to push her outward, her calves straining to support her body on only the front points of her crampons, forearms trembling as the urgency to move quickly is telegraphed from mind to muscle: hurry, this gully feels unsafe, the warmth unseasonable. Why this stillness in the air? This heaviness?

Did she sense the avalanche? The pulse of kinetic energy about to snap? I cannot stop myself from imagining the moment she fell, delivered into the wide hands of that warm, blue air. I know she screamed in terrible frustration – she always screamed, at even the most minor defeat.

This day it was not simply a move she could not make and a fall of a few feet, but her life wrenched from her hands as quickly as she was torn from the ice. Two days later, her body, broken in many places, was discovered half-buried in avalanche debris.

Other climbers have said that she pushed beyond the limits of even her brilliance, that she was somewhere she shouldn't have been, but few climbers can claim never to have found themselves in the wrong place at the wrong time. 'Pushing' is only the natural impulse to grow, to improve. I answer with less than complete assurance: 'I don't think she suffered. She was probably unconscious or dead when she hit the ground.' Maybe it helps my mother to know that some die quickly, although it seems little comfort, given the fact that both her daughters climb and that climbing is a sport in which risks, however carefully considered, are an essential element.

When the mountains claim another life, a single aspect of climbing – the possibility of death – invades and eclipses all other meanings. For we survivors, the significance of her death pales against the fullness of a life anchored in the mountains.

The Olympics, Rainier, the Cascades: whether you climb them or not, the mountains of the Pacific Northwest are impossible to ignore. From the beginning of my life, I heard them praised. Whenever we plowed down a certain hill in the old Rambler, my Dad would say, 'Look at those Cascades!'

Inevitably, on even a vaguely clear day, people will ask, 'Have you seen the mountains?' If the reference is singular – the mountain – they are referring to Rainier, who so dominates her territory that on a sunny day thousands of city workers step outside on their lunchbreaks and turn their heads to the southeast, to the star-white glaciated peak transcending, or is it levitating, above the clouds.

Such a climate of appreciation for the environment produces people who seek immersion in the wilderness. I began climbing my last year in college for the most common reason in the world – because my best friend climbed. She took a course through our college, and it sounded like fun. Because she had shown the potential to become passionately involved in the sport, I knew I'd never see her unless I signed up, too.

It seemed easy then. Beg or borrow the gear, grab someone, set your sights on a place very far or very high – say that humpback peak or the one with a shark-fin ridge or the glacier-frosted cupcake that was Mt. St. Helens – and then do it, by placing one foot in front of the other, over and over and over.

My friend and I and another friend completed that college mountaineering course and did our first climb together. In our desire to make the summit, we made a typical beginner's mistake and neglected to turn back early enough. Benighted, we were forced to descend an entire glacier, honeycombed with crevasses, without headlamps. At eleven p.m., after what seemed an eternity of tenuous footwork, we reached the moraine. With a heavy sigh, Vaughn sat all six long feet of himself down on a rock, looked up at the moon, and cried, 'I want my mother.'

Those early climbs were endurance tests, and we always found ourselves equal to them. What a feeling! We ran up trails just to see how fast we could go, wondering if our legs would accordion under us, if we would ever reach the limit – but we didn't. We discovered we did what we had to do. The climbs were simple, often long snow slogs with a bit of scrambling on rock and more than a bit of tortuous bushwhacking if you lost your way. Climbing The Brothers, a peak in the Olympic range, we got lost on the descent and spent the night first lowering ourselves down a series of small cliffs by swinging on slide alder and, when that was done, swimming through a sea of neck-high foliage, wild spring growth coated with sap that shellacked the hair and tasted sweet when licked off a bare forearm. My companion navigated by the stars, aiming to bisect a foot-wide path, and to my great surprise, the plan worked. On the trail out, I learned to sleep while walking, since we had taken twenty-three hours instead of the usual eight to complete the climb.

I progressed to more technical climbing with a group of women as ignorant as myself. We banded together from a lack of money for instruction, a determination to climb and a desire to learn with other women. Our motivations were as varied as the individuals involved, but we all wanted to take complete responsibility in all aspects of climbing, including leading, and felt that being in a group of women best served that purpose. One spring weekend we packed up and drove across the Cascades to a cluster of sandstone formations set like prehistoric monoliths behind an apple orchard. The area resembled an outdoor jungle gym with a wide range of climbs to choose from. After consulting the guidebook, we chose peacefully named climbs located on gently angling slabs and avoided routes such as Vertigo, Bomb Shelter, Testicle Fortitude, Slender Thread, and Cro-Magnon.

Eventually we felt brave enough to try an imposing hunk called Orchard Rock, scary because of its verticality. I went second on the rope and had an easy time of the first thirty feet, which led to a secure resting place – a ledge with enough room for two feet at once. The crux move lay just beyond this ledge and involved climbing around a corner out onto an exposed face. I made one brave attempt, slipped, and retreated to the ledge. Clearly, it was impossible. How had I gotten into this fix? Because I was being belayed from above, any fall would have been minimal, but that seemed irrelevant. My tongue sealed to the roof of my mouth, and although I was perfectly still, I began to sweat. In short, I was gripped. Ten fingertips made pathetic forays across the rock searching for a decent hold (that is, a big one) but my body would not follow. I was rapidly becoming living sculpture.

Below me, third on the rope, Laura waited patiently. Dusk shadowed her face as her brown eyes gazed with maddening serenity over the orchards and dusty-green fields stitched together with roads and fences. Above me, birds chimed on a sunlit ridge and the air had the feeling of an embrace. 'This really is for the birds,' I muttered. 'That's okay. Take as long as you want,' she responded. I took forty-five minutes. How the hell could she be so calm while I agonized before the fact that this rock wasn't going to move for me. I had to move. With the bloodless precision of a slowly developing photograph, those forty-five minutes of deliberation revealed nearly everything I know about fear. Since then there have only been exquisite refinements.

To the climber, fear serves several purposes. It can make you attentive to possible danger, can warn you, infuse you with energy, serve as a gauge of your mental condition, and prevent you from taking risks beyond your ability. Fear deserves recognition but not one iota more of your attention, though it is usually eager to consume all of it. The natural flow of fear must be channeled or paralysis can result, and paralysis is serious. For me, fear manifests through resistance and hesitation, both of which cause unnecessary energy loss.

Those first few years taught me the simple things: eat before you're hungry and drink even if you don't want water because often the body reacts to stress and cold by erasing the desire for food and water at exactly those times when it is most needed. If you wait until your hands are cold before putting on gloves, they take an immense amount of heat to rewarm, creating an unnecessary energy drain. If you forget even the smallest thing – a spare mitten, an extra bulb for a headlamp – the consequences can be disastrous. If your upper body is so strong that you can haul yourself up a rock with just your arms, instead of using your legs, which are much better suited to hold your weight, you are a wastrel. In the words of Yvon Chouinard, climbing depends on conservation of energy, which translates into economy of movement coupled with reasonable speed.

Those years also taught me the range of movement involved in climbing – from the clumsy ferrying of loads to the base of the 'climb' to the delicate moves or sequences of moves that were the cream and usually took only a fraction of the total time spent out. Yet what I grew to love above all was the pure luxury of spending two uninterrupted days with someone. As a teenager I spent a summer at a hiking camp; I remember being startled and disturbed at how naked people appeared outside the city: no makeup, no fancy clothes or houses, no supporting actors (parents). All the girls were tiny figures, cut and pasted against a background of sea and trees. As an adult I began to appreciate this nakedness. I was no longer disturbed by it and grew less afraid of the emotional exposure climbing creates.

This intimacy, this insight into the wilderness that is another person, is a gift. Not to mention a true test of friendship. Let me count the ways: withstanding the smell of your partner at night, stripped down to her fragrant long underwear and equally fragrant wet socks; the shove she gives you in her sleep, pushing you towards the wall of the tent dripping with condensation; the rude way she steps on you in the middle of the night as she heads out for relief; the hours spent reading to you by candlelight; the bites of chocolate fed to you at each bend of the trail to inspire you onward.

Seven years later I still climb with the woman who couldn't stop laughing at the sight of me splashing in a creek in midwinter like some huge woolly beetle trying to right herself with a pack on her back. From the other side, she offered only these words of consolation: 'I told you not to cross with your snowshoes on.'

Certain climbs are described as 'committed'. Put simply, a committed climb means there is no easy escape: once begun, both ascending and descending are difficult. These climbs require a firm intention to finish, simply because the alternatives are unappealing. Ptarmigan Ridge on Mt. Rainier falls into this category. My partner Kathy, her friend Karl, and I planned to do Ptarmigan Ridge one Memorial Day weekend. It was to be an apprentice climb for me; Kathy and Karl were to share the leading, and I was to go along as a third, knowing it would technically approach my limits. I read the route description with growing apprehension: '. . . steep snow/ice slope . . . snow/ice apron . . . rock buttress . . . steep ice chute . . . crevasse/serac pattern . . . sustained rockfall . . . gentle slope above . . .' Fortunately, preparation left little time for worry.

The day of the climb finally arrived, and we left the parking lot at 7 a.m. After a lengthy approach we at last reached our high camp, a breezy rock perch with just enough space, if we squeezed, for our three bivy sacks. Sleep came easily, and the next morning we were wakened at 3 a.m. by the steady pulse of an electronic alarm. The day promised to be windless and clear – ideal conditions. Karl, propped up on one elbow and still enjoying the warmth of his bag, was kind enough to boil water for coffee. After eating, we packed quickly and set off, arriving at the base of the climb before light. We had agreed to rope up at the start, and happy to shear weight off my load, I took out the Mammut and laid its brilliant, diamond-back coils loosely on the snow. Kathy glanced at our faces, barely defined in the twilight. 'Ready?' she asked. I nodded, palm resting on my ice axe, and waited for the rope to stretch out between us. Cold seconds passed as the steel of the adze bit clear through my woollen mittens to the skin. With agonizing slowness, energy dammed up in my legs and lungs. I wanted desperately to move, to step out of that moment of extreme tension that marks a beginning, and start climbing the mountain.

We all commented on the perfect snow conditions; cramponing was effortless. My primary responsibility was to follow and keep myself on my feet at all times, always a challenge. It seemed my two partners must have tremendous faith in me: if I fell, and I was the most likely candidate, we would all fall. I thought about that a good deal and paid the closest attention to each step, no small task when ascending a thousand feet of snow.

After perhaps an hour, Kathy stopped to rest on a bit of rock. As I drew near her, I detected a difference in texture in the ground ahead, a smooth pond of light in the wind-scored snow. I stood still for a moment, 'testing the water' with a delicately placed front point. ICE. 'Oh, that bit's easy,' said Kathy, between hearty bites of her sandwich, 'and it's just a taste of what's up ahead.' As I was afraid, she was completely right.

We continued to inch upward, in a race between three snails and the sun, which upon reaching its zenith, would begin to warm and dangerously soften our route. At the apex of the slope, we began our traverse of the 'apron'. Each footstep punched in the rotten, icy snow seemed likely to give way with the weight of the next person, but somehow never did.

Just under the rock buttress we stopped for lunch. Removing my gloves, I laid three fingers against the pulse in my throat. 'Hey, it's 120 per minute,' I said. Kathy and Karl were unimpressed, already surveying the next fifty feet – a sheet of ice rounding a hump of rock with a nice, clear view several thousand feet down. Lunch was rather short and strained since we were all anxious to move.

Karl took the lead and danced over the ice with typical, angular ease. Kathy went next. Then he and Kathy waited quietly for me to cross. Too quietly. They seemed to be holding their breath, as though afraid any small draft might prove fatal. Using two tools, I began my crablike traverse and suddenly understood why Gwen Moffat, the famous British climber, titled her book *Space Below My Feet*. Midway through, I panicked and briefly hesitated, but standing still was much more terrifying than moving. I kept on, if only to evade the nasty fall line, making small explosive noises as I tried to place all four points with decision. The hip belt of my pack came unbuckled, and my hat (tied on the belt) began a direct descent. From the corner of my eye, I noticed Kathy wishing it a silent bon voyage.

Breathing deeply, I reached the other side, but there was no time to reflect, as Karl was nearly up the next lead, a narrow icy chute that was actually easier climbing but complicated by a cascade of spindrift, dreamily blowing down. From the top I heard Karl shouting at me to hurry, afraid heavier snow would follow and knock me off. His voice sounded remote, and his directions impossible to follow. I was overcome by the altitude and the odd sensation of moving against the flow. Under a misty white veil, I climbed steadily upward, groping for contact with ice and fighting to maintain my balance, constantly threatened by the swaying of my pack.

The chute led to the crevasse/serac pattern, a section of slopes tiered like a giant, white layer-cake and riddled with crevasses. Probing carefully, Kathy led out and immediately fell into one up to her hips. She climbed out and promptly fell into another. Turning back, she grinned and said, 'Think light.' Somehow we managed to weave our way out to what appeared to be the final tier leading to the fabled 'gentle slope' and to the ridge for which the climb was named. As Kathy made a few tricky moves over the chest-high ice shoulder and onto the slope, Karl and I felt the entire crust shift and drop below our feet. Fired by wildly beating hearts we nearly jumped over the shoulder in our eagerness to reach solid ground.

At last Ptarmigan Ridge resembled a ridge, with that exhilarating combination of firm ground underfoot and airiness on all sides. The worst was over, and I began to relax, although we were at least two hours from the summit with the descent yet to come. As we ascended, clouds blew in and we were forced to use compass bearings for direction. Soon we all needed a rest from the effects of fog and altitude, especially Karl who, exhausted from the lower part of the climb, stumbled and lurched like a drunken man. In the shelter of an overhanging crevasse, we nestled together sharing an ensolite pad and gingersnaps. 'Look at where we are,' I said, 'this is heaven.' 'Now if we could only be sure of that,' Kathy joked.

Suddenly the air cleared and *voilà*, the sun. Kathy and Karl leapt up and scurried off in different directions to see if they could sight any landmarks. Serious business, obviously. Their quick, neat movements temporarily distracted me, but finding myself out of cookies, I began rooting in Kathy's private stash. She'll never know, I reasoned, absorbed in the luxurious ebb and flow of the clouds, teased by views through windows with drifting and torn edges. My reverie was cut short by a shout from Kathy. She had recognized Sunset Amphitheater, an unmistakable western slope of Rainier, scooped out as though to form a gargantuan rock echo chamber.

Greatly encouraged, we slogged forward until the clouds descended again. This time, however, we were certain of our direction and felt our way with the Braille of steps kicked by Kathy, seventy-five feet ahead. By early evening we came upon the false summit, Liberty Cap, and were able to inform several other climbers, who had converged through the whiteout from different routes, of their location. Since we had neither time nor energy to build a snow cave, we scraped out a hollow in a small bank, which protected the lower half of our bodies. Kathy and I shared a bivy sack for warmth. She crawled in right away, uncharacteristically leaving her gear strewn about. As I was relatively refreshed, I put everything away in her pack, then lay awake most of the night, amazed at how warm we were at 14,000 feet with only three thin layers between us and the snow. Kathy slept the twitching, jerking sleep of the exhausted. Since it was impossible to keep the top of the bivy sack closed, downy flakes of snow caught in her red hair and melted slowly. She seemed infinitely vulnerable, protected only by skin that tears so easily. I gently pulled her hat over her head, marveling again at my warmth and the brightness of a night that never seemed to fall.

Climbing, like any exacting activity, draws one deeper and deeper into its own territory, a territory often as narrow as the ice-blue thread of a couloir. In return for this extraordinary sacrifice of energy, the climber receives visions of earth. In the moment before a difficult move, she may turn her head away from what is directly before her and the beauty – or is it the fear – lays her open. Her eyes are the eyes of God, the land flows in and through and from her like a river. As night falls she may gaze across an oceanic glacier rinsed with aqua to yet another sea of black peaks, wreathed by coral clouds. She has a view of earth where everything seems unmasked, naked. Forces corresponding to her own emotions are at work, visible in the sudden rapid devastation of avalanche, in the moraine foaming up and around the tip of a glacier as that tongue of ice furrows through earth, century after century. Something inside says yes, yes, I recognize this. I want to see the earth above all with nothing hidden. The same laws that govern this world govern the life of my body and soul and it is a relief, finally, to see violence and beauty erupt, both parts of the whole.

Venturing into the wilderness the climber inhabits two worlds. Place them side by side, and the contrast makes each distinct. What does it mean to survive in the mountains? What does survival in the city mean? What defines courage in the mountains; when is one courageous in the city? What is the nature of commitment in the mountains? In the city? None of these questions are easily answered. I am a slow learner and understand best through my body. The lessons I learn in the wilderness work into my urban life. When I have moved through fear and taken a risk, such as crossing a stretch of ice unroped at 12,000 feet, other risks, especially emotional ones, become easier.

My survival in the city has not meant physical survival (although there is always the threat of violence against women). I have not gone hungry or been without shelter. Usually I must contend with less tangible forces, such as the volatile energy created by many lives denied expression and many voices silenced. The physical stress of climbing can actually be a reprieve after, for example, the mental stress of searching for work. Both are difficult. One simply gives me the strength to face the other. I need to see success measured in physical terms: climbing a mountain, or weathering storms and changing conditions.

We all know intuitively that our survival depends on each other, but in the city, recognition of our interdependence is often reduced to providing and paying for services. In the mountains, climbers are bound by absolute necessity. We depend on our partners and routinely, through the use of a rope, trust them with our lives.

The climber is vulnerable to her companions the way she is rarely vulnerable in the city. Observing the way in which a woman climbs can be an intimate experience without the exchange of a single word or touch. You may learn more than her mother knows about how she approaches problems and whether she can persevere. You are allowed to witness your friend struggle and eventually reach the top, or fail and learn to accept that failure. You will perfect the art of encouragement: when to speak and when not to, what to say when your partner is frightened, and how to praise her when she succeeds. On occasion, you will be graced by the sight of a woman when everything in her being says yes: when intelligence and skill are transformed into strong, sure movement upon any medium – snow, rock or ice.

I have been asked how I can justify taking risks with my life. I often respond that driving to work scares me more than climbing a pitch of ice. Some days, when asked that question, I remember a thunderous crack that split open a sunny August morning as three women, strung together like pearls, scanned the rocky cliffs for the source of the sound. I remember how I stood perfectly still, keeping mute vigil as, seconds after the crack, a gully directly above my sister and my friend came alive, showering them first with a pressurized spray of snow and rocks and then, after a pause the length of three breaths, with car-sized blocks of ice. During that pause I remember the sense of terror radiating from Nancy's body as she realized she was trapped, and how she moved as though the ice itself burned her. And my sister's face, tilting upward, with an expression I cannot describe. Later she told me, 'I thought I was going to die.'

Why are the three of us alive today? The only answer is grace. We were roped, parallel a yawning crevasse twenty feet below us. If not crushed by rocks and ice, we could easily have been swept into the crevasse. Why did we do it to begin with? For me, that question alone is easy to answer: I climb from a deep love for the wilderness, for my partners, and for my own body and its amazing strength. I don't climb *because* of the risk, although that element must be reckoned with.

Eve Dearborn took a risk, and she lost. But I remember her alive: she climbed hard, she pushed, she had not yet accepted any limits. Many women in the climbing community were influenced and inspired by her. Eve was one strong woman. Clearly, her spirit was a gift to us, and her spirit lives.

Even now, the promise of future climbs and expeditions shapes my days. I try to soak up the Arizona sun and store it like bear fat against the coming sub-zero temperatures. During my daily run I compare road grades to the slopes I will ascend on unknown mountains. I want to sweat out all the poison and worries clinging to my skin. I want to be so tired that my only desire is to put my back against the earth. A ritual of purification? Yes. And I wouldn't trade anything for a bird's wing embossed on the snow or the morning I woke above the clouds to find the spiraling tracks of mountain goats beside my tent. I long to visit again that land between earth and sky, the middle kingdom, to see the red hair of my partner flame in the sun, casting a jeweled light on the white hand of the mountain.

Nine years have passed since I wrote the first part of this essay. Last year, on 28 January 1991, Kathy Phibbs and her partner Hope Barnes died in a climbing accident in the Cascades. Six months later, another member of our community, Nancy Czech, also died in a climbing accident. Hope and Kathy had been friends and climbing partners; Nancy and Kathy had been friends, climbing partners, and lovers. The deaths of these three well-loved women sent waves of shock and grief through Women Climbers Northwest; many of us will feel the reverberations for years to come.

As Eve's death was the occasion for writing the first half of this essay, Kathy's is the occasion for the second. I remember that one of my initial responses to Eve's death was to worry about how my mother would feel if anything should ever happen to me. Recently, I found an eerie echo of that feeling in a letter written by Kathy, days after Eve's death. After describing the accident and the viewing of Eve's body at a funeral home, she gives an account of the memorial service, where she met Mrs. Dearborn for the first time. Talking with Eve's mother, she said, gave her faith for her own mother's strength in a similar situation.

I remember writing the first half of this essay with a kind of desperation, hoping to shift my mother's gaze away from the accident; climbing was about living to me, not death, and I wanted her to understand that. For some, risk is the primary element in climbing's alchemy; for me, it's friendship. Women, adventure, a whole shining world: that's what I wanted to talk about. Then, as now, climbing was surrounded by concentric rings of questions. On the outside, I heard the world asking, 'Why climb?' or 'How can you justify risking your life?' Inside that, I heard myself asking, What does it mean to climb with women? And last, the inner circle, the cauldron: What is the nature of my friendship with this woman? With Kathy? Still, I am most interested in the last questions.

When the first half of this essay was published, I was ready to move in a brand new direction, satisfied that I'd put risk in its place, or at least explained myself to my mother.

It took years, but late last January, I had slogged forward to what I hoped was the end of another essay on climbing. I knew it needed more work, but I was excited because I'd made a start in the direction I'd long since mapped out. I couldn't wait to hear what Kathy thought. The day I finished it, Hope and Kathy fell from Dragontail. Three days later, when the search party went into the mountains, I heard about the accident, and I put the essay away.

Now, shortly after the first anniversary of her death, I find myself completing this, a good-bye to Kathy, and discover that something has changed in the nine intervening years.

In the face of her death, the old questions are raised, and though I still love climbing, I find I don't want to talk about it at all: not to defend it, or explain it, or glorify it. I feel tired when the subject is brought up, because I am more absorbed with her loss than the vehicle of her loss. And this perspective, finally, feels right: climbing was both the means of her death and a wonderful expression of our friendship when she was alive.

When a climber dies, you hear a lot of people say, 'At least she died doing what she loved.' That was never much comfort to me, but I was happy that Kathy spent so much of her life climbing – as Eve did, as Hope did, as Nancy did, as many of us still do.

Now, instead of dreams winging into the future, I have only memories of our friendship and a deepening, pervasive sense of mystery. My last image of Kathy belongs to a cold, wet day in January when I went to Leavenworth, Washington, with several of Kathy's friends to view her body in a funeral home. I had been away on a writing break in Arizona when Kathy died and had flown home immediately when I received the news. A public viewing had not been scheduled, but Mr Phibbs was kind enough to arrange a private one at my request.

I drove to Leavenworth with Saskia, a woman with whom Kathy had recently begun a relationship. Both Saskia and Hope's companion had joined the rescue party that carried the bodies out of the mountains. Through Monroe, Sultan, Startup, Goldbar, Index, the drive we could have done blind, I listened to Saskia describe the accident and how Kathy looked when she found her frozen in the snow beside Colchuck Lake. Seconds ticked by; I scanned the passing sky, the pastures heavy with standing water, the road – all were colored a dull gray-green that worried my eyes with its sameness. Again and again, I came up against the familiar fringe of dark firs corralling the dumb land. On the east side of Stevens Pass, I looked out at the winter forest and wanted something from it – we were so close now to where they had died – but I was met again with silence.

When we arrived at the funeral home, the owner tried to discourage us from seeing Kathy, saying she hadn't been prepared. Nancy spoke to him, politely, but made it clear she would brook no interference. He gave in reluctantly, adding that he was sorry but because of the short notice, he didn't have a room for her – the hallway was the best he could offer.

We filed in one by one, Nancy and Saskia first. They gasped as they walked through the door, then reached out to each other and stepped back, leaning against the wall. Kathy was lying on a hospital gurney in a maroon corduroy body bag zipped up to the neck, a white silk scarf covering her throat. Her head was tilted back slightly, and an agonized expression drew all her features tight. Her face was cut and bruised, and her mouth was open, as if she were still breathing hard and in pain.

Looking down at my friend, I knew I had found what I came for – the story of Kathy's death was written on her face. I could see the anger, the loneliness, and the fear of her last moments. She had fought hard before leaving this world.

The long habit of touching her moved my hands hesitantly towards her, to the cold that had overcome her body, hardening her skin and draining the light from her hair. I was filled with an immense desire to continue loving her even through death.

Yes, she was gone. But this home of flesh and bones was where we had known her, and the only place we could come to say good-bye. Our hands laid gently on her beautiful, strong body, our tears, the words whispered alone to her, were our good-byes, and the first step towards loosening the knot of grief that bound us to her.

We stood in a circle around her, and then each of us spent a few minutes alone with her. While we were all in the room together, Mr Phibbs called and asked Nancy to say good-bye for him and to tell Kathy he was proud of her.

On the drive home, Nancy said it looked as if her death had been as hard as her life, the past year; Donna said she would have liked to stay beside her longer, she would go again to see her if she could; Bill said he'd kept looking up to the corners of the room, thinking he might catch a glimpse of her – he wondered if she was with us.

We'd planned to climb in Alaska in the spring. Instead, I returned to the Southwest, this time to the high desert of northern New Mexico. I think of her constantly, during days so hot that thousands of creamy pods from the elms near my house fall to the ground, fluttering and swooning in dizzy descending circles.

Her death feels like a retort that left me silent. The jokes I had saved to tell her, the new essay I'd written that needed her point of view. Always in these months, I look up to the night sky for signs of her, as if a galaxy might suddenly reshape itself in her image, or a string of stars form the profile I loved – even an ice axe would be welcome. Couldn't you at least do that, I ask.

The cottonwoods, so tall the tips of their branches brush the sky, are closer to her than I am. She is at once everywhere and nowhere, and the words I want to say to her work themselves inside, becoming hard seeds in the muscle of my heart.

Then she finds me, through the memory of a climb. It's almost as if she re-enters the day so that she can leave this life and our friendship on her own terms, as if in death, time has softened between her hands.

The memory is of the day we climbed Sahale. We didn't set out to climb it, we'd planned to do the North Face of Forbidden. It was summer and we slept out on the moraine in just our bags. A small wandering pack of deer woke us before daybreak, happy to find salt in patches of bare dirt near camp, our boots, and our pack straps. Shapely hooves and big, casual licks. Only half-awake, Kathy muttered something about the deer lacking manners, and how it was entirely possible we'd be trampled in our sleep.

It was time to get up anyway, so we rose, ate, and packed. I realized my sore throat had developed into something more serious, but I couldn't bring myself to say anything. We started off and she immediately gained fifty yards on me. Realizing I was too weak to do the climb, I sat down on a rock and cried with shame and disappointment. Her back slowly disappeared into the twilight, then she turned and came back into focus. We decided to go back to bed and get up at a decent hour to climb Sahale. Kathy dispensed a few Sudafeds, her cure-all, and we slept soundly until the sun warmed our bags.

We woke the second time to a blue sky, which grew brighter by leaps. Sahale looked friendly, and Kathy was the best of company with her gift of taking great pleasure in the smallest things – in this case, a bit of tiptoeing between two crevasses, a chance to use an axe like an ice tool, a single move causing a few quick beats of the heart. All ease she was and so pleased with herself she treated me to a running commentary on my style and the 'route'. The fact that we had full packs was not to be forgotten or discounted, indeed, and neither was the proximity of the only two crevasses on the glacier, just inches away, nor the flexibility I demonstrated with my cramponing technique, nor the presence of the ferocious North Cascades, kept at bay for at least one glorious day.

Then we gained the summit, and Kathy, with her ready box of

gingersnaps and red crown of hair, seemed queen of all she surveyed. She talked about routes, first stabbing the air with her finger, then rubbing her hands together in excitement and wiping the sweat off against her legs. So northern, she said, of the rich greens, browns, and grays, and I remembered that unlike me, she knew and loved other ranges.

But the best was yet to come – the walk down Sahale Arm. The day grew bigger and bigger and finally burst into night, shedding the light softly, for a quiet dusk. We descended the sandy, winding path, arm of the giant, through heather where tiny white blooms shone like footlights. All around us rose the night mountains, sisters of the day mountains, but black and splendid and jagged and twice as fierce, baring gleaming slopes of snow and ice.

But we were happy and safe, enjoying the evening's warmth. I will never forget how she walked, the discipline of years showing in her steady stride, always a sense of purpose about her. I didn't ever want the trail to end. I would have followed it with her forever, watching the falling light melt into the snow, happy to carry one more successful climb home.

Once she paused, and when I reached her, she took my hand without words. We continued walking, and everything fell into place – our bodies on the path through meadows among mountains on an earth spinning in an ocean of stars.

Finally we reached Cascade Pass, and this is where the memories diverge. Instead of descending the endless switchbacks as we did on that summer evening, she pauses at the pass, and I notice how the darkness clusters around her, dense and purple. Then she waves, a single wave that doesn't ask for a response, and I understand she is leaving now – this is the moment she's chosen.

She gives me the smile I know so well, the one she saved for summits and hard leads, and I can't help but smile back. Not so much leaving me, she seems to say, but going home, home from this last evening walk in the mountains.

She turns and begins moving away from me, back into her Beloveds, whose sleeping profiles are now barely visible. Her body vanishes, sinking like a torn leaf into the smooth vast darkness.

from Remote People

by Evelyn Waugh

Evelyn Waugh (1903–66) became a climber by accident during a visit to Yemen. The Mr Leblanc in this anecdote resembles some contemporary climbers in his contempt for people who don't share his experience, his skill or his lust for unprotected overhangs.

E veryone was delightfully hospitable, and between meals I made a serious attempt to grasp some of the intricacies of Arabian politics; an attempt which more often than not took the form of my spreading a table with maps, reports, and notebooks, and then falling into a gentle and prolonged stupor. I spent only one really strenuous afternoon. That was in taking 'a little walk over the rocks', with Mr Leblanc and his 'young men'.

Nothing in my earlier acquaintance with Mr Leblanc had given me any reason to suspect what I was letting myself in for when I accepted his invitation to join him in his little walk over the rocks. He was a general merchant, commercial agent, and shipowner of importance, the only European magnate in the Settlement; they said of him that he thrived on risk and had made and lost more than one considerable fortune in his time. I met him dining at the Residency, on my first evening in Aden. He talked of Abyssinia, where he had heavy business undertakings, with keen sarcasm; he expressed his contempt for the poetry of Rimbaud; he told me a great deal of very recent gossip about people in Europe; he produced, from the pocket of his white waistcoat, a Press-cutting about Miss Rebecca West's marriage; after dinner he played some very new gramophone records he had brought with him. To me, rubbed raw by those deadly four days at Dirre-Dowa and Djibouti, it was all particularly emollient and healing.

A day or two afterwards he invited me to dinner at his house in Crater. A smart car with a liveried Indian chauffeur came to fetch me. We dined on the roof; a delicious dinner; iced *vin rosé* – 'It is not a luxurious wine, but I am fond of it; it grows on a little estate of my own in the South of France' – and the finest Yemen coffee. With his very thin gold watch in his hand, Mr Leblanc predicted the rising of a star – I forget which. Punctual to the second, it appeared, green and malevolent, on the rim of the hills; cigars glowing under the night sky; from below the faint murmur of the native streets; all infinitely smooth and civilized.

At this party a new facet was revealed to me in the character of my host. Mr Leblanc the man of fashion I had seen. Here was Mr Leblanc the patriarch. The house where we sat was the top storey of his place of business; at the table sat his daughter, his secretary, and three of his 'young men'. The young men were his clerks, learning the business. One was French, the other two English lately down from Cambridge. They worked immensely hard – often, he told me, ten hours a day; often halfway through the night, when a ship was in. They were not encouraged to go to the club or to mix in the society of Steamer Point. They lived together in a house near Mr Leblanc's; they lived very well and were on terms of patriarchal intimacy with Mr Leblanc's family. 'If they go up to Steamer Point, they start drinking, playing cards, and spending money. Here, they work so hard that they cannot help saving. When they want a holiday they go round the coast visiting my agencies. They learn to know the country and the people; they travel in my ships; at the end of a year or two they have saved nearly all their money and they have learned business. For exercise we take little walks over the rocks together. Tennis and polo would cost them money. To walk in the hills is free. They get up out of the town into the cool air, the views are magnificent, the gentle exercise keeps them in condition for their work. It takes their minds, for a little, off business. You must come with us one day on one of our walks.'

I agreed readily. After the torpid atmosphere of Aden it would be delightful to take some gentle exercise in the cool air. And so it was arranged for the following Saturday afternoon. When I left, Mr Leblanc lent me a copy of Gide's *Voyage au Congo*.

Mr Leblanc the man of fashion I knew, and Mr Leblanc the patriarch. On

Saturday I met Mr Leblanc the man of action, Mr Leblanc the gambler.

I was to lunch first with the young men at their 'mess' – as all communal *ménages* appear to be called in the East. I presented myself dressed as I had seen photographs of 'hikers', with shorts, open shirt, stout shoes, woollen stockings, and large walking-stick. We had an excellent luncheon, during which they told me how, one evening, they had climbed into the Parsees' deathhouse, and what a row there had been about it. Presently one of them said, 'Well, it's about time to change. We promised to be round at the old man's at half-past.'

'Change?'

'Well, it's just as you like, but I think you'll find those things rather hot. We usually wear nothing except shoes and shorts. We leave our shirts in the cars. They meet us on the bathing-beach. And if you've got any rubber-soled shoes I should wear them. Some of the rocks are pretty slippery.' Luckily I happened to have some rubber shoes. I went back to the chaplain's house, where I was then living, and changed. I was beginning to be slightly apprehensive.

Mr Leblanc looked magnificent. He wore newly creased white shorts, a silk openwork vest, and white *espadrilles* laced like a ballet dancer's round his ankles. He held a tuberose, sniffing it delicately. 'They call it an Aden lily sometimes,' he said. 'I can't think why.'

There was with him another stranger, a guest of Mr Leblanc's on a commercial embassy from an oil firm. 'I say, you know,' he confided in me, 'I think this is going to be a bit stiff. I'm scarcely in training for anything very energetic.'

We set out in the cars and drove to a dead end at the face of the cliffs near the ancient reservoirs. I thought we must have taken the wrong road, but everyone got out and began stripping off his shirt. The Leblanc party went hatless; the stranger and I retained our topis.

'I should leave those sticks in the car,' said Mr Leblanc.

'But shan't we find them useful?' (I still nursed memories of happy scrambles in the Wicklow hills.)

'You will find them a great nuisance,' said Mr Leblanc.

We did as we were advised.

Then the little walk started. Mr Leblanc led the way with light, springing steps. He went right up to the face of the cliff, gaily but purposefully as Moses may have approached the rocks from which he was about to strike water. There was a little crack running like fork-lightning down the blank wall of stone. Mr Leblanc stood below it, gave one little skip, and suddenly, with great rapidity and no apparent effort, proceeded to ascend the precipice. He did not climb; he rose. It was as if someone were hoisting him up from above and he had merely to prevent himself from swinging out of the perpendicular, by keeping contact with rocks in a few light touches of foot and hand.

In just the same way, one after another, the Leblanc party were whisked away out of sight. The stranger and I looked at each other. 'Are you all right?' came reverberating down from very far ahead. We began to climb. We climbed for about half an hour up the cleft in the rock. Not once during that time did we find a place where it was possible to rest or even to stand still in any normal attitude. We just went on from foothold to foothold; our topis made it impossible to see more than a foot or two above our heads. Suddenly we came on the Leblanc party sitting on a ledge.

'You look hot,' said Mr Leblanc. 'I see you are not in training. You will find this most beneficial.'

As soon as we stopped climbing, our knees began to tremble. We sat down. When the time came to start again, it was quite difficult to stand up. Our knees seemed to be behaving as they sometimes do in dreams, when they suddenly refuse support in moments of pursuit by bearded women broadcasters.

'We thought it best to wait for you,' continued Mr Leblanc, 'because there is rather a tricky bit here. It is easy enough when you know the way, but you need someone to show you. I discovered it myself. I often go out alone in the evenings finding tricky bits. Once I was out all night, quite stuck. I thought I should be able to find a way when the moon rose. Then I remembered there was no moon that night. It was a very cramped position.'

The tricky bit was a huge overhanging rock with a crumbling flaky surface.

'It is really quite simple. Watch me and then follow. You put your right foot here . . .' – a perfectly blank, highly polished surface of stone – '. . . then rather slowly you reach up with your left hand until you find a hold. You have to stretch rather far . . . so. Then you cross your right leg under your left – this is the difficult part – and feel for a footing on the other side . . . With your right hand you just steady yourself . . . so.' Mr

Leblanc hung over the abyss partly out of sight. His whole body seemed prehensile and tenacious. He *stood* there like a fly on the ceiling. 'That is the position. It is best to trust more to the feet than the hands – push up rather than pull down . . . you see the stone here is not always secure.' By way of demonstration he splintered off a handful of apparently solid rock from above his head and sent it tinkling down to the road below. 'Now all you do is to shift the weight from your left foot to your right, and swing yourself round . . . so.' And Mr Leblanc disappeared from view.

Every detail of that expedition is kept fresh in my mind by recurrent nightmares. Eventually after about an hour's fearful climb we reached the rim of the crater. The next stage was a tramp across the great pit of loose cinders; then the ascent of the other rim, to the highest point of the peninsula. Here we paused to admire the view, which was indeed most remarkable; then we climbed down to the sea. Variety was added to this last phase by the fact that we were now in the full glare of the sun, which had been beating on the cliffs from noon until they were blistering hot.

'It will hurt the hands if you hang on too long,' said Mr Leblanc. 'One must jump on the foot from rock to rock like the little goats.'

At last, after about three hours of it, we reached the beach. Cars and servants were waiting. Tea was already spread; bathing-dresses and towels laid out.

'We always bathe here, not at the club, 'said Mr Leblanc. 'They have a screen there to keep out the sharks – while in this bay, only last month, two boys were devoured.'

We swam out into the warm sea. An Arab fisherman, hopeful of a tip, ran to the edge of the sea and began shouting to us that it was dangerous. Mr Leblanc laughed happily and, with easy powerful strokes, made for the deep waters. We returned to shore and dressed. My shoes were completely worn through, and there was a large tear in my shorts where I had slipped among the cinders and slid some yards. Mr Leblanc had laid out for him in the car a clean white suit, a shirt of green crêpe-de-Chine, a bow tie, silk socks, buckskin shoes, ivory hairbrushes, scent spray, and hair lotion. We ate banana sandwiches and drank very rich China tea.

For a little additional thrill on the way back, Mr Leblanc took the wheel of his car. I am not sure that that was not the most hair-raising experience of all.

from Scrambles Amongst the Alps
by Edward Whymper

Edward Whymper (1840–1911) made seven attempts on the unclimbed Matterhorn between 1861 and 1865. His last attempt involved a hastily assembled party racing to forestall rival climbers. The tragedy that ensued provoked tremendous controversy. Whymper's account of the disaster is both apologia and hymn; some climbers can quote the last passage by heart.

We started from Zermatt on 13 July 1865, at half-past five, on a brilliant and perfectly cloudless morning. We were eight in number – Croz, old Peter Taugwalder and his two sons, Lord F. Douglas, Hadow, Hudson, and I. To ensure steady motion, one tourist and one native walked together. The youngest Taugwalder fell to my share, and the lad marched well, proud to be on the expedition, and happy to show his powers. The wine-bags also fell to my lot to carry, and throughout the day, after each drink, I replenished them secretly with water, so that at the next halt they were found fuller than before! This was considered a good omen, and little short of miraculous.

On the first day we did not intend to ascend to any great height, and we mounted, accordingly, very leisurely; picked up the things which were left in the chapel at the Schwarzsee at 8.20, and proceeded thence along the ridge connecting the Hörnli with the Matterhorn. At half-past eleven we arrived at the base of the actual peak; then quitted the ridge, and clambered round some ledges, on to the eastern face. We were now fairly upon the mountain, and were astonished to find that places which from the Riffel, or even from the Furggen Glacier, looked entirely impracticable, were so easy that we could *run about.*

Before twelve o'clock we had found a good position for the tent, at a height of 11,000 feet. Croz and young Peter went on to see what was above, in order to save time on the following morning. They cut across the heads of the snow-slopes which descended towardss the Furggen Glacier, and disappeared round a corner; but shortly afterwards we saw them high up on the face, moving quickly. We others made a solid platform for the tent in a well-protected spot, and then watched eagerly for the return of the men. The stones which they upset told us that they were very high, and we supposed that the way must be easy. At length, just before 3 p.m., we saw them coming down, evidently much excited. 'What are they saying, Peter?' 'Gentlemen, they say it is no good.' But when they came near we heard a different story. 'Nothing but what was good; not a difficulty, not a single difficulty! We could have gone to the summit and returned today easily!'

We passed the remaining hours of daylight – some basking in the sunshine, some sketching or collecting; and when the sun went down, giving, as it departed, a glorious promise for the morrow, we returned to the tent to arrange for the night. Hudson made tea, I coffee, and we then retired each one to his blanket bag; the Taugwalders, Lord Francis Douglas, and myself, occupying the tent, the others remaining, by preference, outside. Long after dusk the cliffs above echoed with our laughter and with the songs of the guides, for we were happy that night in camp, and feared no evil.

We assembled together outside the tent before dawn on the morning of the 14th, and started directly it was light enough to move. Young Peter came on with us as a guide, and his brother returned to Zermatt. We followed the route which had been taken on the previous day, and in a few minutes turned the rib which had intercepted the view of the eastern face from our tent platform. The whole of this great slope was now revealed, rising for 3,000 feet like a huge natural staircase. Some parts were more, and others were less, easy; but we were not once brought to a halt by any serious impediment, for when an obstruction was met in front it could always be turned to the right or to the left. For the greater part of the way there was, indeed, no occasion for the rope, and sometimes Hudson led, sometimes myself. At 6.20 we had attained a height of 12,800 feet, and halted for half an hour; we then continued the ascent without a break until 9.55, when we stopped for fifty minutes, at a height of 14,000 feet. Twice we struck the north-east ridge and followed it for some little distance – to no advantage, for it was usually more rotten and steep, and always more difficult than the face. Still, we kept near to it, lest stones perchance might fall.

We had now arrived at the foot of that part which, from the Riffelberg or from Zermatt, seems perpendicular or overhanging, and could no longer continue upon the eastern side. For a little distance we ascended by snow upon the arête – that is, the ridge – descending towardss Zermatt, and then, by common consent, turned over to the right, or to the northern side. Before doing so, we made a change in the order of ascent. Croz went first, I followed, Hudson came third; Hadow and old Peter were last. 'Now,' said Croz, as he led off, 'now for something altogether different.' The work became difficult and required caution. In some places there was little to hold, and it was desirable that those should be in front who were least likely to slip. The general slope of the mountain at this part was less than 40°, and snow had accumulated in, and had filled up, the interstices of the rock-face, leaving only occasional fragments projecting here and there. These were at times covered with a thin film of ice, produced from the melting and refreezing of the snow. It was the counterpart, on a small scale, of the upper 700 feet of the Pointe des Ecrins – only there was this material difference; the face of the Ecrins was about, or exceeded, an angle of 50°, and the Matterhorn face was less than 40°. It was a place over which any fair mountaineer might pass in safety, and Mr. Hudson ascended this part, and, as far as I know, the entire mountain, without having the slightest assistance rendered to him upon any occasion. Sometimes, after I had taken a hand from Croz, or received a pull, I turned to offer the same to Hudson; but he invariably declined, saying it was not necessary. Mr. Hadow, however, was not accustomed to this kind of work, and required continual assistance. It is only fair to say that the difficulty which he found at this part arose simply and entirely from want of experience.

This solitary difficult part was of no great extent. We bore away over it at first, nearly horizontally, for a distance of about 400 feet; then ascended directly towardss the summit for about 60 feet; and then doubled back to the ridge which descends towardss Zermatt. A long stride round a rather awkward corner brought us to snow once more. The last doubt vanished! The Matterhorn was ours! Nothing but 200 feet of easy snow remained to be surmounted!

You must now carry your thoughts back to the seven Italians who started from Breuil on 11 July. Four days had passed since their departure, and we were tormented with anxiety lest they should arrive on the top before us. All the way up we had talked of them, and many false alarms of 'men on the summit' had been raised. The higher we rose, the more intense became the excitement. What if we should be beaten at the last moment? The slope eased off, at length we could be detached, and Croz and I, dashing away, ran a neck-and-neck race, which ended in a dead heat. At 1.40 p.m. the world was at our feet, and the Matterhorn was conquered. Hurrah! Not a footstep could be seen.

It was not yet certain that we had not been beaten. The summit of the Matterhorn was formed of a rudely level ridge, about 350 feet long, and the Italians might have been at its farther extremity. I hastened to the southern end, scanning the snow right and left eagerly. Hurrah! again; it was untrodden. 'Where were the men?' I peered over the cliff, half doubting, half expectant, and saw them immediately – mere dots on the ridge, at an immense distance below. Up went my arms and my hat. 'Croz! Croz!! come here!' 'Where are they, Monsieur?' 'There, don't you see them, down there?' 'Ah! the *coquins*, they are low down.' 'Croz, we must make those fellows hear us.' We yelled until we were hoarse. The Italians seemed to regard us – we could not be certain. 'Croz, we must make them hear us; they shall hear us!' I seized a block of rock and hurled it down, and called upon my companion, in the name of friendship, to do the same. We drove our sticks in, and prized away the crags, and soon a torrent of stones poured down the cliffs. There was no mistake about it this time. The Italians turned and fled.

Still, I would that the leader of that party could have stood with us at that moment, for our victorious shouts conveyed to him the disappointment of the ambition of a lifetime. He was *the* man, of all those who attempted the ascent of the Matterhorn, who most deserved to be the first upon its summit. He was the first to doubt its inaccessibility, and he was the only man who persisted in believing that its ascent would be accomplished. It was the aim of his life to make the ascent from the side of Italy, for the honour of his native valley. For a time he had the game in his hands: he played it as he thought best; but he made a false move, and he lost it.

The others had arrived, so we went back to the northern end of the ridge. Croz now took the tent-pole, and planted it in the highest snow. 'Yes,' we said, 'there is the flag-staff, but where is the flag?' 'Here it is,' he answered, pulling off his blouse and fixing it to the stick. It made a poor flag, and there was no wind to float it out, yet it was seen all around. They saw it at Zermatt – at the Riffel – in the Val Tournanche. At Breuil, the watchers cried, 'Victory is ours!' They raised 'bravos' for Carrel, and 'vivas' for Italy, and hastened to put themselves *en fête*. On the morrow they were undeceived. 'All was changed; the explorers returned sad – cast down – disheartened – confounded – gloomy.' 'It is true,' said the men. 'We saw them ourselves – they hurled stones at us! The old traditions are true – there are spirits on the top of the Matterhorn!'

We returned to the southern end of the ridge to build a cairn, and then paid homage to the view. The day was one of those superlatively calm and clear ones which usually precede bad weather. The atmosphere was perfectly still, and free from all clouds or vapours. Mountains fifty – nay a hundred – miles off, looked sharp and near. All their details – ridge and crag, snow and glacier – stood out with faultless definition. Pleasant thoughts of happy days in bygone years came up unbidden, as we recognized the old, familiar forms. All were revealed – not one of the principal peaks of the Alps was hidden. I see them clearly now – the great inner circles of giants, backed by the ranges, chains, and *massifs*. First came the Dent Blanche, hoary and grand; the Gabelhorn and pointed Rothorn; and then the peerless Weisshorn; the towering Mischabelhörner, flanked by the Allalinhorn, Strahlhorn, and Rimpfischhorn; then Monte Rosa – with its many Spitzes – the Lyskamm and the Breithorn. Behind were the Bernese Oberland, governed by the Finsteraarhorn; the Simplon and St. Gotthard groups; the Disgrazia and the Ortler. Towards the south we looked down to Chivasso on the plain of Piedmont, and far beyond. The Viso – one hundred miles away – seemed close upon us; the Maritime Alps – one hundred and thirty miles distant – were free from haze. Then came my first love – the Pelvoux; the Ecrins and the Meije; the clusters of the Graians; and lastly, in the west, glowing in full sunlight, rose the monarch of all – Mont Blanc. Ten thousand feet beneath us were the green fields of Zermatt, dotted with chalets, from which blue smoke rose lazily. Eight thousand feet below, on the other side, were the pastures of Breuil. There were forests black and gloomy, and meadows bright and lively; bounding waterfalls and tranquil lakes; fertile lands and savage wastes; sunny plains and frigid *plateaux*. There were the most rugged forms, and the most graceful outlines – bold, perpendicular cliffs, and gentle undulating slopes; rocky mountains and snowy mountains, sombre and solemn, or glittering and white, with walls – turrets – pinnacles – pyramids – domes – cones – and spires! There was every combination that the world can give, and every contrast that the heart could desire.

We remained on the summit for one hour –

'One crowded hour of glorious life.'

It passed away too quickly, and we began to prepare for the descent.

• • •

Hudson and I again consulted as to the best and safest arrangement of the party. We agreed that it would be best for Croz to go first, and Hadow second; Hudson, who was almost equal to a born mountaineer in sureness of foot, wished to be third; Lord Francis Douglas was placed next, and old Peter, the strongest of the remainder, after him. I suggested to Hudson that we should attach a rope to the rocks on our arrival at the difficult bit, and hold it as we descended, as an additional protection. He approved the idea, but it was not definitely settled that it should be done. The party was being arranged in the above order whilst I was sketching the summit, and they had finished, and were waiting for me to be tied in line, when someone remembered that our names had not been left in a bottle. They requested me to write them down, and moved off while it was being done.

A few minutes afterwards I tied myself to young Peter, ran down after the others, and caught them just as they were commencing the descent of the difficult part. Great care was being taken. Only one man was moving at a time; when he was firmly planted the next advanced, and so on. They had not, however, attached the additional rope to rocks, and nothing was said about it. The suggestion was not made for my own sake, and I am not sure that it even occurred to me again. For some little distance we two followed the others, detached from them, and should have continued so had not Lord Francis Douglas asked me, about 3 p.m., to tie on to old Peter, as he feared, he said, that Taugwalder would not be able to hold his ground if a slip occurred.

A few minutes later, a sharp-eyed lad ran into the Monte Rosa Hotel, to Seiler, saying that he had seen an avalanche fall from the summit of the Matterhorn on to the Matterhorn Glacier. The boy was reproved for telling idle stories; he was right, nevertheless, and this was what he saw.

Michel Croz had laid aside his axe, and in order to give Mr. Hadow greater security, was absolutely taking hold of his legs, and putting his feet, one by one, into their proper positions. So far as I know, no one was actually descending. I cannot speak with certainty, because the two leading men were partially hidden from my sight by an intervening mass of rock, but it is my belief, from the movements of their shoulders, that Croz, having done as I have said, was in the act of turning round, to go down a step or two himself; at this moment Mr. Hadow slipped, fell against him, and knocked him over. I heard one startled exclamation from Croz, then saw him and Mr. Hadow flying downwards; in another moment Hudson was dragged from his steps, and Lord Francis Douglas immediately after him.

All this was the work of a moment. Immediately we heard Croz's exclamation, old Peter and I planted ourselves as firmly as the rocks would permit: the rope was taut between us, and the jerk came on us both as on one man. We held; but the rope broke midway between Taugwalder and Lord Francis Douglas. For a few seconds we saw our unfortunate companions sliding downwards on their backs, and spreading out their hands, endeavouring to save themselves. They passed from our sight uninjured, disappeared one by one, and fell from precipice to precipice on the Matterhorn Glacier below, a distance of nearly 4,000 feet in height. From the moment the rope broke it was impossible to help them.

So perished our comrades! For the space of half an hour we remained on the spot without moving a single step. The two men, paralysed by terror, cried like infants, and trembled in such a manner as to threaten us with the fate of the others. Old Peter rent the air with exclamations of 'Chamonix! Oh, what will Chamonix say?' He meant, Who would believe that Croz could fall? The young man did nothing but scream or sob, 'We are lost! We are lost!' Fixed between the two, I could neither move up nor down. I begged young Peter to descend, but he dared not. Unless he did, we could not advance. Old Peter became alive to the danger, and swelled the cry, 'We are lost! we are lost!' The father's fear was natural – he trembled for his son; the young man's fear was cowardly – he thought of self alone. At last old Peter summoned up courage, and changed his position to a rock to which he could fix the rope; the young man then descended, and we all stood together. Immediately we did so, I asked for the rope which had given way, and found, to my surprise – indeed, to my horror – that it was the weakest of the three ropes. It was not brought, and should not have been employed, for the purpose for which it was used. It was old rope, and, compared with the others, was feeble. It was intended as a reserve, in case we had to leave much rope behind, attached to rocks. I saw at once that a serious question was involved, and made him give me the end. It had broken in mid air, and it did not appear to have sustained previous injury.

For more than two hours afterwards I thought almost every moment that the next would be my last; for the Taugwalders, utterly unnerved, were not only incapable of giving assistance, but were in such a state that a slip might have been expected from them at any moment. After a time, we were able to do that which should have been done at first, and fixed rope to firm rocks, in addition to being tied together. These ropes were cut from time to time, and were left behind. Even with their assurance the men were afraid to proceed, and several times old Peter turned with ashy face and faltering limbs, and said, with terrible emphasis, '*I cannot!*'

About 6 p.m. we arrived at the snow upon the ridge descending towardss Zermatt, and all peril was over. We frequently looked, but in vain, for traces of our unfortunate companions; we bent over the ridge and cried to them, but no sound returned. Convinced at last that they were neither within sight nor hearing, we ceased from our useless efforts; and, too cast down for speech, silently gathered up our things, and the little effects of those who were lost, preparatory to continuing the descent. When, lo! a mighty arch appeared, rising above the Lyskamm, high into the sky. Pale, colourless, and noiseless, but perfectly sharp and defined, except where it was lost in the clouds, this unearthly apparition seemed like a vision from another world; and, almost appalled, we watched with amazement the gradual development of two vast crosses, one on either side. If the Taugwalders had not been the first to perceive it, I should have doubted my senses.* They thought it had some connection with the accident, and I, after a while, that it might bear some relation to ourselves. But our movements had no effect upon it. The spectral forms remained motionless. It was a fearful and wonderful sight; unique in my experience, and impressive beyond description, coming at such a moment.

I was ready to leave, and waiting for the others. They had recovered their appetites and the use of their tongues. They spoke in patois, which I did not understand. At length the son said in French, 'Monsieur.' 'Yes.' 'We are poor men; we have lost our Herr; we shall not get paid; we can ill afford this.'

---

*I can add very little about it to that which is said above. The sun was directly at our backs; that is to say, the fog-bow was opposite to the sun. The time was 6.30 p.m. The forms were at once tender and sharp; neutral in tone; were developed gradually, and disappeared suddenly. The mists were light (that is, not dense), and were dissipated in the course of the evening.

'Stop!' I said, interrupting him, 'that is nonsense; I shall pay you, of course, just as if your Herr were here.' They talked together in their patois for a short time, and then the son spoke again. 'We don't wish you to pay us. We wish you to write in the hotel-book at Zermatt, and to your journals, that we have not been paid.' 'What nonsense are you talking? I don't understand you. What do you mean?' He proceeded – 'Why, next year there will be many travellers at Zermatt, and we shall get more *voyageurs.*'

Who would answer such a proposition? I made them no reply in words, but they knew very well the indignation that I felt. They filled the cup of bitterness to overflowing, and I tore down the cliff, madly and recklessly, in a way that caused them, more than once, to inquire if I wished to kill them. Night fell; and for an hour the descent was continued in the darkness. At half-past nine a resting-place was found, and upon a wretched slab, barely large enough to hold the three, we passed six miserable hours. At daybreak the descent was resumed, and from the Hörnli ridge we ran down to the chalets of Buhl, and on to Zermatt. Seiler met me at his door, and followed in silence to my room. 'What is the matter?' 'The Taugwalders and I have returned.' He did not need more, and burst into tears; but lost no time in useless lamentations, and set to work to arouse the village. Ere long a score of men had started to ascend the Hohlicht heights, above Kalbermatt and Z'Mutt, which commanded the plateau of the Matterhorn Glacier. They returned after six hours, and reported that they had seen the bodies lying motionless on the snow. This was on Saturday; and they proposed that we should leave on Sunday evening, so as to arrive upon the plateau at daybreak on Monday. Unwilling to lose the slightest chance, the Rev. J. M'Cormick and I resolved to start on Sunday morning. The Zermatt men, threatened with excommunication by their priests if they failed to attend the early mass, were unable to accompany us. To several of them, at least, this was a severe trial. Peter Perren declared with tears that nothing else would have prevented him from joining in the search for his old comrades. Englishmen came to our aid. The Rev. J. Robertson and Mr J. Phillpotts offered themselves, and their guide Franz Andermatten; another Englishman lent us Joseph Marie and Alexandre Lochmatter. Frédéric Payot, and Jean Tairraz, of Chamonix, also volunteered.

We started at 2 a.m. on Sunday the 16th, and followed the route that we had taken on the previous Thursday as far as the Hörnli. Thence we went down to the right of the ridge, and mounted through the *séracs* of the Matterhorn Glacier. By 8.30 we had got to the plateau at the top of the glacier, and within sight of the corner in which we knew my companions must be. As we saw one weather-beaten man after another raise the telescope, turn deadly pale, and pass it on without a word to the next, we knew that all hope was gone. We approached. They had fallen below as they had fallen above – Croz a little in advance, Hadow near him, and Hudson some distance behind; but of Lord Francis Douglas we could see nothing. We left them where they fell; buried in snow at the base of the grandest cliff of the most majestic mountain of the Alps.

All those who had fallen had been tied with the Manilla, or with the second and equally strong rope, and, consequently, there had been only one link – that between old Peter and Lord Francis Douglas – where the weaker rope had been used. This had a very ugly look for Taugwalder, for it was not possible to suppose that the others would have sanctioned the employment of a rope so greatly inferior in strength when there were more than two hundred and fifty feet of the better qualities still remaining out of use. For the sake of the old guide (who bore a good reputation), and upon all other accounts, it was desirable that this matter should be cleared up; and after my examination before the court of inquiry which was instituted by the Government was over, I handed in a number of questions which were framed so as to afford old Peter an opportunity of exculpating himself from the grave suspicions which at once fell upon him. The questions, I was told, were put and answered; but the answers, although promised, have never reached me.

Meanwhile, the administration sent strict injunctions to recover the bodies, and upon 19 July, twenty-one men of Zermatt accomplished that sad and dangerous task. Of the body of Lord Francis Douglas they, too, saw nothing; it was probably still arrested on the rocks above. The remains of Hudson and Hadow were interred upon the north side of the Zermatt Church, in the presence of a reverent crowd of sympathizing friends. The body of Michel Croz lies upon the other side, under a simpler tomb; whose inscription bears honourable testimony to his rectitude, to his courage, and to his devotion.

So the traditional inaccessibility of the Matterhorn was vanquished, and was replaced by legends of a more real character. Others will essay to scale its proud cliffs, but to none will it be the mountain that it was to its early explorers. Others may tread its summit-snows, but none will ever know the feelings of those who first gazed upon its marvellous panorama; and none, I trust, will ever be compelled to tell of joy turned into grief, and of laughter into mourning. It proved to be a stubborn foe; it resisted long, and gave many a hard blow; it was defeated at last with an ease that none could have anticipated, but, like a relentless enemy – conquered but not crushed – it took terrible vengeance. The time may come when the Matterhorn shall have passed away, and nothing, save a heap of shapeless fragments, will mark the spot where the great mountain stood; for, atom by atom, inch by inch, and yard by yard, it yields to forces which nothing can withstand. That time is far distant; and, ages hence, generations unborn will gaze upon its awful precipices, and wonder at its unique form. However exalted may be their ideas, and however exaggerated their expectations, none will come to return disappointed!

The play is over, and the curtain is about to fall. Before we part, a word upon the graver teachings of the mountains. See yonder height! 'Tis far away – unbidden comes the word 'Impossible!' 'Not so,' says the mountaineer. 'The way is long, I know; it's difficult – it may be dangerous. It's possible, I'm sure; I'll seek the way; take counsel of my brother mountaineers, and find how they have gained similar heights, and learned to avoid the dangers.' He starts (all slumbering down below); the path is slippery – may be laborious, too. Caution and perseverance gain the day – the height is reached and those beneath cry, 'Incredible; 'tis superhuman!'

We who go mountain-scrambling have constantly set before us the superiority of fixed purpose or perseverance to brute-force. We know that each height, each step, must be gained by patient, laborious toil, and that wishing cannot take the place of working; we know the benefits of mutual aid; that many a difficulty must be encountered, and many an obstacle must be grappled with or turned, but we know that where there's a will there's a way; and we come back to our daily occupations better fitted to fight the battle of life, and to overcome the impediments which obstruct our paths, strengthened and cheered by the recollection of past labours, and by the memories of victories gained in other fields.

I have not made myself either an advocate or an apologist for mountaineering, nor do I now intend to usurp the functions of a moralist; but my task would have been ill performed if it had been concluded without one reference to the more serious lessons of the mountaineer. We glory in the physical regeneration which is the product of our exertions; we exult over the grandeur of the scenes that are brought before our eyes, the splendours of sunrise and sunset, and the beauties of hill, dale, lake, wood, and waterfall; but we value more highly the development of manliness, and the evolution, under combat with difficulties, of those noble qualities of human nature – courage, patience, endurance, and fortitude.

Some hold these virtues in less estimation, and assign base and contemptible motives to those who indulge in our innocent sport.

> 'Be thou chaste as ice, as pure as snow,
> thou shalt not escape calumny.'

Others, again, who are not detractors, find mountaineering, as a sport, to be wholly unintelligible. It is not greatly to be wondered at – we are not all constituted alike. Mountaineering is a pursuit essentially adapted to the young or vigorous, and not to the old or feeble. To the latter, toil may be no pleasure; and it is often said by such persons, 'This man is making a toil of pleasure.' Let the motto on the title-page* be an answer, if an answer be required. Toil he must who goes mountaineering but out of the toil comes strength (not merely muscular energy – more than that), an awakening of all the faculties; and from the strength arises pleasure. Then, again, it is often asked, in tones which seem to imply that the answer must, at least, be doubtful, 'But does it repay you?' Well, we cannot estimate our enjoyment as you measure your wine, or weigh your lead – it is real, nevertheless. If I

---

* 'Toil and pleasure in their natures opposite, are yet linked together in a kind of necessary connection.'—Livy.

could blot out every reminiscence, or erase every memory, still I should say that my scrambles amongst the Alps have repaid me, for they have given me two of the best things a man can possess – health and friends.

The recollections of past pleasures cannot be effaced. Even now as I write they crowd up before me. First comes an endless series of pictures, magnificent in form, effect, and colour. I see the great peaks, with clouded tops, seeming to mount up for ever and ever; I hear the music of the distant herds, the peasant's *jodel*, and the solemn church-bells; and I scent the fragrant breath of the pines: and after these have passed away, another train of thoughts succeeds – of those who have been upright, brave, and true; of kind hearts and bold deeds; and of courtesies received at strangers' hands, trifles in themselves, but expressive of that good will towardss men which is the essence of charity.

Still, the last, sad memory hovers round, and sometimes drifts across like floating mist, cutting off sunshine, and chilling the remembrance of happier times. There have been joys too great to be described in words, and there have been griefs upon which I have not dared to dwell; and with these in mind I say, Climb if you will, but remember that courage and strength are nought without prudence, and that a momentary negligence may destroy the happiness of a lifetime. Do nothing in haste; look well to each step; and from the beginning think what may be the end.

The Only Blasphemy
by John Long

Climbing can be a great teacher, although sometimes its lessons come too late. It taught veteran climber and writer John Long what matters most to him.

At speeds beyond 80 mph, the cops jail you. I cruise at a prudent 79. Tobin [Sorenson] drove 100 – did so till his Datsun blew. It came as no surprise when he perished attempting to solo the North Face of Mt. Alberta. Tobin never drew the line. His rapacious motivation and a boundless fear threshold enamoured him of soloing.

I charge towardss Joshua Tree National Monument, where two weeks prior, another pal had tweeked while soloing. After his fall, I inspected the base of the route, wincing at the grisly blood stains, the grated flesh and tufts of matted hair: soloing is unforgiving. Yet I mull these calamities like a salty dog, considering them avoidable. Soloing is okay I think; you just have to be realistic, not some knave abetted by peer pressure or ego. At 85, Joshua Tree comes quickly, but the stark night drags.

The morning sun peers over the flat horizon, gilding the countless rocks that bespeckle the desert carpet. The biggest stones are little more than 150ft. high. I hook up with John Bachar, probably the world's premier free-climber. John lives at that climbing area featuring the most sun. He has been at Joshua for two months and his soloing feats astonish everyone. It is winter, when school checks my climbing to weekends, so my motivation is fabulous, but my fitness only so-so. Bachar suggests a Half Dome day which translates as: Half Dome is 2,000ft. high, or about twenty pitches. Hence, we must climb twenty pitches to get our Half Dome day. In a wink, Bachar is shod and cinching his waist sling from which his chalk bag hangs. 'Ready?' Only now do I realise he intends to climb all 2,000ft. solo. To save face, I agree, thinking: Well, if he suggests something too asinine, I'll just draw the line.

We embark on familiar ground, twisting feet and jamming hands into vertical cracks; smearing the toes of our skin-tight boots onto tenuous bumps; pulling over roofs on bulbous holds; palming off rough rock and marvelling at it all. We're soloing: no rope. A little voice sometimes asks how good a quarter-inch, pliable hold can be. If you're tight, you set an aquiline hand or pointed toe on that quarter-incher and push or pull perfunctorily.

After three hours, we've disposed of a dozen pitches, feel invincible. We up the ante to 5.10. We slow considerably, but by 2.30, we've climbed twenty pitches. As a finale, Bachar suggests soloing a 5.11, which is a pretty grim prospect for anyone, period; 5.11 is about my wintertime limit . . . when I'm fresh and sharp. But now I am thrashed and stolid from the past 2,000ft., having cruised the last four or five pitches on rhythm and momentum. Regardless, we trot over to Intersection Rock, the 'hang' for local climbers; also, the locale for Bachar's final solo.

He wastes no time and scores of milling climbers freeze like salt statues when he begins. He moves with dauntless precision, plugging his fingertips into shallow pockets in the 105° wall. I scrutinise his moves, taking mental notes on the sequence. He pauses at 50ft. level, directly beneath the crux bulge. Splaying out his left foot onto a slanting rugosity, he pinches a minute wafer and pulls through to a gigantic bucket hold. He walks over the last 100ft. which is only dead vertical.

By virtue of boots, chalk bag, location, and reputation, the crowd, with its heartless avarice, has already committed me. All eyes pan to me, as if to say: Well?! He did make it look trivial, I think, stepping up for a crack.

I draw several audible breaths, as if to convince myself if nobody else. A body length of easy moves, then those incipient pockets which I finger adroitly before yarding with maximum might; 50ft. passes quickly, unconsciously. Then, as I splay my left foot out onto that slanting rugosity, the chilling realisation comes that, in my haste, I have bungled the sequence, that my hands are too low on that puny wafer which I'm now pinching with waning power, my foot vibrating, and I'm desperate, wondering if and when my body will seize and plummet before those heartless salt statues, cutting the air like a swift. A montage of abysmal images floods my brain.

I glance beneath my legs and my gut churns at the thought of a hideous free fall onto the gilded boulders. That 'little' voice is bellowing: 'Do something! Pronto!' My breathing is frenzied while my arms, trashed from the previous 2,000ft., feel like titanium beef steaks. Pinching that little wafer, I suck my feet up so as to extend my arm and jam my hand in the bottoming crack above: the crack is too shallow, will accept only a third of my hand. I'm stuck, terrified, and my whole existence is focused down to a pinpoint which sears my everything like the torrid amber dot from a magnifying glass. Shamefully I understand the only blasphemy: to wilfully jeopardize my own existence, which I've done, and this sickens me. I know that wasted seconds could . . . then a flash, the world stops, or is it preservation instincts booting my brain into hyper gear? In the time it takes a hummingbird to wave its wings – once – I've realised my implacable desire to live, not die!; but my regrets cannot alter my situation: arms shot, legs wobbling, head ablaze. My fear has devoured itself, leaving me hollow and mortified. To concede, to quit would be easy. Another little voice calmly intones: 'At least die trying' . . . I agree and again punch my tremulous hand into the bottoming crack. If only I can execute this one crux move, I'll get an incut jug-hold, can rest on it before the final section. I'm afraid to eyeball my crimped hand, jokingly jammed in the shallow crack. It *must* hold my 190 lb, on an overhanging wall, and this seems ludicrous, impossible.

My body has jittered in this spot for a millennium, but that hummingbird has moved but one centimetre. My jammed hand says 'NO WAY!', but that other little voice adds 'might as well try it.' I pull up slowly – my left foot is still pasted to that sloping edge – and that big bucket hold is right there . . . 'I almost have it, I do!', and simultaneously my right hand rips from the crack and my left foot flies off that rugosity; all my weight hangs from an enfeebled left arm. Adrenalin rockets me atop that Thank God hold when I press my chest to the wall, get that 190 lb over my feet and start quaking like no metaphor can depict.

That hummingbird is halfway to Rio before I consider pushing on. I would rather extract my wisdom teeth with vice grips. Dancing black orbs dot my vision when I finally claw over the summit. 'Looked a little shaky,' Bachar croons, flashing that candid, disarming snicker.

That night, I drove into town and got a bottle, and Sunday, while Bachar went for an El Capitan day (3,000ft.), I listlessly wandered through dark desert corridors, scouting for turtles, making garlands from wild flowers, relishing the skyscape, doing all those things a person does on borrowed time.

acknowledgments

Many people made this anthology.

At Thunder's Mouth Press and Avalon Publishing Group:
Neil Ortenberg and Susan Reich offered vital support and expertise. Dan
O'Connor and Ghadah Alrawi also were indispensable.

At Balliett & Fitzgerald Inc.:
Sue Canavan created the book's look. Maria Fernandez oversaw
production with grace and skill. Paul Paddock and Carol Petino helped
with production. Kathryn Daniels proofread copy with great care and
skill.

At the Thomas Memorial Library in Cape Elizabeth, Maine:
The librarians cheerfully worked to locate and borrow books from
across the country. Karla Sigel deserves special mention.

At the Writing Company:
The versatile Shawneric Hachey led the charge, gathering books,
permissions, facts and photographs; he also scanned and proofread
copy. Meghan Murphy gathered and checked facts, contributed ideas
and helped in many other ways. John Bishop, Nate Hardcastle, Mark
Klimek and Taylor Smith also helped with the book and took up slack
on other projects.

At various publishing companies and literary agencies, many people supported this project.

Among friends and family:
Jennifer Schwamm Willis lent me her judgement – again.
Abner Willis and Harper Willis were patient and sweet.
Jay Schwamm and Judy Mello Schwamm shared the Tetons and showed me a thing or two about generosity and courage.
My friend and teacher Michael Jewell shared his wisdom about climbing and other sacred matters.
Steve Longenecker 25 years ago took me under his wing; he also lent me copies of *Annapurna South Face* and *Direttissma*.
My friend Will Balliett made it a pleasure – again.

Jim Wickwire and Hamish MacInnes shared photographs from their personal collections.

Finally, I am grateful to all of the writers whose work appears in this book.

We gratefully acknowledge all those who gave permission for written material to appear in this book. We have made every effort to trace and contact copyright holders. If an error or omission is brought to our notice we will be pleased to remedy the situation in future editions of this book. For further information, please contact the publisher.

'Moments of Doubt' by David Roberts included with permission of the publisher. ©1986 by David Roberts. Excerpted from the book *Moments of Doubt* by David Roberts, published by The Mountaineers, Seattle, WA. ✤ 'How I (Almost) Didn't Climb Everest' by Greg Child included with permission of the publisher. © 1998 by Greg Child. Excerpted from *Postcards From the Ledge* by Greg Child, published by The Mountaineers, Seattle, WA. ✤ 'The Green Arch' by John Long. © 1994 by John Long. First published in *Summit Magazine*, 1994. Reprinted by permission of the author. ✤ Excerpt from *Addicted to Danger: A Memoir* by James Wickwire and Dorothy Bullitt. © 1998 by James Wickwire and Dorothy Bullitt. Reprinted with the permission of Pocket Books, a Division of Simon & Schuster, Inc. ✤ Excerpt from *The Price of Adventure* by Hamish MacInnes. © 1987 by Hamish MacInnes. Reprinted by permission of author. ✤ 'A Short Walk with Whillans' from *One Man's Mountains* by Tom Patey. U.S. Rights: Reproduced by permission of Curtis Brown London on behalf of the Estate of Tom Patey. © 1978 by Tom Patey. All other rights: Reprinted by permission of Victor Gollancz, Orion Publishing Group Ltd., London. ✤ Excerpt from *Summit Fever* by Andrew Greig. © 1985 by Andrew Greig. Reprinted with permission of Simpson Fox Associates, London. ✤ Excerpt from *Stories Off the Wall* by John Roskelley. © 1993 by John Roskelley. Included with permission of the publisher from *Stories Off the Wall*, by John Roskelley, published by The Mountaineers, Seattle, WA. ✤ Excerpt from *We Aspired: The Last Innocent Americans* by Pete Sinclair. © 1993 by Pete Sinclair. Reprinted by permission of Utah State University Press, Logan, UT. ✤ Excerpt from *High and Wild: A Mountaineer's World* by Galen Rowell. © 1979 by Galen Rowell. Reprinted by permission of Sierra Club Books, San Francisco. ✤ Excerpt from *Looking for Mo* by Daniel Duane. © 1998 by Daniel Duane. Reprinted by permission of Farrar, Straus and Giroux, LLC. ✤ 'Queen of All She Surveys' by Maureen O'Neill from *Leading Out: Women Climbers Reaching for the Top* edited by Rachel da Silva. © 1992 by Maureen O'Neill. Reprinted by permission of Seal Press, Seattle, WA. ✤ Excerpt from *Remote People* by Evelyn Waugh. © 1931 by Evelyn Waugh. Reprinted by

b i b l i o g r a p h y

The selections used in this anthology were taken from the editions listed below. In some cases, other editions may be easier to find. Hard to find or out-of-print titles often can be acquired through inter-library loan services or through Internet booksellers.

The Armchair Mountaineer. David Reuther and John Thorn, editors. Birmingham, AL: Menasha Ridge Press, 1989 (for 'Little Mother up the Mörderberg' by H. G. Wells).

Child, Greg. *Postcards from the Ledge.* Seattle: The Mountaineers, 1998.

Duane, Daniel. *Looking For Mo.* New York: Farrar, Straus and Giroux, 1998.

Greig, Andrew. *Summit Fever.* Seattle: The Mountaineers, 1997.

Leading Out: Women Climbers Reaching for the Top. Rachel da Silva, editor. Seattle: Seal Press, 1992 (for 'Queen of All She Surveys' by Maureen O'Neill).

Long, John. 'The Green Arch'. From *Summit Magazine*, Summer 1994.

Long, John. *Gorilla Monsoon.* Everclear, CO: Chockstone Press, 1984 (for 'The Only Blasphemy').

MacInnes, Hamish. *The Price of Adventure.* Seattle: The Mountaineers, 1987.

Patey, Tom. *One Man's Mountains.* London: Victor Gollancz Ltd., 1989.

Roberts, David. *Moments of Doubt and Other Mountaineering Writings.* Seattle: The Mountaineers, 1986.

Roskelley, John. *Stories Off the Wall.* Seattle: The Mountaineers, 1993.

Rowell, Galen. *High and Wild: A Mountaineer's World.* San Francisco: Sierra Club Books, 1979.

Sinclair, Pete. *We Aspired: The Last Innocent Americans.* Logan, Utah: Utah State University Press, 1993.

Waugh, Evelyn. *Remote People.* New York: The Ecco Press, 1990.

Whymper, Edward. *Scrambles Amongst the Alps.* New York: C. Scribner's Sons, 1937.

Wickwire, Jim and Dorothy Bullitt. *Addicted to Danger: A Memoir.* New York: Simon & Schuster, 1998.

Clint Willis, a climber and an armchair mountaineer since he was ten years old, is series editor of Adrenaline™ Books. His seven anthologies for the series also include *Epic: Stories of Survival from the World's Highest Peaks; High: Stories of Survival from Everest and K2; Wild: Stories of Survival from the World's Most Dangerous Places;* and *Ice: Stories of Survival from Polar Exploration.* He is at work on *Dark: Stories to Scare You to Death.* Clint lives with his wife and two sons in Maine.